ELECTRICIAN

Electrician's Helper

Edited by

Hy Hammer, Chief of
Examining Service Division
New York City Department
of Personnel, (Ret.)

PRENTICE
HALL
PRESS

New York   London   Toronto   Sydney   Tokyo   Singapore

Fifth Edition

 PRENTICE HALL PRESS

Simon & Schuster, Inc.
15 Columbus Circle
New York, NY 10023

An Arco Book
Published by Prentice Hall Press

Prentice Hall Press and colophons are
registered trademarks of Simon & Schuster, Inc.

Manufactured in the United States of America

10   11   12   13   14   15   16

Library of Congress Cataloging-in-Publication Data

Main entry under title:
    Electrician—electrician's helper.

    At head of title: The complete study guide for scoring
high.
    1. Electric engineering—Examinations, questions, etc.
I. Hammer, Hy. II. Arco Publishing.
TK169.H35   1982   621.3'076   82-11405
ISBN 0-668-05492-1 (pbk.)

CONTENTS

HOW TO USE THIS INDEX
Slightly bend the right-hand edge
of the book. This will expose
the corresponding Parts
which match the index, below.

PART

PART ONE
REQUIREMENTS AND TEST PREPARATION

PART TWO
A SELF-INSTRUCTIONAL COURSE
TO HELP YOU MASTER THE WORK AND PASS THE
TEST

1

2

3

PART THREE
PREVIOUS EXAMINATIONS FOR PRACTICE

WHAT THIS BOOK WILL DO FOR YOU

ARCO Publishing, Inc. has followed testing trends and methods ever since the firm was founded in 1937. We specialize in books that prepare people for tests. Based on this experience, we have prepared the best possible book to help *you* score high.

To write this book we carefully analyzed every detail surrounding the forthcoming examination . . .
- the job itself
- official and unofficial announcements concerning the examination
- all the previous examinations, many not available to the public
- related examinations
- technical literature that explains and forecasts the examination

CAN YOU PREPARE YOURSELF FOR YOUR TEST?

You want to pass this test. That's why you bought this book. Used correctly, your "self-tutor" will show you what to expect and will give you a speedy brush-up on the subjects tested in your exam. Some of these are subjects not taught in schools at all. Even if your study time is very limited, you should:

- Become familiar with the type of examination you will have.
- Improve your general examination-taking skill.
- Improve your skill in analyzing and answering questions involving reasoning, judgment, comparison, and evaluation.

- Improve your speed and skill in reading and understanding what you read—an important part of your ability to learn and an important part of most tests.

This book will tell you exactly what to study by presenting in full every type of question you will get on the actual test.

This book will help you find your weaknesses. Once you know what subjects you're weak in you can get right to work and concentrate on those areas. This kind of selective study yields maximum test results.

This book will give you the *feel* of the exam. Almost all our sample and practice questions are taken from actual previous exams. On the day of the exam you'll see how closely this book follows the format of the real test.

This book will give you confidence *now,* while you are preparing for the test. It will build your self-confidence as you proceed and will prevent the kind of test anxiety that causes low test scores.

This book stresses the multiple-choice type of question because that's the kind you'll have on your test. You must not be satisfied with merely knowing the correct answer for each question. You must find out why the other choices are incorrect. This will help you remember a lot you thought you had forgotten.

After testing yourself, you may find that you are weak in a particular area. You should concentrate on improving your skills by using the specific practice sections in this book that apply to you.

ELECTRICIAN

THE KIND OF WORK YOU WILL BE DOING

ELECTRICIANS   (CONSTRUCTION)

Nature of the Work

Heat, light, power, air-conditioning, and refrigeration components all operate through electrical systems that are assembled, installed, and wired by construction electricians. These workers also install electrical machinery, electronic equipment, controls, and signal and communications systems. Construction electricians follow blueprints and specifications for most installations. To install wiring in factories and offices, they may bend and fit conduit (pipe or tubing) inside partitions, walls, or other concealed areas. They then pull insulated wires or cables through the conduit to complete the circuit between outlets and switches. In lighter construction, such as housing, plastic-covered wire is usually used rather than conduit. In any case, electricians connect the wiring to circuit breakers, transformers, or other components. Wires are joined by soldering or mechanical means. When the wiring is finished, they test the circuits for proper connections and grounding.

Electricians, for safety reasons, must follow National Electrical Code regulations and, in addition, must fulfill requirements of State, county, and municipal electrical codes.

Electricians generally furnish their own tools, including screwdrivers, pliers, knives, and hacksaws. Employers furnish heavier tools, such as pipe threaders, conduit benders, and most test meters and power tools.

Places of Employment

Most electricians work for electrical contractors. Many others are self-employed contractors. A small number of electricians worked for government agencies or business that do their own electrical work. Construction electricians are employed throughout the country, but are concentrated in industrialized and urban areas.

Training, Other Qualifications, and Advancement

Most training authorities recommend the completion of a 4-year apprenticeship program as the best way to learn the electrical trade. However, some people learn the trade informally by working for many years as electricians' helpers. Many helpers gain additional knowledge through trade school or correspondence courses, or through special training in the Armed Forces.

Apprenticeship programs are sponsored through and supervised by local union-management committees. These programs provide 144 hours of classroom instruction each year in addition to comprehensive on-the-job training. In the classroom, apprentices learn blueprint reading, electrical theory, electronics, mathematics, and safety and first-aid practices. On the job, under the supervision of experienced electricians, apprentices must demonstrate mastery of electrical principles. At first, apprentices drill holes, set anchors, and set up conduit. In time and with experience, they measure, bend, and install conduit, as well as install, connect, and test wiring. They also learn to set up and draw diagrams for entire electrical systems.

To qualify for an apprenticeship, an applicant must be at least 18 years old and usually must be a high school or vocational school graduate with 1 year of algebra. Courses in electricity, electronics, mechanical drawing, science, and shop provide a good background. Although physical strength is not essential, manual dexterity, agility, and good health are important. Good color vision is necessary because electrical wires frequently are identified by color.

To obtain a license, which is necessary for employment in most cities, an electrician must pass an examination which requires a thorough knowledge of the craft and of State and local building codes.

Experienced construction electricians can advance to supervisors, superintendents, or contract estimators for contractors on construction jobs. Many electricians start their own contracting businesses. In most large urban areas, a contractor must have a master electrician's license.

Employment Outlook

Employment of construction electricians is expected to increase faster than the average for all occu-pations through the mid-1980's. As population and business grow, more electricians will be needed to install electrical fixtures and wiring in new homes, offices, and other buildings. In addition to jobs created by employment growth, many openings will arise as experienced electricians retire, die, or transfer to other occupations.

While employment in this field is expected to grow over the long run, it may fluctuate from year to year due to ups and downs in construction activity. When construction jobs are not available, however, electricians may be able to transfer to other types of electrical work. For example, they may find jobs as maintenance electricians in factories, or jobs as electricians in shipbuilding or aircraft manufacturing.

Earnings and Working Conditions

Apprentice wage rates start at from 40 to 50 percent of the rate paid to experienced electricians and increase periodically.

Construction electricians are not required to have great physical strength, but they frequently must stand for long periods and work in cramped quarters. Because much of their work is indoors, electricians are less exposed to unfavorable weather than are most other construction workers. They risk electrical shock, falls from ladders and scaffolds, and blows from falling objects. However, safety practices have helped to reduce the injury rate.

A large proportion of construction electricians are members of the International Brotherhood of Electrical Workers.

Sources of Additional Information

For details about electrician apprenticeships or other work opportunities in this trade, contact local electrical contractors; a local union of the International Brotherhood of Electrical Workers; a local union-management apprenticeship committee, or the nearest office of the State employment service or State apprenticeship agency.

For general information about the work of electricians, contact:

International Brotherhood of Electrical Workers, 1125 15th St. NW., Washington, D.C. 20005.

National Electrical Contractors Association, 1730 Rhode Island Ave. NW., Washington, D.C. 20036.

National Joint Apprenticeship and Training Committee for the Electrical Industry, 1730 Rhode Island Ave. NW., Washington, D.C. 20036.

MAINTENANCE ELECTRICIANS

Nature of the Work

Maintenance electricians keep lighting systems, transformers, generators, and other electrical equipment in good working order. They also may install new electrical equipment.

Duties vary greatly, depending on where the electrician is employed. Electricians who work in large factories may repair particular items such as motors and welding machines. Those in office buildings and small plants usually fix all kinds

S3522

of electrical equipment. Regardless of location, electricians spend much of their time doing preventive maintenance—periodic inspection of equipment to locate and correct defects before breakdowns occur. When trouble occurs, they must find the cause and make repairs quickly to prevent costly production losses. In emergencies, they advise management whether continued operation of equipment would be hazardous, necessitating a shutdown.

repairs by replacing items such as fuses, circuit breakers, or switches. When installing new or replacing existing wiring, they splice wires and cut and bend conduits (pipes) through which the wires are run.

Maintenance electricians sometimes work from blueprints, wiring diagrams, or other specifications. They use meters and other testing devices to locate faulty equipment. To make repairs they use pliers, screwdrivers, wirecutters, drills, and other tools.

Electricians Training Center
2300 Hampton, St. Louis, MO
63139, last 5 days every month
Age-18-24 or explain why your
still young enough in a letter
(314) 644-3587

Peoria Local 34, Jan. application
period (309) 692-7830

Champaign Electrical Workers
Apprentice Committee (217) 352-
3704

ELECTRICIAN

PART ONE

Requirements and Test Preparation

SAMPLE NOTICE OF EXAMINATION
ELECTRICIAN'S HELPER

Qualification Requirements

MINIMUM REQUIREMENTS:

(1) Three years of full-time paid experience   acquired within the last
fifteen years as an Electrician's Helper; or

(2) Not less than one and one-half years of such experience acquired
within the last ten years plus sufficient full-time paid experience
as a helper or apprentice or training of a relevant nature acquired
in an approved trade or vocational high school to make up the
equivalent of three years of acceptable experience. Six months
of acceptable experience will be credited for each year of helper
or apprentice experience or approved trade or vocational high school;

(3) A satisfactory equivalent.

The minimum requirements must be met by the last date for the receipt of
applications.

EXPERIENCE PAPER FORM A MUST BE FILED WITH THE APPLICATION. The experience
paper must be filled out completely and in detail.

At the time of appointment and at the time of investigation, eligibles must
present all the official documents and proof required to qualify. Failure
to present required documents, including proof of education or experience
requirement, will result in disqualification for appointment or a direction
to terminate services.

All candidates who file an application will be summoned for the written
test prior to the determination of whether they meet the above requirements.
Only the experience papers of passing candidates will be examined with
respect to meeting these requirements.

JOB DESCRIPTION

DUTIES AND RESPONSIBILITIES: Under direct supervision, assists an electrician
in installing, repairing, replacing and maintaining of electric wiring systems,
appliances, apparatus and equipment according to the provisions of the Electrical
Code and approved plans and specifications; performs related work.

EXAMPLES OF TYPICAL TASKS: Assists electricians in the erection and placing of
components of electrical systems. Helps electricians in pulling wires and testing
electrical systems. Replaces defective light switches, plugs, lighting fixtures,
and checks signal systems. Keeps electricians supplied with materials, tools,
and supplies. Cleans working areas, machines, tools and equipment. Performs
routine machine operations.

TEST INFORMATION

TESTS: Written, qualifying, 70% required; practical-oral, 70% required. The written test will be of the multiple-choice type and may include questions on basic electric circuit theory; fundamentals of electrical machinery and controls; installation and maintenance of interior wiring systems; electrical instruments, measurements and testing; tools and materials of the trade; rudiments of the Electrical Code; safety and other related areas. The practical-oral test may include questions on the hookup of electrical equipment; electrical instruments; panelboards; wire gauges and measurement of wire sizes; electrical diagrams and general knowledge of equipment.

Eligibles will be required to pass a medical test prior to appointment. An eligible will be rejected for any current medical and/or psychiatric impairment which impairs his or her ability to perform the duties of the class or positions.

PROMOTION OPPORTUNITIES

Employees in the title of Electrician's Helper are accorded promotional opportunities, when eligible, to the title of Electrician.

SAMPLE NOTICE OF EXAMINATION
ELECTRICIAN

In conjunction with the holding of this examination, a promotion examination will be held. The names appearing on the promotion list will receive prior consideration in filling vacancies. However, it is expected that there will be sufficient vacancies so that the open-competitive list will be used as well.

It is expected that the list resulting from this examination will be used to fill vacancies in the various City departments and in the Health and Hospitals Departments.

PROMOTION OPPORTUNITIES: Employees in the title of Electrician are accorded promotion opportunities when eligible to the title of Foreman Electrician.

MINIMUM REQUIREMENTS: (A) Five years of full-time paid experience in or on buildings as an electrician working on the installation, repair, or maintenance of high or low potential electrical systems for light, heat and power; or (B) not less than three years of experience as specified in (A) plus sufficient helper or apprentice experience, or educational training in an approved trade or vocational school to make a total of five years of acceptable experience. Six months of acceptable experience will be credited for each year of helper or apprentice experience or for each school year of approved educational training.

All candidates who file an application will be summoned for the written test prior to the determination of whether they meet the above requirements. Only the experience papers of passing candidates will be evaluated with respect to meeting these requirements.

The minimum requirements must be met by the last date for the receipt of applications.

EXPERIENCE PAPER FORM A MUST BE FILED WITH THE APPLICATION: Applicants must print their Social Security Number in the box labeled Application Number on the Experienc Paper Form A.

> At the time of appointment and at the time of investigation, candidates must present all the official documents and proof required to qualify as stated in this Notice of Examination.

> Failure to do so will result in a refusal to qualify for appointment or a direction to terminate services.

DUTIES AND RESPONSIBILITIES: Under direction, works as an electrician on the installation, repair and maintenance of high or low tension electrical systems for light, heat and power in or on buildings and/or on highways; performs related work.

EXAMPLES OF TYPICAL TASKS: Installs, repairs, replaces and maintains electric wiring systems and components, equipment and apparatus in or on buildings or structures in accordance with the provisions of the Electrical Code, pertinent plans and specifications or job orders. Installs, repairs, replaces, and maintains electric wiring systems and components and traffic signals and controllers. Installs conduit, raceway, and electrical conductors. Makes tests on existing installations to determine faults and makes necessary repairs. Keeps job and other records. May supervise assigned personnel.

TESTS: Written, qualifying, 70% required; practical-oral, qualifying, 70% required. The qualifying written test will be of the multiple choice type and may include questions on electrical theory, A.C. Machinery, D.C. Machinery, applied electronics, electrical maintenance and repairs, wiring systems and associated equipment, Electrical Code, safety, supervision and other related areas. In the practical-oral test the candidate may be required to hook up electrical circuits, use electrical instruments, perform panelboard circuit testing, make wire size measurements, read electrical diagrams, demonstrate his knowledge of electrical equipment, and perform in other related areas.

Eligibles will be required to pass a qualifying medical test prior to appointment. An eligible will be rejected for any current medical and/or psychiatric impairment which impairs his or her ability to perform the duties of the class or position.

HOW TO BE A MASTER TEST TAKER

SCORING PAPERS BY MACHINE

A typical machine-scored answer sheet is shown below, reduced from the actual size of 8¼ x 11 inches. Since it's the only one that reaches the office where papers are scored, it's important that the blanks at the top be filled in completely and correctly.

You'll have to mark your answers on one of these sheets. Consequently, we've made it possible for you to practice with them throughout this book.

SAMPLE ANSWER SHEET

EXAM TITLE		TODAY'S DATE	
SCHOOL OR BUILDING		ROOM NO.	SEAT NO.

PRINT WITH SOFT PENCIL ONLY. Print, with pencil, your SOCIAL SECURITY NO. and the EXAM. NO. in the boxes at the tops of the columns. ONE NUMBER IN A BOX. In each column, darken (with pencil) the oval containing the number in the box at the top of the column. Only ONE OVAL in a COLUMN should be darkened. Then, using your pencil, print in the: Exam. Title, School or Building, Room No., Seat No., and Today's Date.

Follow the instructions given in the question booklet. Mark nothing ▶ but your answers in the ovals below.

SAMPLE QUESTION: When we add 5 and 3 we get: (A) 11 (B) 9 (C) 8 (D) 2. Since the answer is 8, your answer should be marked like this: ⓐ ⓑ ● ⓓ

WARNING: Be sure that the oval you fill in is in the row numbered the same as the question you are answering. Use a No. 2 pencil (soft pencil).

BE SURE YOUR PENCIL MARKS ARE HEAVY AND BLACK. ERASE COMPLETELY ANY ANSWER YOU WISH TO CHANGE. DO NOT make stray pencil dots, dashes or marks ANYPLACE on this SHEET.

YOUR SOCIAL SECURITY NO.   EXAM NO.

START HERE

FOLLOW DIRECTIONS CAREFULLY

It's an obvious rule, but more people fail for breaching it than for any other cause. By actual count there are over a hundred types of directions given on tests. You'll familiarize yourself with many of them in the course of this book. And you'll also learn not to let your guard down in reading them, listening to them, and following them. Right now, before you plunge in, we want to be sure that you have nothing to fear from the answer sheet and the way in which you must mark it; from the most important question forms and the ways in which they are to be answered.

HERE'S HOW TO MARK YOUR ANSWERS ON MACHINE-SCORED ANSWER SHEETS:

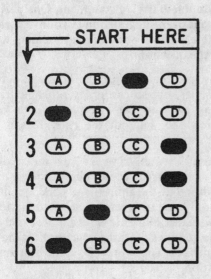

Make only ONE mark for each answer. Additional and stray marks may be counted as mistakes. In making corrections, erase errors COMPLETELY. Make glossy black marks.

(a) Each pencil mark must be heavy and black. Light marks should be retraced with the special pencil.

(b) Each mark must be in the space between the pair of dotted lines and entirely fill this space.

(c) All stray pencil marks on the paper, clearly not intended as answers, must be completely erased.

(d) Each question must have only one answer indicated. If multiple answers occur, all extraneous marks should be thoroughly erased. Otherwise, the machine will give you *no* credit for your correct answer.

MULTIPLE CHOICE METHODS

Multiple choice questions offer you four or five possible answers. Your job is to select *only* the *best* answer. Even the incorrect answers are frequently *partly* correct. They are inserted to force you to think ... and prove that you know the right answer.

THE BEST WAY TO ANSWER MULTIPLE CHOICE QUESTIONS:

1. Read each question carefully to see what the examiner is after. Re-read always.
2. Forget about answers that are clearly wrong.
3. You should be suspicious of choices which contain broad statements using words like "all," "always," "never" and "only."

4. A well-constructed **multiple choice** item will avoid obviously incorrect choices. The good examiner will try to write a cluster of answers, all of which are plausible. Use the clue words to help yourself pick the *most* correct answer.

5. In the case of items where you are doubtful of the answer, you might be able to bring to bear the information you have gained from previous study. This knowledge might be sufficient to indicate that some of the suggested answers are not so plausible. Eliminate such answers from further consideration.

6. Then concentrate on the remaining suggested answers. The fewer answers you have to consider, the better your chances of getting the item right.

7. If the item is in the form of an incomplete statement, it sometimes helps to try to complete the statement before you look at the suggested answers. Then see if the way you have completed the statement corresponds with any of the answers provided. If one is found, it is likely to be the correct one.

8. Use your head! Make shrewd inferences. Sometimes, with a little thought, and the information that you have, you can reason out the answer. We're suggesting a method of intelligent guessing in which you can become quite expert with a little practice. It's a useful method that may help you with some debatable answers.
debatable answers.

NOW, LET'S TRY THESE METHODS OUT ON A SAMPLE MULTIPLE-CHOICE QUESTION.

1. Leather is considered the best material for shoes chiefly because
   (A) it is waterproof
   (B) it is quite durable
   (C) it is easily procurable
   (D) it is flexible and durable
   (E) it can be easily manufactured in various styles.

Here we see that every one of the answer statements is plausible: leather is waterproof if treated properly; it is relatively durable; it is relatively easily procurable; it bends and is shaped easily, and is, again, durable; it constantly appears in various styles of shoes and boots.

However, we must examine the question with an eye toward identifying the key phrase which is: *best* for shoes *chiefly*.

Now we can see that (A) is incorrect because leather is probably not the *best* material for shoes, simply because it is waterproof. There are far bet-

ter waterproof materials available, such as plastics and rubber. In fact, leather must be treated to make it waterproof. So by analyzing the key phrase of the question we can eliminate (A).

(B) seems plausible. Leather is durable and durability is a good quality in shoes. This answer may be correct.

(C) Leather is comparatively easy to procure; but would that make it *best* for shoes? And would that be the *chief* reason why it is used for making shoes? Although the statement in itself is quite true, it does not fit the key phrase of the question and we must, reluctantly, eliminate it.

(D) is a double-barreled statement. One part, the durability, has been suggested in (B) above. Leather is also flexible, so both parts of the statement would seem to fit the question.

(E) It is true that leather can be manufactured in various styles, but so can many other materials. Again, going back to the key phrase, this could be considered one, but not the *chief* reason why it is *best* for shoes.

So, by carefully analyzing the *key* phrase of the question we have narrowed our choices down to (B) and (D). Although durability is a good quality in shoes, it is only one of several. The combination of durability with flexibility provides a more exact definition of the qualities of leather that make it the best material for shoes. Therefore, (D) is the best answer to this question.

The same question, by slightly altering the answer choices, can also call for a *negative* response. Here, even more so, the identification of the key phrase becomes vital in finding the correct answer. Suppose the question and its responses were worded thus:

2. Leather is considered the best material for shoes chiefly because
   (A) it is waterproof
   (B) it is easily colored
   (C) it is easily procurable
   (D) it can easily be manufactured in various styles
   (E) none of these.

We can see that the prior partially correct answer (B) has now been changed, and the doubly-correct answer eliminated. Instead we have a new response possibility (E), "none of these."

We have analyzed three of the choices previously and have seen the reason why none of them is the *chief* reason why leather is considered the *best* material for shoes. The two new elements are (B) "easily colored," and (E) "none of these."

If you think about it, leather *can* be easily colored and often is, but this would not be the chief reason why it is considered *best*. Many other materials are just as easily dyed. So we must come to the conclusion that *none* of the choices are *completely* correct—none fit the key phrase. Therefore, the question calls for a negative response (E).

We have now seen how important it is to identify the key phrase. Equally, or perhaps even more important, is the identifying and analyzing of the key *word*—the qualifying word—in a question. This is usually, though not always, an adjective or adverb. Some of the key words to watch for are: *most, best, least, highest, lowest, always, never, sometimes, most likely, greatest, smallest, tallest, average, easiest, most nearly, maximum, minimum, chiefly, mainly, only, but* and *or*. Identifying these key words is usually half the battle in understanding and, consequently, answering all types of exam questions.

Rephrasing the Question

It is obvious, then, that by carefully analyzing a question, by identifying the key phrase and its key words, you can usually find the correct answer by logical deduction and, often, by elimination. One other way of examining, or "dissecting," a question is to restate or rephrase it with each of the suggested answer choices integrated into the question.

For example, we can take the same question and rephrase it.

(A) The chief reason why leather is considered the best material for shoes is because it is waterproof.
or
(A) Because it is waterproof, leather is considered the best material for shoes.
or
(A) Chiefly because it is waterproof, leather is considered the best material for shoes.

It will be seen from the above three new versions of the original statement and answer that the question has become less obscure because it has been, so to speak, illuminated from different angles. It becomes quite obvious also in this rephrasing that the statement (A) is incorrect, although the *original* phrasing of the question left some doubt.

The rules for understanding and analyzing the key phrase and key words in a question, and the way to identify the *one* correct answer by means of intelligent analysis of the important question-answer elements, are basic to the solution of all the problems you will face on your test.

In fact, perhaps the *main* reason for failing an examination is failure to *understand the question.* In many cases, examinees *do* know the answer to a particular problem, but they cannot answer correctly because they do not understand it.

PART TWO

2

A Self-Instructional Course to Help You Master the Work and Pass the Test

THE ELECTRICAL SELF-TUTOR

The following chapters on electrical work are an important contribution to the literature of the job. Every relevant topic is covered, from Kirchoff's laws to the wiring and maintenance of complicated electrical equipment.

All of the questions in these chapters have been culled from actual previous examinations given to professional electricians. Naturally, in reviewing these exams, we found many more questions than actually appear in the book. How then, did we choose which questions to include—which to discard?

The most important part of the selection process is to find out what lies behind the examiner's method of preparing an actual exam. Our book could hardly be useful if it did not duplicate, in essence, the approach and the subject matter of the exam as it is conceived by the examiner.

The questions are first read and classified according to the particular branch of the science that was covered. Then classified again according to their approach to the subject—were they judgment questions, method questions, general knowledge questions, or another type altogether?

Then the questions are reviewed once again with the idea in mind of preparing a study guide. What is most important? How should the chapters be organized to provide a logical, useful and systematic approach to the subject? These are the questions that are asked and answered. Usually chapters on theory, background, general intelligence and vocabulary are included at the beginning of the book; questions on work and methodology at the end.

In assembling the chapters great care is taken to eliminate duplicate or near duplicate questions, except in cases where reiteration seemed so important that certain questions could be included in different chapters. Many questions were discarded because they were unclear or unanswerable; many because they were of so specific a nature as to be useless; many simply because they were obsolete. The result, of course, is that the book provides a concise selection of the most frequently recurring and crucial questions, each very important and each to be seriously studied.

THE PROVEN Q & A METHOD

We are all familiar with the parent's frustration because of his continued inability to answer the many questions put to him by his children. The questions are frustrating because they cover so wide a field, but they are, nevertheless, the best way for the child, who cannot read well yet, to learn about the world around him. Even when we are grown up questions and answers continue to fascinate us: crossword puzzles and newspaper contests are popular for reasons far deeper than the possibility of winning money: perhaps it is because, as we grow older, it becomes more difficult to question.

Questions have an immediate relationship to answers; solutions to work problems are much nearer when we can imagine the work laid out in front of us. This is what an ARCO book does; it lays the work out in front of us, makes the problem to be solved more appealing because it is a problem, stimulates our interest and makes studying easier and more pleasurable.

THE SELF-TUTORING SCHEME

Each chapter is divided into sections, sometimes sections are divided into sub-sections. Key answers follow immediately after each section, after each sub-section if it is particularly large. Concentrate upon one group of questions and answers at a time, check your answers, calculate if you are weak or strong, and brush up on your weaknesses before going on to the next section. Don't peek at the answers before time —you'll nullify the whole purpose of the book, to help you find out what you don't know. After you have finished using the study guide, answer the questions on the sample tests.

DIRECTIONS FOR ANSWERING QUESTIONS

DIRECTIONS: For each question read all the choices carefully. Then select that answer which you consider correct or most nearly correct. Write the letter preceding your best choice next to the question. Should you want to answer on the kind of answer sheet used on machine-scored examinations, we have provided several such facsimiles. On some machine-scored exams you are instructed to "place no marks whatever on the test booklet." In other examinations you may be instructed to mark your answers in the test booklet. In such cases you should be careful that no other marks interfere with the legibility of your answers. It is always best NOT to mark your booklet unless you are sure that it is permitted. It is most important that you learn to mark your answers clearly and in the right place.

To help you understand exactly how to answer multiple choice questions, we give you a sample item.

The unit for measuring electrical capacity is:
    (A) volt
    (B) farad
    (C) ohm
    (D) watt
The only answer is (B) since volt is a measure of electromotive force; ohm is a unit of electrical resistance; and a watt is a unit of electrical power. Mark this answer on the answer sheet:

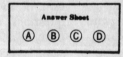

Answer Sheet
(A) (B) (C) (D)

ELECTRICAL THEORY AND WORK

Definition of Electricity. Electricity is an invisible force which we only know about through the effects it produces. While the exact nature of electricity is not known, the laws governing electrical phenomena are clearly understood and defined, just as the laws of gravitation are known, although we cannot define the nature of gravity.

The Movement of Electricity. In many ways electricity in motion is like flowing water, and electrical phenomena can be more easily understood if this analogy is borne in mind. In dealing with the flow of electricity and the flow of water, we consider three factors: (a) Current (Flow of electricity, usually along a conductor). (b) Pressure (that which causes the current to flow). (c) Resistance (that which regulates the flow of current).

Electrical Current or Flow. If we want to know about the flow of water in a pipe, we would determine how many gallons of water flow through the pipe in a second. In exactly the same way, the electrician determines the number of *coulombs* of electricity that flow through a wire in a second. Just as the gallon is a measure of the quantity of water, the coulomb is a measure of the quantity of electricity. There is an abbreviated method of describing the flow of electrical current. The electrician speaks of the *ampere,* which means one coulomb per second, and is thus saved the trouble of saying "per second" every time he wants to describe the current flow.

Electrical Pressure. Water pressure is measured in pounds per square inch. There is also a measure of electrical pressure. This electrical pressure has a definite effect upon the number of amperes flowing along a wire. The electrical unit of pressure is the volt. A volt means the same thing in speaking of a current of electricity that a pound-per-square-inch pressure does in speaking of a current of water. Just as a higher pressure is required to force the same current of water through a small pipe than through a large pipe, so a higher electrical pressure is required to force the same current of electricity through a small wire than through a large wire. The voltage (pressure) between two points in an electric circuit is sometimes spoken of as the difference in potential, or the drop in potential, or merely the "drop" between those two points.

The distinction between amperes and volts should now be plain. The amperes represent the amount of the current flowing through a circuit; the volts represent the pressure causing it to flow.

Electrical Resistance. The electrical unit of resistance is the ohm. We say a wire has one ohm resistance when a pressure of one volt forces a current of one ampere through it.

Ohm's Law. In any circuit through which a current is flowing, the three following factors are present: (1) The pressure or potential difference, expressed in volts, causing the current to flow. (2) The opposition or resistance of the circuit, expressed in ohms, which must be overcome. (3) The current strength, expressed in amperes, which is maintained in the circuit as a result of the pressure overcoming the resistance. A definite and exact relation exists between three factors; pressure, current strength, and resistance in any circuit, whereby the value of any one factor may always be calculated when the values of the other two factors are known. This relation, known as Ohm's Law, is very important, since it forms the basis for all calculations in electrical engineering. It may be summarized as follows:

The current in any electric circuit is equal to the electromotive force applied to the circuit, divided by the resistance of the circuit.

Let E — E. M. F. or available pressure, expressed in volts, applied to any circuit.

R — resistance of the circuit, expressed in ohms,

I — current strength, expressed in amperes, to be maintained through circuit.

Then, by the above statement of Ohm's Law,

$$\text{Current} = \frac{(\text{Pressure})}{\text{Resistance}}$$

$$\text{or Amperes} = \frac{\text{volts}}{\text{ohms}} \quad \text{or } I = \frac{E}{R}$$

The Circuit. Electricity is not as simple as water in that it can not be piped from one point to another. In order to flow, electricity must be sent along a closed circuit. Except through a generator or a battery cell, electricity always flows from a higher to a lower level. The higher level, or positive, is marked +, and the lower level, or negative, is marked —, in order to indicate the direction in which the current is flowing. A given point is + to all points below its level, and — to all points above its level.

If any of the wires leading from the + to the — terminal is broken, the current cannot flow, for the circuit has been interrupted and is incomplete.

Measuring Electrical Current. In order to find out how much current is flowing through an electric circuit, we insert a current meter into the circuit so that all the current which we wish to measure flows through the meter. Since an instrument which measures an electric current must read in amperes, such a current meter is called an ammeter. The ammeter must be of very low resistance in order not to hinder the current. Such an instrument is very delicate and must be handled carefully.

Measurement of Electrical Pressure. When it is necessary to measure the pressure which is causing an electric current to flow through a circuit, the terminals of a *voltmeter* are tapped on to that circuit in such a way that the voltmeter is made to register not current but pressure. The method of attaching a voltmeter is different from that used in attaching an ammeter. The ammeter becomes a part of the circuit. The voltmeter does not become a part of the circuit.

Measurement of Electrical Resistance. In order to find the resistance of an electrical piece, the voltmeter reading is divided by the ammeter reading.

Regulating and Controlling Electrical Current. The usual method of regulating and controlling the current required for various electrical purposes is by inserting or removing resistance from a circuit. An adjustable resistance, or any apparatus for changing the resistance without opening the circuit, is called a rheostat. The function of a rheostat is to absorb electrical energy; and this energy, which appears as heat, is wasted instead of performing any useful work. A rheostat may be constructed of coils of iron wire, iron plates or strips; of carbon, either pulverized in tubes or in the form of solid rods or disks; German silver, platinoid, or wires of other alloys wound on spools; columns of liquids, as water and mercury, etc. The cross-sectional area of the material must be sufficient to carry the current without excessive heating. In rheostats used for regulating the current in commercial electrical circuits no great degree of accuracy of the resistance coils is required, as is the case with laboratory rheostats.

The Effects of a Current. A current of electricity is believed to be a transfer of electrons through a circuit, and since these carriers are so minute, a direct measurement of them is impractical. Consequently, an electric current is measured by the effects it produces, all of which are commercially utilized. The effects manifested by a current of electricity are: Heating Effect, Magnetic Effect, Chemical Effect, and Physiological Effect.

Heating Effect. Every wire which conducts a current of electricity becomes heated to some extent as a result of the current, because the best conductors offer some opposition (resistance) to the flow of the current, and it is in overcoming this resistance that the heat is developed. If the wire is large in cross-sectional area and the current small, the heat developed will be so small in amount as not to be recognized by the touch; nevertheless, the wire releases some heat energy. On the other hand, with a small wire and a large current, it becomes quite hot.

Magnetic Effect. A wire carrying a current of electricity deflects a magnetic needle. When the wire is insulated and coiled around an iron core, the current magnetizes the core.

Chemical Effect. Electrical current is capable of decomposing certain chemical compounds when it is passed through them, breaking up the compounds into their constituent parts. In the production of electrical energy by a simple primary cell, electrolytic decomposition takes places inside the cell when the current is flowing. Electroplating, or the art of depositing a coating of metal upon any object, is based upon the principles of electrolytic decomposition.

Physiological Effect. A current of electricity passed through the body produces muscular contractions which are due to the physiological effects of an electrical current. Electrotherapeutics deals with the study of this effect.

Direct and Alternating Current. A direct or continuous current flows always in the same direction. In many cases it has a constant strength for definite periods of time. A pulsating current has a uniform direction, but the current strength varies. Most direct current generators furnish pulsating current; but since the pulsations are very small, the current is practically constant.

An alternating current of electricity is one that changes its direction of flow at regular intervals of time. These intervals are usually much shorter than one second. During an interval, the current strength is capable of varying in any way. In practice, the strength rises and then falls smoothly. Most electricity today comes in the form of alternating current. This is so because high voltage can more easily be obtained with alternating current than with direct current. High voltages, of course, are much more cheaply transmitted over power lines than are low voltages.

The Dynamo and Electromagnetic Induction. The electrical generator and the electric motor are intimately related. The term dynamo is applied to machines which convert either mechanical energy into electrical energy or electrical energy into mechanical energy by utilizing the principle of electromagnetic induction. A dynamo is called a generator when mechanical energy supplied in the form of rotation is converted into electrical energy. When the energy conversion takes place in the reverse order the dynamo is called a motor. Thus a dynamo is a reversible machine capable of operation as a generator or motor as desired.

The generator consists fundamentally of a number of loops of insulated wires revolving in a strong magnetic field in such a way that these wires cut across the lines of magnetic force. This cutting of the lines of force sets up an electromotive force along the wires.

We have shown that wherever there is an electric current present, there is also present a magnetic field. It is not true that wherever a magnetic field exists, there also exists an electric current, in the ordinary sense; but we can say that wherever a conductor moves in a magnetic field in such a way as to cut lines of force, an electromotive force is set up. It is on this principle that the electric generator works.

THE WORKING ELECTRICIAN

DIRECTIONS: Below we present a number of representative jobs. Although the correct steps for each job are given, they are not placed in the proper order. Examine each job and decide which step should come first. In the space at the right, place the number of this step. Then insert the numbers of the remaining steps, so that when you have finished the numbers can be read in proper job order.

1. In soldering an electric cable, you are assigned to tin the soldering copper.

    (1) The copper should be properly heated.

    (2) Ammonium chloride should be applied to soldering copper together with the solder until copper is tinned.

    (3) Copper should be wired until shiny on an emery cloth.

    (4) The copper should be cleaned and polished with ammonium chloride solution and filed.

2. In the rewinding of an electric motor, you are assigned to wind an electromagnet. What procedure would you employ?

    (1) Polarity of magnet should be determined.

    (2) Core should be wound with No. 20 d.c.c. wire.

    (3) Wire should be attached to the plus and minus terminals.

    (4) A soft iron core that has no magnetism should be selected.

    (5) Core should be tested to find whether it is non-magnetic.

3. You are assigned to a job which requires splicing the ends of connecting wires in an outlet box. What would be the correct method for you to follow?

    (1) Joint should be properly protected by friction tape.

    (2) Wires should be securely entwined.

    (3) Solder joint so that flux and solder run smoothly on heated wires.

    (4) Scrape insulation from cable.

    (5) Joint should be properly protected by rubber plate.

    (6) Remove oxides from surface of wire.

4. You are working on a job when a fuse in a lighting circuit blows out. You have to discover and put in another fuse in its place. What method would you employ in carrying out this task?

    (1) The fuse which has blown out should be removed from the fuse block.

    (2) The line should be traced and the fuse block discovered.

    (3) The bulb which no longer gives light should be investigated for a defective filament.

    (4) The fuses should be carefully examined for defects.

    (5) A new fuse which has the same amperage should be screwed in.

    (6) The circuit should be closed in order to determine whether the new fuse operates properly.

5. An important assignment has been given to you to carry out. You are told that two door bells are to be put in, using a parallel circuit. Further instructions state that both bells are to be operated from one push button and two dry cells. After careful consideration, in what manner would you proceed to carry out this assignment?

    (1) The binding post nuts should be carefully examined in order to see that they are properly tightened.

    (2) Since an electric doorbell requires a current, the button should be pushed and the circuit tested.

(3) The binding posts should be connected with the wires which have been provided.

(4) The length of No. 18. d.c.c., which is the bell wire best suited for his purpose, is to be decided upon.

(5) The staples which have been insulated should be driven in place to carry out the job properly.

(6) The door bells should be mounted, then the button pushed to see if they work properly and the cells sufficiently dried.

TRY THESE MULTIPLE CHOICE QUESTIONS

DIRECTIONS: For each question read all choices carefully. Then select that answer which you consider correct or most nearly correct. Write the letter preceding your best choice next to the question

6. Alternating currents may be increased or decreased by means of
 (A) a generating machine
 (B) a dynamo
 (C) a transformer
 (D) a motor.

7. The best of the following conductors of electricity is
 (A) silver wire
 (B) mica
 (C) nickel and chromium wire
 (D) gold.

8. Different amounts of resistance in a circuit may be introduced by means of
 (A) a voltmeter
 (B) an electromagnet
 (C) an ammeter
 (D) a good connection.

9. In sockets, extension cord is protected by means of the .... knot
 (A) sheepshank
 (B) clove hitch
 (C) fire
 (D) underwriters'.

10. The fuse plug contains a safety element composed of
 (A) a piece of metal that has a high resistance and a low melting point
 (B) a piece of metal that has a low resistance and a high melting point
 (C) a piece of metal that has a low resistance
 (D) a piece of metal that has a high melting point.

11. Storage battery electrolite is formed by the dissolving of .... acid in water
 (A) hydrochloric
 (B) sulphuric
 (C) acetic
 (D) atric.

12. The electric pressure or electromotive force is measured by
 (A) the volt
 (B) the electric meter
 (C) the watt
 (D) kilowatt.

13. The unit of measurement for electrical resistance to currents is
 (A) the ohm
 (B) the ampere
 (C) the volt
 (D) the watt.

14. Electricity is sold by the kilowatt which equals .... watts.
 (A) 1,000
 (B) 2,000
 (C) 10,000
 (D) 100.

15. The unit for measuring electrical capacity is
 (A) farad
 (B) volt
 (C) ohm
 (D) watt.

16. The central terminal of a dry cell is said to be
    (A) positive
    (B) negative
    (C) neutral
    (D) charged.

17. The spark-plug used in automobiles produces electrical energy at .... voltage
    (A) high
    (B) low
    (C) medium
    (D) no.

18. A D.C. series motor that has the current reversed, turns in the .... direction
    (A) opposite
    (B) same
    (C) reverse
    (D) wrong.

19. The current used for charging storage batteries is
    (A) direct
    (B) alternating
    (C) negative
    (D) positive.

20. The starting motor of an automobile requires a high
    (A) amperage
    (B) voltage
    (C) capacity
    (D) degree of insulation.

21. Receptacles in a house-lighting system are regularly connected in
    (A) parallel
    (B) series
    (C) diagonal
    (D) perpendicular.

22. Wire connections should encircle binding posts in the .... manner the nut turns to lighten.
    (A) opposite
    (B) same
    (C) reverse
    (D) different.

23. The headlights to automobiles are found to be connected ordinarily in
    (A) parallel
    (B) series
    (C) diagonal
    (D) perpendicular.

24. The average dry cell gives a voltage approximately

(A) 1.5
(B) 1.3
(C) 1.1
(D) 1.7.

25. Grounding the metallic cover of Greenfield, content or B.X. is for protection
    (A) against open field circuits
    (B) against shock or injury
    (C) against storms
    (D) against change of rate of speed.

26. To install spark-producing equipment on a switchboard situated in a garage, the best place to place it is
    (A) 5 feet above the floor
    (B) 8 feet above the floor
    (C) 4 feet above the floor
    (D) 7 feet above the floor.

27. A load is missing from a D.C. shunt wound motor. If you happen to open the field circuit
    (A) the speed of the motor will slow down greatly
    (B) the speed of the motor will be much greater
    (C) the speed will be the same
    (D) the motor will cease to operate

28. The instrument which is used to determine electric current is
    (A) the scanner drum
    (B) constant-speed racket
    (C) an ammeter
    (D) voltmeter.

29. In lights controlled by three-way switches, the switches should be treated and put in as
    (A) flush switches
    (B) single pole switches
    (C) three double pole switches
    (D) three pole switches.

30. A set of lights coming from three different places can be controlled by .... switches.
    (A) two 3-way and one 4-way switches
    (B) two 3-way and one 2-way
    (C) 2 single pole switches
    (D) four pole switches.

31. Is it a sound principle to install direct current and alternating current conductors in one pull box
    (A) yes—if soldered
    (B) no
    (C) yes—if covered with rubber
    (D) yes—in dry places.

32. Low Potential is a trade term which refers to
    (A) 700 volts
    (B) 600 volts or less
    (C) 1200 volts
    (D) 900 volts.

33. An electrical condenser is best defined as
    (A) a coil of wire
    (B) a coil of wire with layers of metal foil
    (C) a wrapping of many layers of metal foil set apart by waxed paper
    (D) a wrapping of layers of metal foil.

34. Prior to placing stranded wires up to B and D, excluding flexible cords beneath clamps or binding posts, the wire are to be
    (A) shaped and soldered
    (B) shaped and bound
    (C) scraped and grounded
    (D) entwined and soldered.

35. To speed up a D.C. compound wound motor to more than its name plate rating, it is necessary to
    (A) connect resistance in the shunt field circuit
    (B) connect resistance in the armature circuit
    (C) connect a shunt across the armature circuit
    (D) connect resistance coil in line leads.

36. A megger is a tool used for the purpose of
    (A) polarizing the system
    (B) shunting the system
    (C) determining high resistances
    (D) determining amperes.

37. The instruments used to connect electrical apparatus to lath and plastered ceilings are
    (A) meggers
    (B) wood plugs
    (C) wood screws
    (D) toggle bolts.

38. Determining a positive wire on a Single Phase line
    (A) is possible with a voltmeter
    (B) is possible with an ammeter
    (C) is an impossibility
    (D) is possible with a wattmeter.

39. The instrument used in fastening electrical apparatus to terra-cotta walls is
    (A) megger
    (B) ammeter
    (C) toggle bolts
    (D) lead shields.

40. Is it proper procedure to ground the frame of a portable motor?
    (A) No
    (B) No, if it is A.C.
    (C) Yes, unless the tool is specifically designed for use without a ground
    (D) Yes, if the operation takes place at less than 150 volts.

41. A single set of fuses of — amperes or less may protect a group of motors each protected by thermal cutouts
    (A) 40
    (B) 35
    (C) 30
    (D) 45.

42. Neutral wire can be quickly recognized by the
    (A) greenish color
    (B) bluish color
    (C) natural or whitish color
    (D) black color.

43. The instrument by which electric power may be measured is a
    (A) rectifier
    (B) scanner drum
    (C) ammeter
    (D) wattmeter.

44. To determine directly whether all finished wire installations possess resistance between conductors, and between conductors and ground, use
    (A) clamps
    (B) set screws
    (C) shields
    (D) megger.

45. If no change were possible in the voltage and frequency of the supply or mains, to speed up a 3-phase synchronous motor it would be necessary to
    (A) connect a shunt across the field circuit
    (B) connect a shunt against line leads
    (C) do nothing as it is impossible to change the speed
    (D) connect a shunt across the series field.

46. The instruments used to connect electrical apparatus to a concrete ceiling or wall are
(A) toggle bolts
(B) toggle bolts and wooden screws
(C) screws and shields
(D) shields.

47. The most accurate method to employ in finding the circular mil area of a piece of stranded wire is to
(A) multiply the number of strands by the circular mil area of one strand
(B) square the area of the number of strands
(C) use a footage meter
(D) use a micrometer.

48. The appropriate lighting fixture for a room used to keep gasoline and paints is a
(A) vapor proof fixture plus porceltain socket
(B) vapor proof fixture plus mogul socket
(C) vapor proof fixture plus vapor proof globe
(D) porcelain fixture plus mogul socket.

49. To wire according to the Wooden Paceway or Moulding method is valuable
(A) when wire is to carry 33 amperes
(B) when wire is to carry 65 amps
(C) when wire is to carry 45 amps
(D) in no case whatsoever.

50. A "mil" measures
(A) an eighth of an inch
(B) a millionth of an inch
(C) a thousandth of an inch
(D) a ten-thousandth of an inch.

51. S_3 is a symbol used in wiring which indicates that the kind of switch required is a
(A) flush switch
(B) two pole switch
(C) tour pole switch
(D) three way switch.

52. An incandescent lamp of 1000 watt type P. S. requires a base mainly of
(A) rubber
(B) tie wire
(C) mogul
(D) metal.

53. The ground wire of the conduit system in a factory must have a connection with
(A) a floor outlet
(B) a ceiling outlet
(C) a water main, located on the street side of the meter
(D) sewer main.

54. The current through a d.c. arc lamp can be controlled by a
(A) scanner drum
(B) rectifier
(C) rheostat
(D) wattmeter.

Answer Key

(Please make every effort to answer the questions on your own before looking at these answers. You'll make faster progress by following this rule.)

Theory and Work

1.1423	8.B	15.A	22.B	29.B	36.C	43.D	49.D
2.42351	9.D	16.A	23.A	30.A	37.D	44.D	50.C
3.462351	10.A	17.D	24.A	31.B	38.C	45.C	51.D
4.324156	11.B	18.B	25.B	32.B	39.C	46.C	52.C
5.435126	12.A	19.A	26.C	33.C	40.C	47.A	53.C
6.C	13.A	20.A	27.B	34.D	41.C	48.C	54.C
7.D	14.A	21.A	28.C	35.A	42.C		

Symbol test in electricity

DIRECTIONS : Symbols are an important part of the electrician's vocabulary. Column I consists of often-used symbols. Column II is a list of the instruments or conditions for which these symbols stand. Select the letter in Column II which correctly identifies the symbol in Column I. Write that letter next to the numbered symbol in Column I.

COLUMN I

COLUMN II

A POTENTIOMETER	T LOUDSPEAKER, PERMANENT MAGNET
B CONDENSER OR CAPACITOR | FIXED	U PLUG
C CONDENSER OR CAPACITOR | VARIABLE	V JACK, OPEN CIRCUIT
	W JACK, CLOSED CIRCUIT
D GROUND	X CONTACTS | NORMALLY OPEN
E ANTENNA	
F FUSE	Y CONTACTS | NORMALLY CLOSED
G LAMP	Z HEADPHONES
H DIODE, DIRECTLY HEATED CATHODE	AA SWITCH, SINGLE POLE, SINGLE THROW
I DIODE, INDIRECTLY HEATED CATHODE	BB SWITCH, DOUBLE POLE, SINGLE THROW
J TRIODE, INDIRECTLY HEATED CATHODE	CC SWITCH, DOUBLE POLE, DOUBLE THROW
K ARMATURE ONLY (D.C. MOTOR GENERATOR)	DD SWITCH, ROTARY
L D.C. GENERATOR	EE METER SHUNT
M D.C. MOTOR	FF GALVANOMETER
N A.C. GENERATOR OR ALTERNATOR	GG AMMETER
O A.C. MOTOR	HH VOLTMETER
	II CELL
P TRANSFORMER, AIR CORE	JJ BATTERY
Q TRANSFORMER, IRON CORE	KK CONNECTIONS
	LL NO CONNECTIONS
R COIL, AIR CORE	MM RESISTOR OR RESISTANCE | FIXED
S COIL, IRON CORE	NN RHEOSTAT

Answer Key

1. FF	5. JJ	9. NN	13. D	17. H	21. L	25. P	29. T	33. Z	37. BB
2. GG	6. KK	10. A	14. E	18. I	22. M	26. Q	30. U	34. X	38. CC
3. HH	7. LL	11. B	15. F	19. J	23. N	27. R	31. V	35. Y	39. DD
4. II	8. MM	12. C	16. G	20. K	24. O	28. S	32. W	36. AA	40. EE

VOCABULARY FOR ELECTRICIANS

The words used in electrical work are derived from the vocabulary of science and from the vocabulary of tools and mechanics. Although their meaning is often determined by convention, for the most part they have been established by laws, such as the various Electrical Codes.

DIRECTIONS: Use a separate, blank sheet to write out your answers to these questions. Try to write independently, without looking at our answers. After you have done your best on your own you'll be able to go back and review, comparing your answers with ours.

The answer for each question is given with the question. In addition to the answer we have provided more extended explanations, wherever we felt they would be helpful.

Electrical code review

(The following questions are based on the electrical code generally used throughout the country. While these questions may be typical, enough variations in codes compel you to review the code for your particular area.

Q. 1. Explain meanings of (A) Low potential (B) High potential (C) Extra high potential.

A.   (A) 600 volts or less (B) between 601 and 5,000 volts (C) over 5,000 volts.

Q. 2. Give five factors to be considered in determining whether to use a device, fitting, apparatus or electrical appliance.

A.   (1) suitability for installation and use in conformity with the Electrical Code (2) mechanical strength and durability (3) electrical insulation (4) heating effects under normal and abnormal conditions (5) arcing effects.

Q. 3. Describe a satisfactory base on which live parts are to be mounted.

A.   Of insulating material, designed to withstand the most severe conditions liable to arise in service. Holes for supporting screws countersunk or located to allow ½ inch between the screw head and nearest live metal part. Nuts or screw heads on underside of the base countersunk and sealed with waterproof compound.

Q. 4. What compounds may be used as a lubricant in inserting conductors in raceways?

A.   Graphite, talc, or other approved compounds.

Q. 5. What general principles should be followed in laying out an installation.

A.   Work should be started from a center of distribution and the switches and cutouts, controlling and connected with the branches, be grouped together in a safe and easily accessible place where they can readily be reached for repairs or attention. The load should be divided as evenly as possible among the branches and all complicated and unnecessary wiring avoided.

Q. 6. Overhead service conductors, at the point of attachment to a building, shall be not less than .... feet above the ground.

A. Fifteen.

Q. 7. A wooden pole 35 feet long supporting overhead wires should be buried in the ground to a depth of .... feet.

A. Five.

Q. 8. Give the minimum clearance above ground of wires (A) above alleys and driveways on other than residential property (B) supplying lights in automobile parking lots (C) between buildings on residential property.

A. (A) Eighteen feet (B) twelve feet (C) ten feet.

Q. 9. What precautions should be followed in preparing a string of lights for temporary festoon lighting?

A. The voltage between any two conductors should not be over 300 volts. Wiring must be arranged so that not more than 15 amperes will be placed on a branch circuit fuse. Socketsets and receptacles must be of approved moulded composition, waterproof type. All joints must be substantially soldered and covered with both rubber and friction tape and then painted with insulating paint. No. 14 or larger wire must be used with standard sockets, No. 18 or larger with intermediate and smaller size lamps. Lighting strings must not be supported from fire escapes or drainpipes and must be insulated from their supports by strain insulators.

Q. 10. How would you run service conductors from overhead supply wires underground to a building?

A. Should be run in approved, threaded rigid metallic conduit (not enamel conduit) and the portion of the wire underground, and to a point at least eight feet above ground, must be lead covered or have similar approved protection.

Q. 11. What type of conduit must be used for wiring on exterior of buildings?

A. Threaded rigged metallic conduit made of weatherproof material.

Q. 12. What size wire must be used in service entrance conductors?

A. Not smaller than No. 8.

Q. 13. Describe three ways in which a service switch may be installed.

A. (1) As an air-break or oil-immersed switch mounted on a switchboard or panelboard which is accessible to qualified persons only (2) As an air-break or oil-immersed switch enclosed in a metal case. An enclosed service switch of 600 amperes or less must be externally operable and readily accessible (3) Where the current of a circuit or group of circuits is separately metered, switch and cutout must be installed to control each separately: switch and cutout enclosed: switch externally operable.

Q. 14. How should wires be located in damp locations?

A. Open wires in damp places shall be located to permanently maintain an air space between them and pipes which they cross. Wire run in proximity to water pipes or tanks are considered exposed to moisture. Wires must be run over, rather than under pipes on which moisture may gather, or which may leak.

Q. 15. When may link fuses be used?

A. On switches of over 600 amperes capacity.

Q. 16. How are plug fuses of 15 ampere capacity or less distinguished from those of larger capacity?

A. By a hexagonal (eight-sided) opening in the cap through which the mica window shows; or a hexagonal recess in the cap; or some other prominent eight-sided feature of construction.

Q. 17. What is the general requirement for the use of overcurrent devices (automatic overcurrent protection)?

A. In general, overcurrent devices must be provided in all constant-potential interior wiring systems and so placed as to protect each ungrounded conductor; must be located at the point where the conductor receives its supply.

Q. 18. When is a conductor considered as properly protected?

A. By use of fuses or circuit breakers of the time-delay-thermal type with fixed settings or ratings not higher than the allowable carrying capacity of the wires; when circuit breakers of the instantaneous or time-delay magnetic type are used with a setting not greater than 125 per-cent of the instantaneous or allowable capacity of the wires.

Q. 19. What is the maximum allowable rating of fuses or setting of over-current breakers or controllers when used as motor running protective devices in terms of motor full-load current?

A. One hundred and twenty-five per-cent of the motor full load current.

Q. 20. Under what conditions may the controller for a D.C. motor serve as the motor running protective device?

A. If it is equipped with a suitable number of over-current units (trip coils, relays or thermal cutouts) and these over-current units are operative in both the starting and running positions.

Q. 21. Describe the conductor to be grounded in the following alternating current interior wiring systems (A) single-phase, 2 wire (B) single-phase 3 wire (C) multiphase systems having one wire common to all phases (D) multiphase systems having one phase grounded (E) multiphase systems in which one phase is used as in (B) above. How would you identify the grounded conductor?

A. (A) the identified conductor (B) the identified neutral conductor (C) the identified common conductor (E) the identified neutral conductor, one phase only can be grounded. The grounded conductor should be the white wire.

Q. 22. Describe four ways in which to assure the electrical continuity of a raceway system containing a conductor at more than 150 volts to the ground.

A. (A) Threaded fittings with joints made up tight (B) threadless fittings, made up tight, including fittings for rigid conduit, electrical metallic tubing, armored cable and flexible conduit (C) bonding jumpers of a size equal to that specified for the grounding conductor for interior conduit, with proper fittings (D) two locknuts, one inside, one outside of boxes or cabinets.

Q. 23. Describe a satisfactory grounding electrode to be used where a continuous metallic underground water piping system is not available.

A. An electrode of plate copper at least .06 inch thick, or iron or steel plate at least 1/4 inch thick, presenting two square feet of surface to the soil, and buried below permanent moisture level.

Q. 24. What information should appear on the nameplate of a generator or motor?

A. Maker's name, rating in kilowatts or kilovolts amperes, normal volts and amperes corresponding to the rating and revolutions per minute, for generators. For motors, maker's name, rating in horsepower, volts and amperes, including those for the secondary of a wound rotor type motor, the normal full load speed and the interval during which it can operate starting cold, before reaching its rated temperature.

Q. 25. Under what conditions may a single disconnecting means serve a group of motors?

A. If the motors drive the different parts of a single machine or apparatus (metal or woodworking machines for example) groups or motors under the protection of one set of automatic overcurrent protective devices; groups of motors in a single room and within sight of the disconnecting means.

Q. 26. What information should appear on the nameplate of a transformer?

A. Maker's name, rating in kilovolt amperes, primary and secondary voltage ratings, frequency and number of phases. If the liquid-filled type, the liquid capacity. Each capacitor for power correction must be provided with a plate carrying the maker's name, k.v.a., voltage, frequency and number of phases.

Q. 27. What general principles should be followed in installing switches?

A. They should not be placed where exposed to mechanical injury or in the vicinity of easily ignitable material or where exposed to inflammable dust or flying of combustible materials, except those of the oil immersed type which should be enclosed in metal boxes and cabinets. All switches operating over 100 volts to the ground other than those mounted on switchboards, open control panels and reversing switches must be enclosed in metal boxes or cabinets and must be of the externally operable type, if of 800 amperes or less, except oil switches, circuit breakers and similar devices which have casings.

Q. 28. What precaution should be taken in installing a knife switch?

A. Should not be placed where they might be closed by gravity. Double throw knife switches may be mounted for either vertical or horizontal throw, but if vertical, a locking device must be provided to assure the blade remaining in the open position when so set.

Q. 29. Give five rules which determine the location of switchboards?

A. (1) Should be so placed as to reduce danger of fire, space behind the board must not be used for storage (2) leave three feet between the top of the board and the ceiling (3) must be accessible from all sides when the connections are on the back (4) should not be exposed to moisture (5) switchboard frame should be grounded.

Q. 30. Explain the regulations which control the installation of lighting fixtures?

A. Metal fixtures on circuits above 150 volts and metal electrical fixtures used with conduit, armored cable or metal raceways must be grounded. Gas piping to which fixtures are attached must be grounded. Combination gas-electric fixtures may not be installed. Fixtures are considered grounded when mechanically connected, permanently and effectively to a metal conduit, tubing, armored cable, or a metal raceway system. Fixtures and supports should have adequate mechanical strength and supports should consist of suspension from the gas piping or special hangar by means of a hickey or support from the outlet box (ceiling or side wall fixtures) by means of a fixture stud or by metal straps fastened to studs or lugs in the outlet box. Fixtures weighing five pounds or less may be supported by straps and secured to strap by two machine screws. Fixtures weighing 50 pounds or more must be supported independent of the outlet box, by a hangar. Gas pipes shall be covered with insulating tubing back of the blind hickey. Fixtures must be installed so that the connections between the fixtures and the branch circuit wires will be available for inspection without disconnecting any portion of the wiring, unless the fixture is attached by an approved plugging device.

Q. 31. What precautions should be taken in installing a lamp holder in a closet?

A. Flexible cord pendant lamps in closets (other than linen and clothes closets) should be of such length that the lamps cannot be left in contact with combustible material and should not be exposed to mechanical injury. Lamp holding devices in clothes or linen closets must be installed on the wall or ceiling and controlled by wall or door switch or pull chain socket receptacle.

Q. 32. What precautions should be taken in installing a fixture in a bath room?

A. It should be equipped with a keyless type lamp holder and controlled by a wall switch. Metal pull chains of porcelain fixtures must be provided with insulating links.

Q. 33. Give seven rules regulating the control of electric ranges rated at over 1,650 watts.

A. (1) Controlling switch must be located within sight of and not more than 15 feet from the range between 30 inches and 5 feet from the floor (2) The switch may be part of the range assembly provided it is located as near as possible to the point where the conductor enters the range (3) Range disconnect switch shall not control lighting, motors or other appliances which are not part of the range assembly (4) A single polarized attachment plug and connector receptacle having a rating of not over 50 amperes may be used instead of a switch if it is designed so that it may be pulled out without leaving any live parts exposed (5) Each individual heating element must be controlled by a switch with "Off," "High," "Medium" and "Low" indications (6) Single pole switches may not be used in any grounded conductor (7) Where the switch controls a motor operated appliance, it must be within sight of the appliance.

Q. 34. What size wire must be used in a circuit containing a Mogul lamp holder?

A. No. 12 or larger.

Q. 35. Explain the outlet requirements for 15 ampere circuits.

A. Generally, not more than eight outlets are connected to a 15 ampere circuit in a store or show window, and must be wired with slow-burning wire, type SB. Show counter and display cases must be wired with No. 16 or larger and protected by a separate cutout. Unless No. 14 wire is installed to sockets, not more than 700 watts shall be supplied through one over-current protective device.

In residential buildings, one outlet shall be provided for each 15 linear feet of wall per room, except unfinished attics, kitchens or bathrooms. At least one 10 ampere outlet shall be provided in each kitchen and either in breakfast or dining room.

Oil burner, automatic stoker and air conditioner shall be supplied by an individual

15 ampere circuit or appliance branch circuit.

Necessary outlets in a building are: one in attic controlled by switch at foot of stairs; one in basement controlled by switch at head of stairs; one to illuminate front of furnace; one over, or within three feet of permanently located laundry tub in basement.

Q. 36. Describe Class I, Class II and Class III hazardous locations.

A. Class I—Where inflammable, volatile liquids, gases or mixtures are manufactured or used or handled outside of their original containers. Such as work rooms in dry-cleaning plants, gasoline pumps and discharge pedestals at service stations, pump houses or gasoline storage tanks, varnish manufacturing plants, spray-paint shops, etc.

Class II—Where inflammable dust or flyers collect, such as flour mills, feed mills, grain elevators, sugar cocoa or coal pulverizing plants, cotton and textile mills, clothing manufacturing plants, woodworking plants, etc.

Class III—Where combustible fibres are stored such as warehouses in which cotton, cotton linters, cotton waste, jute, baled waste, kapok, excelsior, etc., are stored.

Q. 37. How would you install a fuse in a Class I hazardous location? In a Class II hazardous location?

A. Class I—Must be mounted in an explosion proof enclosure. Fuse cutout bases and enclosures must be of type approved for use in explosive atmosphere. Class II—Must be enclosed in dust-tight metal cases or cabinets and circuit breakers must be of dust-tight or dust-tight oil-immersed type.

Q. 38. How would you provide service for a private garage from a house.

A. By a lead covered conductor run in threaded rigid iron conduit and buried at least 18 inches below the surface of the ground. An approved switch (snap, flush or externally operated knife switch) at the entrance of the service conductor, arranged to cut off all ungrounded conductors in the garage. Service conductors protected by fuses or circuit breakers at cut out cabinet where the conductors leave the house.

Q. 39. What restrictions are placed by the NYC Electrical Code on motors operating at more than 7,500 volts.

A. They may not be installed except in substations and fire-resistive motor rooms.

Q. 40. What preliminary steps must be taken before installation of a high tension vertical distribution system.   (6731)

A. Special permission must be obtained from the Department of Water Supply, Gas and Electricity and work must not begin until a complete plan of the system has been approved.

**(NOTE ON ELECTRICAL CODES. Electrical codes have been changing with great rapidity in recent times. Code items in this section may be obsolete even as this book goes to print. Before taking your examination, review the latest edition of your local code, and try to become familiar with the standards of the National Board of Fire Underwriters.)

ELECTRICAL CODE DEFINITIONS

The words used in electrical work are derived from the vocabulary of science and from the vocabulary of tools and mechanics. Although their meaning is often determined by convention, for the most part they have been established by laws, such as the various Electrical Codes.

DIRECTIONS: Use a separate, blank sheet to write out your answers to these questions. Try to write independently, without looking at our answers. After you have done your best on your own you'll be able to go back and review, comparing your answers with ours.

Can You Define These Terms?

1. Accessible; (A) as applied to wiring methods; (B) as applied to equipment means
2. Adjustable speed motor is one in which
3. Appliances are
4. An Automatic Door is one which
5. Automatic over current protection means use of a device such as
6. Branch Circuit is
7. Cable is
8. Certificate of Inspection is
9. Circuit Breaker is
10. Concealed refers to wires which
11. Conductor is
12. Controller is
13. Cutout Box is an enclosure
14. Dead-front (as applied to switchboards and panel boards) means
15. Demand Factor of any system or part of a system is
16. Device is
17. Different Systems are those which
18. Dustproof means
19. Dusttight means
20. Continuous Duty is
21. Intermittent Duty is
22. Periodic Duty is
23. Short-time Duty is
24. Varying Duty is
25. Enclosed means
26. Equipment is a general term including
27. Explosion-proof means
28. Exposed means
29. An Externally Operable switch is one which
30. Factory Yard is
31. Feeder is
32. Fitting is an accessory such as
33. Flexible Conduit is
34. Flexible Cord is
35. General Use Switch is one
36. Grounding Conductor is
37. Guarded means
38. Hazardous Locations are
39. Hoistway is
40. Isolated means
41. Isolated Plant is
42. Isolating Switch is
43. Lighting Outlet is
44. License is
45. Main Distribution Board or Center consists of
46. Mains are
47. Manually Operable means
48. Master Electrician is
49. Master Service means
50. Motor Control Equipment includes
51. Motor Installation includes
52. Motor Room is

53. Service Conductors are
54. Service Conduit is
55. Service Drop is
56. Service Entrance Conductors are
57. Service Equipment consists of
58. Service Raceway is
59. Setting (of circuit breaker) is
60. Sub-station is

61. Switchboard is
62. System Ground Conductor is
63. Totally Enclosed Motor is a motor which is
64. Vapor-tight means
65. Ventilated means
66. Voltage (of a circuit) is
67. Voltage to Ground means
68. Weatherproof means

Here's What We Think They Mean!

Here are the official definitions of the terms you
have just given your explanations for, according to
the electrical code. Check your answers with these.
Don't try to memorize these definitions but you
should understand the full meaning of each term.

1. (A) Not permanently closed in by the structure or finish of the building, capable of being removed without disturbing the building structure or finish (B) admitting close approach because not guarded by locked doors, elevation or other effective means.

2. The speed can be varied gradually over a considerable range, but when once adjusted remains practically unaffected by the load, such as shunt motors designed for a variation of field strength.

3. Current-consuming equipment, fixed or portable.

4. Closes automatically by means of a device operated by heat.

5. A fuse or current breaker by which the electrical continuity of a circuit will be automatically broken by overcurrent or voltage.

6. That portion of a wiring system extending beyond the final overcurrent device protecting the circuit.

7. A stranded conductor (single conductor cable) or a combination of conductors insulated from one another (multiple conductor cable).

8. The certificate of the Bureau of WSG & E that the installation, alteration or repair of electric wiring or appliances for light, heat or power in or on a building, specified in such certificate has been inspected and is approved by the department either temporarily or finally.

9. A device designed to open a current-carrying circuit without injury to itself, only on the occurrence of abnormal conditions. The term, as used in the Code, applies only to the automatic type designed to trip on a predetermined overload of current.

10. Are rendered inaccessible by the structure or finish of the building. Wires in concealed raceways are considered concealed even though they may become accessible by withdrawing them.

11. A wire or cable or other form of metal suitable for carrying electrical energy.

12. A device or group of devices, which serve to govern, in some predetermined manner, electric power delivered.

13. Designed for surface mounting and having swinging doors or covers secured directly to and telescoping with the walls of the box proper.

14. Boards that are so designed and constructed that current-paying parts are not exposed in such manner that persons are liable to come into contact with them while operating the switches or renewing fuses, and so that persons cannot come into contact with the current carrying parts at any time without using special means to gain access to such parts.

15. The ratio of the maximum demand of the system, or part of the system, to the total connected load of the system, or of the part of the system under consideration.

16. A unit of an electrical system other than a conductor which is intended to carry but not consume electrical energy.

17. Derive their supply from (1) different sources of current (2) transformers connected to separate primary circuits, or (3) transformers having different maximum secondary voltages (4) sources of different voltage where the voltage of one circuit is over three hundred percent greater

    than the other, or (5) where one circuit is protected by a different over-current protection device from another, and the difference between these devices is more than seven hundred percent.

18. So constructed or protected that an accumulation of dust will not interfere with its successful operation.

19. So constructed that dust will not enter the enclosing case.

20. A requirement of service that demands operation at a substantially constant load for an indefinitely long time.

21. A requirement of service that demands operation for alternate intervals of (1) load and no load or (2) load and rest, or (3) load, no load and rest.

22. A type of intermittent duty in which the load conditions are regularly recurrent.

23. A requirement of service that demands operation at a substantially constant load for a short and definitely specified time.

24. A requirement of service that demands operation at loads, and for intervals of time, both of which may be subjected to wide variation.

25. Surrounded by a case which will prevent accidental contact with live parts.

26. Material, fittings, devices, appliances, fixtures, apparatus and the like, used as a part of, or in connection with an electrical installation.

27. Enclosed in a case which is designed and constructed to withstand an explosion of a specified gas or dust which may occur within it, and to prevent ignition of the specified gas or dust surrounding the enclosure by sparks, flashes or

explosions of the specified gas or dust, which may occur within the enclosure.

28. Accessible, not concealed.

29. Capable of being operated without exposing the operator to contact with live parts. (This term is applied to equipment such as a switch that is enclosed in a case or cabinet).

30. A plot containing an assemblage of buildings served by an isolated plant, or by a substation, or by a master service and permitting access from building to building within the yard.

31. Any conductor of a wiring system between the main switchboard or point of distribution, and the branch circuit over-current device.

32. Such as a locknut, bushing or other part of a wiring system which is intended primarily to perform a mechanical rather than an electrical function.

33. A flexible metal tube made up of strips of metal wound in a close spiral.

34. A small flexible cable consisting of two or more conductors, separately insulated, each made up of a number of strands of very small wire. The two or more separately insulated conductors are usually twisted together to form the cord (twisted cord); in some cases are parallel to each other and are surrounded by an outer braid or covering (parallel cord).

35. Which is intended for use in a general distribution and branch circuit. It is rated in amperes and is capable of interrupting its rated voltage.

36. A conductor which is used to connect the equipment device or wiring system with a grounding electrode or electrodes.

37. Covered, shielded, fenced, enclosed or otherwise protected by means of suitable covers or casings, barriers, rails or screens, mats or platforms, to prevent dangerous contact or approach by persons or objects to a point of danger.

38. Premises, locations, rooms or portions thereof in which (A) inflammable gases, inflammable volatile liquids, mixtures or other inflammable substances are manufactured or used or are stored in other than original containers, or **(B)**

where combustible dust or flyings are liable to be present in quantities sufficient to produce an explosive or combustible mixture or (C) where easily ignitible fibres or materials producing combustible flyings are handled, manufactured, stored or used.

39. Any shaftway, hatchway, well hole or other vertical opening or space in which an elevator or dumbwaiter is designed to operate.

40. Not readily accessible to persons unless special means for access are used.

41. A private electrical installation deriving energy from its own generator driven by a prime mover.

42. A switch intended for isolating a circuit from its source of power. It is to be operated only when the circuit has been opened by some other means.

43. An outlet intended for the direct connection of a lampholder, a lighting fixture, or a pendant cord terminating in a lampholder.

44. The written authorization of the Commissioner of the Bureau of WSE & G to an individual, partnership or corporation to engage in the business of installing, altering or repairing electric wiring or appliances for light, heat or power in or on any building or premises or lot in the city.

45. One or more cutouts or switches and cutouts supplied by service entrance conductors and controlling feeders, sub-feeders or branch circuits.

46. Conductors of a wiring system between the lines of the public utility company and other source of supply and the main switchboard or point of distribution.

47. Operated by a person or by personal intervention. A manual operation may be the initial operation of a certain series in which the subsequent operations may be automatic. Manually operated devices are of two classes—those which are operated directly by hand, such as an ordinary knife switch, and those which are auto-manual, in which the action is initiated by hand but carried out automatically, such as a magnetically operated switch, the opening and closing of which is controlled by manually operated push buttons.

48. Any person, partnership or corporation who engages in or carries on as his or its regular business of installing, erecting, altering, extending, maintaining or repairing electrical wiring, apparatus, fixtures, devices, appliances or equipment utilized or designed for the utilization of electricity for light, heat or power purposes or for signalling systems operating on fifty volts or more, exclusive of interior fire alarm systems and their attachments under the jurisdiction of the Fire Department and the Board of Standards and Appeals, and who carries on such business as an independent contractor having the final determination and the full responsibility for the manner in which the work is done, for the materials used and for the selection, supervision and control of any persons employed on the work engaged in by said person, partnership or corporation.

49. The service conductors and service equipment supplying a group of buildings under one management.

50. Apparatus and the devices immediately accessory thereto for starting, stopping, regulating, controlling or protecting electrical motors. Switches or circuit breakers which are used, or intended to be used, for motor starting are to be considered as motor control equipment. Where the equipment mounted on switchboards, panelboards, etc., is used essentially or primarily for starting, stopping, regulating and controlling motors, it is to be considered as motor control equipment.

51. The motor and its control equipment together with all necessary wiring.

52. A building, room or separate space within which a motor installation is located and which has such construction or arrangement as to prevent the entrance of unauthorized persons, or interference by them with the equipment inside and which has all entrances not under the observation of a qualified attendant kept locked, and which has signs, prohibiting entrance to unauthorized persons, conspicuously displayed at entrance. An enclosure which is not of sufficient size to permit the entrance of attendants and to afford safe access and working space within the enclosure cannot be considered as a motor room.

53. That portion of the supply, conductors which extend from the street main or duct to the

service equipment of the building supplied. For overhead conductors, this includes the conductors from the last line pole to the service equipment.

54. The conduit or duct that contains underground service conductors and extends from the junction with outside supply wires into the consumer's premises.

55. That portion of overhead service conductors between the last line pole and the first point of attachment to the building.

56. That portion of service conductors between the terminals of service equipment and a point outside the building, clear of building walls, where joined by tap or splice to the service drop or to street mains or other source of supply.

57. The necessary equipment, usually consisting of circuit breaker or switch and fuses and their accessories, located near point of entrance of supply conductors to a building and intended to constitute the main control and means of cutoff for the supply to that building.

58. The rigid steel conduit that encloses service entrance conductors.

59. The setting of an instantaneous trip circuit breaker is the current value in amperes at which it will trip; the setting of a time-delay circuit breaker is the value of current in amperes, which it will carry indefinitely and beyond which it will trip at specified values of overload and time.

60. A building, room, or enclosure, in which is installed transformers or generating equipment or other sub-station apparatus. The term generally includes isolated generating stations on the premises of the consumers.

61. A single panel, frame or assembly of panels, on which are mounted on the face or back, or both, switches, overcurrent and other protective devices, buses, and usual instruments. Switchboards are generally accessible from the rear as well as the front and are not intended to be installed in cabinets.

62. An auxiliary, grounded conductor used for connecting together the individual grounding conductors throughout a given area, but which is not part of a circuit wire.

63. So completely enclosed by integral or auxiliary covers as to practically prevent the circulation of air in the interior. Such a motor is not necessarily air-tight.

64. So enclosed that vapor will not enter the enclosure.

65. Provided with means to permit circulation of the air sufficiently to remove an excess of heat, fumes or vapors.

66. The greatest effective difference of potential between any two conductors of the circuit concerned.

67. In grounded circuits, the voltage between the given conductor and that point of the conductor of the circuit which is grounded: in ungrounded circuits, the greatest voltage between the given conductor and any other conductor of the circuit.

68. So constructed or protected that exposure to the weather will not interfere with successful operation.

ELECTRICIAN

ELECTRICAL CODE PROBLEMS

The words used in electrical work are derived from the vocabulary of science and from the vocabulary of tools and mechanics. Although their meaning is often determined by convention, for the most part they have been established by laws, such as the various Electrical Codes.

1. In most cities, the local public utility company has no jurisdiction over
   (A) location and type of service to be supplied to a building
   (B) wiring installations for light and power in buildings
   (C) location and type of service switch and metering equipment to be installed in buildings
   (D) maximum permissible starting current of motors when started directly across the line.

2. Most city Electrical Codes state that electrical metallic tubing shall not be used for interior wiring systems of more than 600 volts, nor for conductors larger than
   (A) No. 6   (B) No. 4
   (C) No. 2   (D) No. 0.

3. According to the Code, in order that armored cable will not be injured, the radius of the curve of the inner edge of any bend must be not less than
   (A) 3 times the diameter of the cable
   (B) 5 times the diameter of the cable
   (C) 7 times the diameter of the cable
   (D) 10 times the diameter of the cable.

4. The Code states that feeders over 40' in length supplying two branch circuits shall be not smaller than
   (A) 2 No. 14 AWG   (B) 2 No. 12 AWG
   (C) 2 No. 10 AWG   (D) 2 No. 8 AWG.

5. In accordance with the Code, circuit breakers for motor branch circuits protection shall have continuous current ratings not less than
   (A) 110% of the full load current of the motor
   (B) 115% of the full load current of the motor
   (C) 120% of the full load current of the motor
   (D) 125% of the full load current of the motor.

6. In accordance with the Code all wiring is to be installed so that when completed, the system will be free from shorts or grounds. A circuit installation of #12 wire with all safety devices in place, but lampholders, receptacles, fixtures and or appliances not connected, shall have a resistance between conductors and between all conductors and ground not less than
   (A) 10,000 ohms   (B) 100,000 ohms
   (C) 250,000 ohms   (D) 1,000,000 ohms.

7. The Code states that wires, cables and cords of all kinds except weather-proof wire shall have a
   (A) distinctive marking so that the maker may be readily identified
   (B) tag showing the minimum working voltage for which the wire was tested or approved
   (C) tag showing the maximum current passed through the conductor under test
   (D) tag showing the ultimate tensile strength.

8. The Code states that conductors supplying an individual motor shall have a minimum carrying capacity of
   (A) 110% of the motor full load current
   (B) 120% of the motor full load current
   (C) 125% of the motor full load current
   (D) 135% of the motor full load current.

9. For not more than three conductors in raceway, "based on a room temperature of 86°F" the allowable current carrying capacity, in amperes, of a No. 12, AWG type R conductor is
   (A) 15   (B) 20
   (C) 30   (D) 40.

S1111

10. In accordance with the Code, the grounding connection for interior metal raceways and armored cable shall be made at a point
    (A) not greater than 5 feet from the source of supply
    (B) not greater than 10 feet from the source of supply
    (C) as far as possible from the source of supply
    (D) as near as practicable to the source of supply.

11. In accordance with the Code, a grounding conductor for a direct current system shall have a current carrying capacity not less than that of the largest conductor supplied by the system and in no case less than that of
    (A) No. 12 copper wire
    (B) No. 10 copper wire
    (C) No. 8 copper wire
    (D) No. 6 copper wire.

12. In accordance with the Code, the number of No. 14 AWG type R conductors running through or terminating in a 1½" x 3¼" octagonal outlet or junction box, should not be greater than
    (A) 5
    (B) 6
    (C) 7
    (D) 8.

13. In accordance with the Code, motors
    (A) may be operated in series multiple
    (B) may be operated in multiple series
    (C) shall not be operated in series multiple
    (D) shall not be operated in multiple.

14. Two ¼ h.p. motors, under the protection of a single set of over-current devices and with or without other current consuming devices in the current, are considered as being sufficiently protected if the rating or setting of the over-current devices does not exceed
    (A) 15 amperes at 250 volts
    (B) 15 amperes at 125 volts
    (C) 30 amperes at 125 volts
    (D) 30 amperes at 250 volts.

Answer Key

(You'll learn more by writing your own answers before comparing them with these.)

Electrical Code Problems

1. B	5. B	9. B	13. C
2. D	6. D	10. D	14. B
3. B	7. A	11. C	
4. C	8. C	12. A	

SCRAMBLED DICTIONARY OF ELECTRICAL TERMS

The following alphabetical list of terms is intended for use both as a dictionary and as a testing device. For your convenience we have divided the list into a series of brief tests. As you go on to other sections in this book, you will find these terms being used over and over again. Familiarize yourself with them now, and help insure a high test score later.

SEVENTEEN TEST-TYPE QUIZZES FOR PRACTICE

ANSWER KEY APPEARS AFTER EACH TEST

TEST ONE

DIRECTIONS: In this test the numbered TERMS *in Column I are listed in alphabetic order. Select the correct* DEFINITION *in Column II and place the corresponding number next to the definition in Column I. To fix the meanings firmly in your mind, repeat the test until you are familiar with every term.*

COLUMN I

1. A— (A minus)
2. A+ (A plus)
3. Adapter
4. Admittance
5. Air Gap
6. Alloy
7. Alternating Current
8. A.M.
9. Ambient Temperature
10. Ammeter

Answer Key

(You'll learn more by writing your own answers before comparing them with these.)

1.	8	3.	9	5.	7	7.	6	9.	4
2.	1	4.	2	6.	10	8.	3	10.	5

COLUMN II

1. The point to which the positive terminal of the supply is to be connected.
2. The measure of ease with which an alternating current flows in a circuit.
3. Amplitude Modulation.
4. The temperature of air or other medium surrounding an electrical device.
5. Measures the current flow in amperes in a circuit.
6. An electric current which reverses its direction of flow at regular intervals.
7. A path for electrical energy through air between two electrodes or core sections of a transformer.
8. The point to which the negative terminal of the supply is to be connected.
9. A device used to change, temporarily or permanently, the terminal connections of a circuit or part.
10. A mixture of two or more metals.

TEST TWO

DIRECTIONS: In this test the numbered TERMS *in Column I are listed in alphabetic order. Select the correct* DEFINITION *in Column II and place the corresponding number next to the definition in Column I. To fix the meanings firmly in your mind, repeat the test until you are familiar with every term.*

TERMS	DEFINITION
COLUMN I	COLUMN II

11. Ampere

12. Ampere-Hour

13. Ampere-Turn

14. Amplitude

15. Apparent Power

16. Arc

17. Armature

18. Armored Cable

19. Artificial Ground

20. Auto-Transformer

1. The maximum departure of an alternating current or voltage from zero value, measured in either direction from zero.

2. The movable portion of a magnetic circuit.

3. A luminous discharge of electricity between separated conductors.

4. The unit of electrical current flow. If a one ohm resistance is connected to a one volt source, one ampere will flow.

5. A transformer in which part of the primary winding serves also as the secondary, or in which part of the secondary winding is also in the primary circuit.

6. Two or more individually insulated conductors, wrapped in an insulating cover and enclosed within an interlocking spirally-wound galvanized steel cover.

7. A grounding electrode, metal plate or pipe, buried in the earth.

8. The product of volts and amperes in an alternating current circuit whose voltage and current are not in phase, measured by volt-amperes.

9. A unit of magnetizing force equal to the number of amperes of current multiplied by the number of turns in the winding in which it flows.

10. A current of one ampere flowing for one hour.

Answer Key

(Please make every effort to answer the questions on your own before looking at these answers. You'll make faster progress by following this rule.)

11. 4	13. 9	15. 8	17. 2	19. 7
12. 10	14. 1	16. 3	18. 6	20. 5

TEST THREE

DIRECTIONS: In this test the numbered TERMS *in Column I are listed in alphabetic order. Select the correct* DEFINITION *in Column II and place the corresponding number next to the definition in Column I. To fix the meanings firmly in your mind, repeat the test until you are familiar with every term.*

TERMS COLUMN I	DEFINITION COLUMN II
21. B— (B minus)	1. The point in a circuit to which the negative terminal of the plate supply is to be connected.
22. B+ (B plus)	2. An electric charge which remains in an insulated conductor due to a nearby charge of opposite polarity.
23. B & S Gauge	3. A condenser, grid bias voltage and Centigrade temperature scale.
24. Bipolar	4. Two parallel paths connected between a common source of potential, with each path divided into two at intermediate junction points, and with an indicating element (galvanometer) bridged from one of the junctions to the other.
25. Booster	5. The standard gauge used in the United States to specify wire sizes. (Brown & Sharpe)
26. Bound Charge	6. The voltage at which the insulation between two conductors will break down.
27. Breakdown Voltage	7. A protective enclosure for buses (conductors formed by large cross-section bars or rods).
28. Bridge Circuit	8. The point in a circuit to which the positive terminal of the plate supply is to be connected.
29. Busway	9. A transformer or generator inserted in a circuit to increase the voltage to overcome line drop.
30. C	10. Having two magnetic poles, north and south; two-pole.

Answer Key

(Please make every effort to answer the questions on your own before looking at these answers. You'll make faster progress by following this rule.)

21. 1	23. 5	25. 9	27. 6	29. 7
22. 8	24. 10	26. 2	28. 4	30. 3

TEST FOUR

DIRECTIONS: In this test the numbered TERMS *in Column I are listed in alphabetic order. Select the correct* DEFINITION *in Column II and place the corresponding number next to the definition in Column I. To fix the meanings firmly in your mind, repeat the test until you are familiar with every term.*

TERMS COLUMN I	DEFINITION COLUMN II
31. C— (C minus)	1. The point in a vacuum tube circuit to which the negative terminal of the grid bias source is to be connected.
32. C+ (C plus)	2. The effect of capacitance in opposing the flow of alternating or pulsating current.
33. Candelbra Lampholder	3. A lampholder having a nominal screw diameter of 1/2 inch.
34. Candlepower	4. A unit of light equal to the intensity from a standard candle.
35. Capacitance	5. The electrical size of a condenser determining the amount of electrical energy which can be stored by a given voltage.
36. Capacitive Circuit	6. A fuse enclosed with an insulating and protective covering and provided with connections at its ends.
37. Capacitive Reactance	7. A split-phase motor in which a condenser displaces part of the current in phase from the remainder in order that the motor may be self-starting on single phase supply current.
38. Capacitor Motor	8. One containing more capacitive reactance than inductive reactance.
39. Capacity	9. Electrostatic capacity.
40. Cartridge Fuse	10. The point in a vacuum tube circuit to which the positive terminal of the grid bias source is to be connected.

Answer Key

(Please make every effort to answer the questions on your own before looking at these answers. You'll make faster progress by following this rule.)

31. 1	33. 3	35. 9	37. 2	39. 5
32. 10	34. 4	36. 8	38. 7	40. 6

TEST FIVE

DIRECTIONS: In this test the numbered TERMS *in Column I are listed in alphabetic order. Select the correct* DEFINITION *in Column II and place the corresponding number next to the definition in Column I. To fix the meanings firmly in your mind, repeat the test until you are familiar with every term.*

TERMS COLUMN I	DEFINITION COLUMN II
41. Cellular Metal Floor Raceway	1. A ring of insulated copper segments connected to the windings of an armature, which bear brushes connecting the armature winding to the outside circuits to change the induced alternating current of the armature to direct current in the output.
42. Centigrade	2. A unit of cross-sectional-area; equals the area of a circle with a diameter of one mil or 1/1,000 inch.
43. Centimeter	3. The greatest effective difference of potential between any two conductors in a given circuit.
44. Circuit	4. Unit of metric system of measurement, equals approx. .39 inch; 1/100th of a meter.
45. Circuit-Breaker	5. A raceway formed in the hollow spaces of cellular metal floors, together with its fittings.
46. Circuit Voltage	6. The European scale of measuring temperature. 0 represents temperature of melting ice, 100 the temperature of boiling water at sea level.
47. Circular Mil	7. A complete path over which an electric current can flow.
48. Circular Mil Foot	8. A device to automatically open a circuit in case of over-current, sometimes in case of under-voltage.
49. Commutation	9. A unit of conductor size, equal to a portion of the conductor having a cross-sectional area of one circular mil and length of one foot.
50. Commutator	10. Conversion of alternating current to direct current.

Answer Key

(Please make every effort to answer the questions on your own before looking at these answers. You'll make faster progress by following this rule.)

41. 5	43. 4	45. 8	47. 2	49. 10
42. 6	44. 7	46. 3	48. 9	50. 1

TEST SIX

DIRECTIONS: *In this test the numbered* TERMS *in Column I are listed in alphabetic order. Select the correct* DEFINITION *in Column II and place the corresponding number next to the definition in Column I. To fix the meanings firmly in your mind, repeat the test until you are familiar with every term.*

TERMS	DEFINITION
COLUMN I	COLUMN II

51. Compound Winding

52. Compound Wound Generator

53. Compound Wound Motor

54. Conductance

55. Conductivity

56. Conduit

57. Connector

58. Contact

59. Control Panel

60. Coulomb

1. Any substance in which a difference of voltage between two points causes current to flow between those points; wires, cables, etc.
2. A metallic enclosure for conductors.
3. A device to join conductors by soldering or mechanical means.
4. In a common magnetic circuit, the winding connecting in series with the load.
5. A direct current motor having a series and shunt winding for its field.
6. A unit of electrical charge; the quantity of electricity passing in one second through a circuit in which the rate of flow is one ampere.
7. A terminal to which a connection can be made.
8. An exposed or enclosed upright panel carrying switches and other protective, controlling and measuring devices for electric machinery or equipment.
9. The measure of ease with which a substance conducts electricity, measured in ohms.
10. A direct current generator having a series and shunt winding for its field.

Answer Key

(Please make every effort to answer the questions on your own before looking at these answers. You'll make faster progress by following this rule.)

51. 4	53. 5	55. 1	57. 3	59. 8
52. 10	54. 9	56. 2	58. 7	60. 6

TEST SEVEN

DIRECTIONS: In this test the numbered TERMS *in Column I are listed in alphabetic order. Select the correct* DEFINITION *in Column II and place the corresponding number next to the definition in Column I. To fix the meanings firmly in your mind, repeat the test until you are familiar with every term.*

TERMS COLUMN I	DEFINITION COLUMN II
61. Current	1. Switch or device connected to both sides of a circuit, or controlling both sides of a circuit.
62. Current Transformer	2. The ratio of the maximum demand of a system to the total connected load; maximum watts used at any time, divided by the total wattage of all equipment connected to the system.
63. Cycle	3. Direct current.
64. D.C.	4. The movement of electrons through a conductor; measured in amperes: milliamperes and micro-amperes.
65. Dead End	5. A complete reversal of alternating current, passing through a complete set of changes or motions in opposite directions, from a rise to maximum, return to zero, rise to maximum in the other direction, and another return to zero.
66. Demand Factor	6. The ends of circuit wires which are connected to supports, but do not carry an electric load.
67. Direct Current	7. The capacity distributed between conducting elements; distinguished from capacity concentrated in a condenser.
68. Distributed Capacity	8. One which simultaneously opens or closes two separate circuits or both sides of the same circuit.
69. Double Pole	9. An electric current that always flows in the same direction in its circuit.
70. Double Pole Switch	10. An instrument transformer with primary winding in series with a current-carrying conductor and secondary winding connected to a meter or device which is actuated by conductor current and current changes.

Answer Key

(Please make every effort to answer the questions on your own before looking at these answers. You'll make faster progress by following this rule.)

61. 4	63. 5	65. 6	67. 9	69. 1
62. 10	64. 3	66. 2	68. 7	70. 8

TEST EIGHT

DIRECTIONS: In this test the numbered TERMS *in Column I are listed in alphabetic order. Select the correct* DEFINITION *in Column II and place the corresponding number next to the definition in Column I. To fix the meanings firmly in your mind, repeat the test until you are familiar with every term.*

TERMS	DEFINITION
COLUMN I	**COLUMN II**

71. Double Throw Switch

72. Drop

73. D.S.C.

74. Duty Cycle

75. E

76. Edison Base

77. Effective Current

78. Efficiency

79. Electrochemistry

80. Electronics

1. The voltage drop developed across a resistor due to current flow through it.
2. Double silk insulation on a wire.
3. The percentage of total time during which an electrical device carries current.
4. The value of alternating current that will cause the same heating effect as a given value of direct current.
5. The ratio of energy output to energy input, expressed as a percentage.
6. The production or separation of chemical elements and compounds by the action of electric currents.
7. The science and art dealing with the flow of electricity or electrons through vacuums and gases confined within the envelopes of tubes or tanks.
8. The standard screw base used for light bulbs.
9. Voltage.
10. One which connects one circuit terminal to either of two other circuit terminals.

Answer Key

(Please make every effort to answer the questions on your own before looking at these answers. You'll make faster progress by following this rule.)

71. 10	73. 2	75. 9	77. 4	79. 6
72. 1	74. 3	76. 8	78. 5	80. 7

TEST NINE

DIRECTIONS: In this test the numbered TERMS *in Column I are listed in alphabetic order. Select the correct* DEFINITION *in Column II and place the corresponding number next to the definition in Column I. To fix the meanings firmly in your mind, repeat the test until you are familiar with every term.*

TERMS COLUMN I	DEFINITION COLUMN II
81. Farenheit	1. The basic measuring unit of capacity.
	2. Any conductor of a system between the service equipment (or the generator switchboard of an isolated plant) and the overcurrent devices that protect branch circuits.
82. Farad	
	3. A unit of illumination; the degree of illumination produced by a lumin-luminous flux of one lumen per square foot of surface area.
83. Feedback	
	4. A wire used to connect equipment or a wiring system with ground, or to a grounding electrode buried in the earth.
84. Feeder	
	5. A conductor providing electrical connection between the equipment and circuit and the earth; the metal portions of a support when used as a conductor.
85. Foot-Candle	
86. Four-Way Switch	6. A strip of wire or metal which, when it carries an excess of current over its rated capacity will burn out. Also called a cutout.
	7. The United States' temperature measuring system. 32 degrees is the temperature of freezing water; 212 the temperature of boiling water at sea level.
87. Fuse	
	8. Transfer of electric energy from one point in a system to a preceding point.
88. Gang Switch	9. One used in a circuit that permits a single lamp to be controlled from any of three or more positions: it has four terminals which alternately are joined together in different pairs.
89. Ground	
	10. Two or more rotary switches on one shaft and operated by the same control.
90. Grounding Conductor	

Answer Key

(Please make every effort to answer the questions on your own before looking at these answers. You'll make faster progress by following this rule.)

81. 7	83. 8	85. 3	87. 6	89. 5
82. 1	84. 2	86. 9	88. 10	90. 4

TEST TEN

DIRECTIONS: In this test the numbered TERMS *in Column I are listed in alphabetic order. Select the correct* DEFINITION *in Column II and place the corresponding number next to the definition in Column I. To fix the meanings firmly in your mind, repeat the test until you are familiar with every term.*

TERMS	DEFINITION
COLUMN I	COLUMN II

91. I

92. Impedance

93. Impulse

94. Induction motor

95. Inductive Circuit

96. Inductive Coupling

97. Inductor

98. Insulation is a material which

99. Intermediate Lampholder

100. Internal Resistance

1. A momentary increase in the current or voltage in a circuit.
2. A circuit containing more inductive reactance than capacitive reactance; such as one with many devices having iron core coils and windings; induction motors, etc.
3. A form in which energy is transferred from a coil in one circuit to a coil in another by induction.
4. A coil, with or without an iron core, which opposes changes in current because of its self-inductance.
5. The resistance of conductors inside electrical equipment, measured between terminal connections.
6. Current.
7. An A.C. motor in which energy from the stationary windings is transferred to conductors on the rotor by electromagnetic induction, and in which the rotor receives no current through any conductive contacts.
8. The total opposition which a circuit offers the flow of alternating current at a given frequency; combination of resistance and reactance, measured in ohms.
9. Has an electrical resistance high enough to allow of its use for separating one electrical circuit from another.
10. One with a screw diameter of 21/32 inch.

Answer Key

(Please make every effort to answer the questions on your own before looking at these answers. You'll make faster progress by following this rule.)

91. 6	93. 1	95. 2	97. 4	99. 10
92. 8	94. 7	96. 3	98. 9	100. 3

TEST ELEVEN

DIRECTIONS: In this test the numbered TERMS *in Column I are listed in alphabetic order. Select the correct* DEFINITION *in Column II and place the corresponding number next to the definition in Column I. To fix the meanings firmly in your mind, repeat the test until you are familiar with every term.*

TERMS COLUMN I	DEFINITION COLUMN II
101. Joule	1. Sum of all voltage sources acting in a complete circuit must be equal to the sum of all the voltage drops in the circuit.
102. Jumper	2. Switch in which one or more metal blades (usually copper), pivoted at one end, serve as the moving parts.
103. Kilocycle	3. An inductance or coil.
104. Kilowatt	4. A wire used as temporary connection.
105. Kilowatt-Hour	5. 1,000 watts.
106. Kirchoff's Current Law	6. The sum of all currents flowing to a point in a circuit must be equal to the sum of all currents flowing away from that point.
107. Kirchoff's Voltage Law	7. A measure of electrical energy; a power of one watt for one second; the work done by sending one ampere through a resistance of one ohm for one second.
108. Knife Switch	8. 1,000 cycles per second.
109. L	9. A unit of electric energy equal to the power rate of one kilowatt continuing for one hour.
110. Lagging Current	10. A.C. current (in an inductive circuit) whose zero values and maximum values in a given direction occur later than the zeros and corresponding maximums of the A.C. voltage in the same circuit.

Answer Key

(Please make every effort to answer the questions on your own before looking at these answers. You'll make faster progress by following this rule.)

101. 7	103. 8	105. 9	107. 1	109. 3
102. 4	104. 5	106. 6	108. 2	110. 10

TEST TWELVE

DIRECTIONS: In this test the numbered TERMS *in Column I are listed in alphabetic order. Select the correct* DEFINITION *in Column II and place the corresponding number next to the definition in Column I. To fix the meanings firmly in your mind, repeat the test until you are familiar with every term.*

TERMS COLUMN I	DEFINITION COLUMN II
111. Lampholder	1. The greatest value reached by A.C. current or voltage during any point in the cycle.
112. Leading Current	2. A value of multiplication by 1,000; 25M means 25,000.
113. Line Starter	3. A small strip of metal placed on a terminal screw or riveted to make a site for a soldered wire connection.
114. Line Voltage	4. A.C. current (in a capacitive circuit) whose zero values and maximum values in a given direction occur before the zeros and corresponding maximums of the A.C. voltage in the same circuit.
115. Load	5. The voltage at a wall outlet or terminal of a power line system.
116. Lug	6. One with a screw diameter of one inch.
117. M	7. A screw-shell device for receiving the screw base of a lamp bulb or other part; a lamp socket.
118. Maximum Value	8. A motor starter which applies full line voltage to motor immediately on operation of the starter.
119. Medium Lampholder	9. The total of equipment or consuming devices connected to a battery, generator or supply circuit; measured in watts, watt-hours. Ohms, amperes, volts.
120. Megohm	10. A resistance of 1,000,000 ohms.

Answer Key

(Please make every effort to answer the questions on your own before looking at these answers. You'll make faster progress by following this rule.)

111. 7	113. 8	115. 9	117. 2	119. 6
112. 4	114. 5	116. 3	118. 1	120. 10

TEST THIRTEEN

DIRECTIONS: In this test the numbered TERMS *in Column I are listed in alphabetic order. Select the correct* DEFINITION *in Column II and place the corresponding number next to the definition in Column I. To fix the meanings firmly in your mind, repeat the test until you are familiar with every term.*

TERMS COLUMN I	DEFINITION COLUMN II
121. Mogul Lampholder	1. An insulating material; one which offers extreme opposition to the flow of electricity.
122. Multipolar	2. An alloy of nickel, iron and chromium with high resistance and capable of standing high temperature; used in heating elements.
123. Mutual Inductance	3. An electric circuit in which the parts are connected in some special manner and cannot be classed as in series, in parallel, or series-parallel.
124. N.E.C.	4. National Electric Code.
125. Negative	5. One with a screw diameter of 1 1/2 inches.
126. Negative Charge	6. The property of a circuit which permits the action of mutual induction; the production of varying or alternating emf in one circuit by movement across its conductors of field lines rising from another nearby circuit with varying current.
127. Neutral	7. Neither positive nor negative; having zero potential; having electric potential intermediate between the potentials of other associated parts of the circuit, positive with reference to some parts, negative with reference to others.
128. Network	8. A machine having more than two magnetic poles; two-pole type is known as bipolar or two pole.
129. Michrome	9. A potential less than that of another potential or of the earth.
130. Non-Conductor	10. The condition in which a body has more than the normal quantities of negative electrons; more negative electricity than an uncharged or neutral body.

Answer Key

121. 5	123. 6	125. 9	127. 7	129. 2
122. 8	124. 4	126. 10	128. 3	130. 1

TEST FOURTEEN

DIRECTIONS: In this test the numbered TERMS *in Column I are listed in alphabetic order. Select the correct* DEFINITION *in Column II and place the corresponding number next to the definition in Column I. To fix the meanings firmly in your mind, repeat the test until you are familiar with every term.*

TERMS
COLUMN I

131. Non-Inductive

132. Non-Magnetic

133. Non-metallic Sheated Cable

134. Non-Metallic Surface Extension

135. Non-Metallic Waterproof Wiring

136. No-Voltage Release

137. Ohm

138. Ohm's Law

139. Open Wiring

140. Parallel Connection

DEFINITION
COLUMN II

1. The relationship between voltage, current and resistance in a D.C. circuit or the relationship between voltage, current and impedance in A.C. circuits.

2. A switch held by an electromagnet in a closed position and released when voltage across the magnet winding drops to a pre-determined minimum.

3. A multiple-conductor, rubber sheathed cable used for exposed wiring in wet locations where exposed to mild corrosive fumes or vapors.

4. A connection of two or more circuits, or parts of circuits, between the same terminals of a source of current so that the same voltage difference is applied to all parts and the current through each is proportionate to the overall voltage and the resistance of the individual part.

5. Wire or cable covered by insulating compounds and fabric braids in layers providing some mechanical strength.

6. Insulated wires supported on knobs, cleats, or other insulators, but without any other enclosure or covering.

7. The unit of electrical resistance. Resistance is one ohm when a D.C. voltage of one volt will send a current of one ampere through.

8. Two individually insulated conductors attached to a fabric or other device arranged for convenient fastening to walls or other exposed surface.

9. Materials such as paper, glass, wood, etc., which are not affected by magnetic fields.

10. So placed that the effects of self-induction are caused to cancel and to leave a negligible remaining self-induction.

Answer Key

131. 10	133. 5	135. 3	137. 7	139. 6
132. 9	134. 8	136. 2	138. 1	140. 4

TEST FIFTEEN

DIRECTIONS: In this test the numbered TERMS *in Column I are listed in alphabetic order. Select the correct* DEFINITION *in Column II and place the corresponding number next to the definition in Column I. To fix the meanings firmly in your mind, repeat the test until you are familiar with every term.*

TERMS COLUMN I	DEFINITION COLUMN II
141. Peak	1. One end of a magnet, one electrode of a battery.
142. Period	2. The electrical condition of a body which has less than the normal quantity of negative electrons.
143. Phillips Screw	3. The term used to describe a terminal with fewer electrons than normal so that it attracts electrons. Electrons flow into the positive terminals of a voltage source.
144. Pigtail	4. A motor which operates from a supply system of more than one phase.
145. Polarity in a circuit	5. The maximum instantaneous value of a varying voltage or current.
146. Pole	6. The time required for a complete cycle of alternating current or voltage; for 60 cycles per second, would be 1/60 second.
147. Polyphase	7. A flexible connection between a stationary terminal and a part which has a short range of motion.
148. Polyphase Motor	8. A screw having an indented cross in its head in place of the slot.
149. Positive	9. The quality of having two opposite charges, one positive, one negative.
150. Positive Charge	10. Having two or more alternating currents and potentials acting at the same time.

Answer Key

(Please make every effort to answer the questions on your own before looking at these answers. You'll make faster progress by following this rule.)

141.	5	143.	8	145.	9	147.	10	149.	3
142.	6	144.	7	146.	1	148.	4	150.	2

TEST SIXTEEN

DIRECTIONS: In this test the numbered TERMS in Column I are listed in alphabetic order. Select the correct DEFINITION in Column II and place the corresponding number next to the definition in Column I. To fix the meanings firmly in your mind, repeat the test until you are familiar with every term.

TERMS
COLUMN I

151. Potential

152. Potential Gradient

153. Potential Transformer

154. Power Factor

155. Power Factor Corrections

156. Power Level

157. Pulsating Current

158. Pulse

159. Q Factor

160. R

DEFINITION
COLUMN II

1. Resistance.
2. The addition of capacitance to alternating current circuit containing a great deal of inductance to lessen the amount of current that does no useful work; or, inductance might be added to a circuit containing excessive capacitance.
3. An instrument transformer with its primary connected between opposite sides of a line or between points having a potential difference, and with its secondary connected to a meter or other device which is actuated by the potential difference of the line.
4. The rate of change of potential with respect to the distance between two points.
5. A characteristic of a point in an electrical circuit based on its electric charge in comparison with the charge at some other reference point; would be more positive or more negative than the reference point.
6. The ratio of the voltage and current, or volt-amperes, that do useful work in an alternating current circuit or equipment, to the total voltage and current, volt-amperes, flowing in the circuit.
7. The amount of electrical power passing through a given point in a circuit; may be expressed in watts, decibels or volume units.
8. A rating used to indicate characteristics of coils and resonant circuits; reactance divided by ohmic resistance.
9. A current which changes in value but not in direction; direct current combined with a smaller value of alternating current.
10. A momentary sharp change in voltage or current.

Answer Key

151. 5	153. 3	155. 2	157. 9	159. 8
152. 4	154. 6	156. 7	158. 10	160. 1

TEST SEVENTEEN

DIRECTIONS: In this test the numbered TERMS *in Column I are listed in alphabetic order. Select the correct* DEFINITION *in Column II and place the corresponding number next to the definition in Column I. To fix the meanings firmly in your mind, repeat the test until you are familiar with every term.*

TERMS	DEFINITION
COLUMN I	COLUMN II

161. Radiosonde

162. Reactance

163. Regulation

164. Relay

165. Repulsion-Induction Motor

166. Repulsion Motor

167. Repulsion Start Induction Motor

168. R.M.A. Color Guide

169. Rotor

170. Rotary Switch

1. The change in voltage which takes place between a condition of no load and of full load, or rated load, in a transformer, generator or other source.
2. An A.C. motor in which rotor is turned by repulsion between magnetic fields induced by supply current in stator windings and other fields induced in rotor winding. Supply current only to stator windings.
3. One which is operated by turning a control knob.
4. A radio meteorograph.
5. An A.C. motor that starts as a repulsion motor and after attaining speed runs as an induction motor; change over by automatic switch.
6. A standard method of designating resistor values by colored markings. (Radio Manufacturers Ass'n.)
7. The member that rotates in a machine, generator or motor.
8. An A.C. motor with two windings on the rotor, one a squirrel-cage type, the other repulsion-start induction type.
9. Opposition offered to the flow of alternating current by the inductance or capacity of a part; measured in ohms; designated by letter X.
10. An electro-magnetic device which permits control of current in one circuit by a much smaller current in another circuit.

Answer Key

(Please make every effort to answer the questions on your own before looking at these answers. You'll make faster progress by following this rule.)

161. 4	163. 1	165. 8	167. 5	169. 7
162. 9	164. 10	166. 2	168. 6	170. 3

ELECTRICIAN

SAFETY AND JUDGMENT IN ELECTRICAL WORK

DIRECTIONS: For each question read all choices carefully. Then select that answer which you consider correct or most nearly correct. Write the letter preceding your best choice next to the question

1. An electrician should consider all electrical equipment "alive" unless he definitely knows otherwise. The main reason for this practice is to avoid
   (A) doing unnecessary work
   (B) energizing the wrong circuit
   (C) personal injury
   (D) de-energizing a live circuit.

2. When working on live 600-volt equipment where rubber gloves might be damaged, an electrician should
   (A) work without gloves
   (B) carry a spare pair of rubber gloves
   (C) reinforce the fingers of the rubber gloves with rubber tape
   (D) wear leather gloves over the rubber gloves.

3. When connecting a lamp bank or portable tool to a live 600-volt d.c. circuit, the best procedure is to make the negative or ground connection first and then the positive connection. The reason for this procedure is that
   (A) electricity flows from positive to negative
   (B) there is less danger of accidental shock
   (C) the reverse procedure may blow the fuse
   (D) less arcing will occur when the connection is made.

4. If a live conductor is contacted accidentally, the severity of the electrical shock is determined primarily by
   (A) the size of the conductor
   (B) the current in the conductor
   (C) whether the current is a.c. or d.c.
   (D) the contact resistance.

5. A corroded electrical connection in a circuit generally has a tendency to develop a high spot temperature. This is because the corrosion

(A) increases the flow of current through the connection
(B) decreases the voltage drop across the connection
(C) increases the voltage drop across the connection
(D) decreases the effective resistance of the connection.

6. With respect to the safety value of insulation on electrical maintenance tools it can be said properly that
   (A) they insure the safety of the user
   (B) the insulation provides very little real protection
   (C) they are of value mainly to the new helper
   (D) the insulation should not be used as the only protective measure.

7. Before using rubber gloves on high tension work they should be
   (A) given to the helper and he should try them out
   (B) treated with Neats Foot Oil
   (C) washed inside and out
   (D) tested to withstand the required voltage.

8. Metal cabinets used for lighting circuits are grounded to
   (A) eliminate electrolysis
   (B) assure that the fuse in a defective circuit will blow
   (C) reduce shock hazard
   (D) simplify wiring.

9. When working near lead acid storage batteries extreme care should be taken to guard against sparks, essentially to avoid
   (A) overheating the electrolyte
   (B) an electric shock
   (C) a short circuit   (D) an explosion.

10. To prevent accidental starting of a motor which is to be worked on
    (A) remove the fuses
    (B) connect a lamp across the motor leads
    (C) ground the frame
    (D) ground the motor leads.

11. Most electric power tools, such as electric drills, come with a third conductor in the power lead which is used to connect the case of the tool to a grounded part of the electric outlet. The reason for this extra conductor is to
    (A) protect the user of the tool should the winding break down to the case
    (B) prevent accumulation of a static charge on the case
    (C) provide for continued operation of the tool should the regular grounded line-wire open
    (D) eliminate sparking between the tool and the material being worked upon.

12. A good practical test that can be used in the field for detecting punctures in rubber gloves just before putting them on is to
    (A) seal the gloves by rolling down the cuffs, and then compress them against a flat surface
    (B) fill the gloves with water, hang them up, and watch for leaks
    (C) tie the cuffs to compressed-air line outlets and slowly inflate
    (D) dip the gloves in soap suds and then blow into them, watching for bubbles.

13. It is always essential that a foreman in charge of a crew of men preparing to work on a low tension circuit caution them to

    (A) wait until the circuit has been killed
    (B) work only when the load is zero
    (C) consider the circuit alive at all times
    (D) never work on any circuit alone.

14. With respect to the safety value of insulation on electrical maintenance tools it can be said properly that
    (A) they insure the safety of the user
    (B) the insulation provides very little real protection
    (C) they are of value mainly to the new helper
    (D) the insulation should not be used as the only protective measure.

15. It is best as a safety measure, not to use water to extinguish fires involving electrical equipment. The main reason is that water
    (A) may damage wire insulation
    (B) will not extinguish an electrical fire
    (C) may transmit shock to the user
    (D) will turn to steam and hide the fire.

16. When cleaning the insulation of electrical equipment in confined quarters it is *least* desirable to do the cleaning by
    (A) wiping with a dry cloth
    (B) blowing with compressed air
    (C) wiping with a cloth moistened with carbon-tetrachloride
    (D) wiping with a cloth moistened with water.

17. A steel measuring tape is undesirable for use around electrical equipment. The *least* important reason is the
    (A) magnetic effect
    (B) short circuit hazard
    (C) shock hazard
    (D) danger of entanglement in rotating machines.

Answer Key

(You'll learn more by writing your own answers before comparing them with these.)

Safety

1. C	6. D	10. A	14. D
2. D	7. D	11. A	15. C
3. B	8. C	12. A	16. C
4. D	9. D	13. C	17. A
5. C			

ELECTRICAL JUDGMENT

DIRECTIONS: For each question read all choices carefully. Then select that answer which you consider correct or most nearly correct. Write the letter preceding your best choice next to the question

1. Of the following statements, the one that is correct is
   (A) A "running light test" performed on rotating electrical machinery is for the purpose of checking for electrical faults
   (B) If a circuit carries both A.C. and D.C., the type of ammeter best suited to measure the effective value of the combined currents is the permanent magnet type
   (C) Drawings are generally considered as a part of the specifications for any job
   (D) The unit of light intensity may be defined as footcandles per square foot of illuminated area.

2. Which of the following statements is correct?
   (A) Of the common D.C. motors, the one which is least adaptable for traction work is the series motor
   (B) Two 3-way switches cannot be used to control a lamp from two separate locations
   (C) Emergency lighting systems in buildings should preferably be connected to two separate sources of power
   (D) A Fire Underwriter's label on electrical materials may be accepted as proof that it is "approved material" for use on city projects.

3. An electrical code requires that all the conductors connecting an A.C. bus to a load be placed in a single metal conduit, tube or equivalent and does not approve using one conduit for each wire. The principal reason for this requirement is
   (A) a single conduit installation is cheaper
   (B) it makes testing of the wires easier
   (C) it is easier to pull the wires through a single conduit
   (D) currents would circulate through the individual conduits.

4. The blueprint of a switchboard which is being installed under your supervision shows certain connections which you believe to be wrong. Your proper procedure is to
   (A) have the connections made according to the print but be prepared to make the changes if ordered
   (B) report the apparent errors to your supervisor but continue with the remainder of the job
   (C) hold the job until you have checked with the man whose initials are on the blueprint
   (D) have the connections made properly and then return the blueprint marked to show the changes.

5. Assume there have been several reports of lamps in a particular five-light series burning out shortly after renewal. However, the circuit fuse does not blow, and inspections and tests fail to show a reason for this condition. It would probably be best to
   (A) renew the series wiring of the circuit.
   (B) re-test the circuit each time the lamps burn out
   (C) request someone else to keep a close check on the lamps
   (D) take no further action since you have no definite indication.

6. A newly appointed helper has made a blunder which has resulted in injury to another workman. As a foreman you should certainly
   (A) recommend the dismissal of the new helper
   (B) ignore the incident if it is the first offense
   (C) study the accident for remedial action
   (D) reprimand your partner for not properly instructing the helper.

7. As Foreman in charge of operations you have twice reported that an important piece of equipment is very defective but the repair crew has made no move to correct the defect. Under such conditions, you should
   (A) make another inspection to be sure you are right
   (B) attempt to make repairs yourself when the unit is out of service
   (C) keep the unit out of service and explain the reason in your operating logs
   (D) do nothing but keep unit in service as best as possible.

8. A complex maintenance operation has been broken down into smaller and simpler jobs and a job is to be assigned to each subordinate. Each job may be done in a number of different ways. The practical supervisory procedure would be to instruct each subordinate
   (A) to do his job in a specified way
   (B) in several ways of doing his job
   (C) to devise his own way of doing his job
   (D) how to do all jobs.

9. An electrician should always make sure that his tools are kept in good condition because
   (A) a good job can never be done without perfect tools
   (B) defective tools may cause accidents or damage
   (C) tools that are in good condition require no care
   (D) there is less possibility of the tools being lost.

10. When reporting minor trouble orally to your foreman, the most important information he would require from you would be
    (A) the exact time you discovered the trouble
    (B) the type of trouble and its exact location
    (C) the names of all the men with you when you discovered the trouble
    (D) exactly what you were doing when you noticed the trouble.

11. An electrician has been assigned to a certain job and has been told that it is essential that it be finished by a certain time. If, after working diligently for some time, he realizes that he cannot finish the job in time, he should
    (A) notify his foreman immediately
    (B) continue working and get as much done as possible
    (C) skip what he considers minor parts of the job
    (D) take it easy since the job cannot be done in time.

Question 12 refers to the statement below:
"The ampere-turns acting on a magnetic circuit are given by the product of the turns linked by the amperes flowing through these turns. Magnetomotive force tends to drive the flux through the circuit and corresponds to e.m.f. in the electric circuit. It is directly proportional to the ampere-turns and only differs from the numerical value of the ampere-turns by the constant factor 1.257 and the product of this factor and the ampere-turns equals the magnetomotive force. This unit of m.m.f. is the gilbert."

12. One pole of a D.C. motor is wound with 500 turns of wire, through which a current of 2 amperes flows. Under these conditions, the m.m.f., in gilberts, acting on this magnetic circuit is most nearly
    (A) 1,000
    (B) 1,257
    (C) 500
    (D) 628.

Answer Key

(You'll learn more by writing your own answers before comparing them with these.)

Judgment

1. C	4. B	7. C	10. B
2. C	5. A	8. A	11. A
3. D	6. C	9. B	12. B

ELECTRICIAN

SCRAMBLED DICTIONARY OF EQUIPMENT AND USAGE

The following tests cover equipment with which you should be familiar. You are expected to know how to use this equipment and how to solve everyday problems requiring its use. The quizzes measure your current knowledge and allow you to discover your weaker areas. Repeat each quiz until you have confidence in your ability to handle the material covered, when it appears on the "real" test.

TEST ONE

DIRECTIONS: Each DEFINITION *in Column I refers to one of the* TERMS *in Column II. Select the letter which corresponds to the defined* TERM *and write that letter next to the appropriate* DEFINITION *in Column I.*

Column I - DEFINITION

1. Current consuming equipment fixed or portable.
2. That portion of a wiring system extending beyond the final overcurrent device protecting the circuit.
3. Any conductors of a wiring system between the main switchboard or point of distribution and the branch circuit overcurrent device.
4. Not readily accessible to persons unless special means for access are used.
5. A point on the wiring system at which current is taken to supply fixtures, lamps, heaters, motors and current consuming equipment.
6. The rigid steel conduit that encloses service entrance conductors.
7. That portion of overhead service conductors between the last line pole and the first point of attachment to the building.
8. Conductors of a wiring system between the lines of the public utility company or other source of supply and the main switchboard or point of distribution.
9. A wire or cable or other form of metal suitable for carrying electrical energy.
10. Surrounded by a case which will prevent accidental contact with live parts.

Column II - TERM

A. Mains
B. Switchboard
C. Fuse
D. Outlet
E. Service raceway
F. Feeder
G. Isolated

H. Appliances
J. Branch Circuit
K. Fitting
L. Conductor
M. Enclosed
N. Surrounded
O. Service drop.

Answer Key

(You'll learn more by writing your own answers before comparing them with these.)

1. H	3. F	5. D	7. O	9. L
2. J	4. G	6. E	8. A	10. M

TEST TWO

DIRECTIONS: In this test the numbered MATERIALS *in Column I have corresponding* USES, *which are lettered in Column II. Next to each* MATERIAL *in Column I write the letter of its most appropriate* USE.

Column I - MATERIALS

11. Silver
12. Mica
13. Porcelain
14. Phosphor bronze
15. Transite

Column II - USES

(A) strain insulators
(B) arch shields
(C) heater wire
(D) commutators
(E) batteries
(H) relay contact points
(J) relay springs

Answer Key

(You'll learn more by writing your own answers before comparing them with these.)

11. H	13. A	15. B
12. D	14. J	

TEST THREE

DIRECTIONS: In this test the numbered MATERIALS *in Column I are to be matched up with the* ELECTRICAL EQUIPMENT PARTS *listed and lettered in Column II. Next to each of the* MATERIALS *in Column I write the letter of the corresponding Column II* PART.

Column I - MATERIALS

16. Steel
17. Lead
18. Mica
19. Porcelain
20. Rubber
21. Copper
22. Carbon

Column II - ELECTRICAL EQUIPMENT PARTS

(A) acid storage battery plates
(B) transformer cores
(C) d.c. motor brushes
(D) insulating tape
(E) cartridge fuse cases
(H) commutator insulation
(J) strain insulators
(K) knife-switch blades

Answer Key

(You'll learn more by writing your own answers before comparing them with these.)

16. B	18. H	20. D	22. C
17. A	19. J	21. K	

TEST FOUR

DIRECTIONS: In this test each numbered PART *in Column I is commonly associated with one of the* PIECES OF ELECTRICAL EQUIPMENT *listed and lettered in Column II. You are supposed to match up the* PARTS *in Column I with the* PIECES *in Column II. Next to each of the* PARTS *in Column I write the letter of the* PIECE *with which it is most commonly associated.*

Column I - PARTS

23. Current setting plug
24. Lead connectors
25. Closing solenoid
26. Thermostat
27. Pothead

Column II - PIECES OF ELECTRICAL EQUIPMENT

(A) oil circuit breaker
(B) A.C. power cable
(C) induction overload relay
(D) storage battery
(E) electric water heater

Answer Key

(You'll learn more by writing your own answers before comparing them with these.)

23. C	25. A	27. B
24. D	26. E	

TEST FIVE

DIRECTIONS: In this quiz Column I consists of numbered EQUIPMENT PARTS, *each of which is made from one of the* MATERIALS *listed and lettered in Column II. You are to match up the* PARTS *in Column I with their corresponding* MATERIALS *in Column II. Write next to the numbered* PART *in Column I, the letter of the* MATERIAL *from which it is commonly made.*

Column I - EQUIPMENT PARTS

28. d.c. circuit breaker arcing-tips
29. cartridge fuse casing
30. pig-tail jumpers for contacts
31. commutator bars
32. bearing oil-rings
33. cores for wound heater-coils
34. center contact in screw lamp-sockets
35. acid storage battery terminals
36. arc chutes
37. operating sticks for disconnecting switches

Column II - MATERIALS

(A) copper
(B) silver
(C) porcelain
(D) carbon
(E) transite
(H) wood
(J) lead
(K) brass
(L) phosphor bronze
(M) fiber

Answer Key

28. D	30. A	32. K	34. L	36. E
29. M	31. A	33. C	35. J	37. H

TEST SIX

DIRECTIONS: Column I lists various JOB DESCRIPTIONS *in numerical order. Column II lists a variety of* TOOLS, *one of which is used for each of the* JOBS *in Column I. You're supposed to match up the* TOOLS *in Column II with the* JOBS *in Column I. Write next to each* JOB *the letter preceding the proper* TOOL *to use for that job.*

Column I - JOB DESCRIPTIONS

38. Testing an armature for a shorted coil
39. Measurement of electrical pressure
40. Measurement of electrical energy
41. Measurement of electrical power
42. Direct measurement of electrical insulation resistance
43. Direct measurement of electrical resistance (1 ohm to 10,000 ohms)
44. Direct measurement of electrical current
45. Testing to find if supply is D.C. or A.C.
46. Testing the electrolyte of battery
47. Cutting an iron bar
48. Soldering a rat-tail splice
49. A standard for checking the size of wire

Column II - TOOLS

A. Neon light
B. Growler
C. Iron-vane Voltmeter
D. Ohmmeter
E. Wattmeter
F. Hot-wire Ammeter
G. Megger
H. Watthour Meter
J. Manometer
K. Cable clamp pliers
L. Pair of test lamps
M. Hack Saw
N. Hydrometer
O. Electrician's blow-torch
P. American wire gage
Q. Micrometer
R. Hygrometer
S. Rip Saw

Answer Key

(Please make every effort to answer the questions on your own before looking at these answers. You'll make faster progress by following this rule.)

38. B	41. E	44. F	47. M
39. C	42. G	45. A	48. O
40. H	43. D	46. N	49. P

TEST SEVEN

DIRECTIONS: In this test Column I lists a number of DEVICES *which are properly associated in operations with the* CONDITIONS *listed in Column II. You are asked to match up the* CONDITIONS *in Column II with the* DEVICES *in Column I. Write next to each of the* DEVICES *in Column I the letter preceding the* CONDITION *in Column II with which that device is properly associated.*

Column I - DEVICES

50. Transformer
51. Rectifier
52. Rotary converter
53. Storage battery
54. Induction motor
55. Tungsten lamp
56. Soldering iron
57. Generator exciter

Column II - CONDITIONS

(A) Alternating current only
(B) Direct current only
(C) Both alternating *and* direct current
(D) Either alternating current *or* direct current

Answer Key

(You'll learn more by writing your own answers before comparing them with these.)

50. A	52. C	54. A	56. D
51. C	53. B	55. D	57. B

TEST EIGHT

DIRECTIONS: Column I lists various JOB DESCRIPTIONS *in numerical order. Column II lists a variety of* TOOLS, *one of which is used for each of the* JOBS *in Column I. You're supposed to match up the* TOOLS *in Column II with the* JOBS *in Column I. Write next to each* JOB *the letter preceding the proper* TOOL *to use for that job.*

Column I - JOB DESCRIPTIONS

58. Check brush pressure
59. Check contact area between the contact and contact studs of a D.C. breaker
60. Check contact between fingers and blade of an O.C.B.
61. Measure insulation resistance of a lead covered cable
62. Measure resistance of ammeter shunts

Column II - TOOLS

(A) Micrometer
(B) Megger
(C) Wheatstone bridge
(D) (O-6 lbs.) spring balance
(E) Feeler gauge

Answer Key

58. D	60. E	62. C
59. E	61. B	

TEST NINE

DIRECTIONS: In this test Column I lists, in numerical order, several ITEMS *which are frequently represented by the* SYMBOLS *listed in Column II. You are asked to match up the* SYMBOLS *with the* ITEMS *they stand for. Write next to each* ITEM *in Column I the letter preceding the* SYMBOL *in Column II which stands for that item.*

Column I - ITEMS   Column II - SYMBOLS

63. Lighting panel
64. Special purpose outlet
65. Floor outlet
66. Three-way switch
67. Normally closed contact
68. Resistor
69. Watt hour meter
70. Two pole electrically operated contactor with blowout coil
71. Capacitor
72. Bell

A.
B.
C. S_3
D.
E.
F.

G.
H.
J.
K.
L.
M.

Answer Key

63. B	65. E	67. F	69. K	71. H
64. D	66. C	68. G	70. J	72. A

TEST TEN

DIRECTIONS: In this quiz Column I lists in numerical order TERMS *which are used to rate the* DEVICES *listed in Column II. You are asked to match up each* TERM *with the* DEVICE *it rates. Write next to each of the* RATING TERMS *in Column I the letter preceding the one* DEVICE *in Column II to which it is properly applied.*

Column I - RATING TERMS

73. 11,000 to 110 volts
74. 440 volts;   5 H.P.
75. 120 volts; 1000 watts
76. 1000 ohms; 10 watts
77. 100 amperes; 50 millivolts
78. 120 ampere-hours
79. 5 amperes;   2 seconds

Column II - DEVICES

(A) motor   (E) heater
(B) relay   (H) meter shunt
(C) storage battery (J) resistor
(D) transformer

Answer Key

73. D	75. E	77. H	79. B
74. A	76. J	78. C	

TOOLS, EQUIPMENT AND INSTALLATION METHODS

1. Mica is commonly used in electrical construction for
   (A) commutator bar separators
   (B) switchboard panels
   (C) strain insulators
   (D) heater cord insulation.

2. The purpose of having a rheostat in the field circuit of a d.c. shunt motor is to
   (A) control the speed of the motor
   (B) minimize the starting current
   (C) limit the field current to a safe value
   (D) reduce sparking at the brushes.

3. A frequency meter is constructed as a potential device, that is, to be connected across the line. A logical reason for this is that
   (A) only the line voltage has frequency
   (B) a transformer may then be used with it
   (C) the reading will be independent of the varying current
   (D) it is safer than a series device.

4. The cross sectional area of the bus bar shown is
   (A) 1 square inch
   (B) 3 square inches
   (C) 9 square inches
   (D) 12 square inches.

(4)

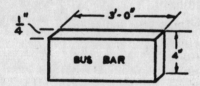

5. The electrical connector shown would most likely be used in a power plant to connect
   (A) two branch cables to a main cable
   (B) a single cable to the terminals of two devices
   (C) a single cable to a flat bus bar
   (D) a round bus bar to a flat one.

(5)

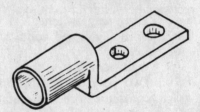

6. The fitting shown is used in electrical construction to
   (A) clamp two adjacent junction boxes together
   (B) act as a ground clamp for the conduit system
   (C) attach flexible metallic conduit to a junction box
   (D) protect exposed wires where they pass through a wall.

(6)

7. The diameter of a bare solid #14 A.W.G. copper wire is approximately
   (A) 0.064 mils
   (B) 0.64 mils
   (C) 6.4 mils
   (D) 64 mils.

8. A direct-current supply may be obtained from an alternating-current source by means of
   (A) a frequency changer set
   (B) an inductance-capacitance filter
   (C) a tungar bulb rectifier
   (D) none of the devices mentioned above.

9. To measure the value of armature circuit resistance corresponding to rated current for a 100-H.P., direct-current, 240-volt, compound motor you would use

(A) a 0-50 millivoltmeter and a 0-500 milli-

(B) A 0-50 millivoltmeter and a 0-500 milli-ammeter

(C) a 0-15 voltmeter and a 0-500 ammeter

(D) a megger.

10. The current-carrying capacity of a No. 2 rubber-insulated aluminum wire as compared to that of a No. 2 rubber-insulated copper wire is

(A) 80 percent

(B) 84 percent

(C) 74 percent

(D) 88 percent.

11. The minimum size of grounding conductor for a direct or alternating-current system is

(A) No. 14

(B) No. 10

(C) No. 8

(D) No. 6

12. The following equipment is required for a "2-line return-call" electric bell circuit:

(A) 2 bells, 2 metallic lines, 2 ordinary push-buttons, and one set of batteries

(B) 2 bells, 2 metallic lines, 2 return-call push-buttons and 2 sets of batteries

(C) 2 bells, 2 metallic lines, 2 return-call push-buttons and one set of batteries

(D) 2 bells, 2 metallic lines, one ordinary push-button, one return-call push-button and one set of batteries.

13. The convenience outlet that is known as *polarized* outlet is number

(A) 1

(B) 2

(C) 3

(D) 4.

(13)

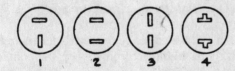

14. A polarized plug generally has

(A) two parallel prongs of the same size

(B) prongs at an angle with one another

(C) magnetized prongs

(D) prongs marked plus and minus.

15. The outlet which will accept the plug is

(A) 1

(B) 2

(C) 3

(D) 4.

(15)

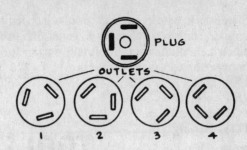

16. The standard colors of the outer coverings of wires used in series lighting circuits are

(A) Positive—black; Negative—white; Series—red

(B) Positive—black; Negative—red; Series—white

(C) Positive—white; Negative—black; Series—red

(D) Positive—red; Negative—white; Series—black.

17. In comparing Nos. 00, 8, 12 and 6 A.W.G. wires, the smallest of the group is

(A) No. 00

(B) No. 8

(C) No. 12

(D) No. 6.

18. An electrician who counts 64 turns of wire on a reel that is 2 feet in diameter knows that the length of wire on the reel is nearest to

(A) 100 feet

(B) 200 feet

(C) 400 feet

(D) 600 feet.

19. The letters RIWP when applied to electrical wire indicate the wire

(A) has a solid conductor

(B) has rubber insulation

(C) is insulated with paper

(D) has lead sheath.

20. The core of an electro-magnet is usually

(A) aluminum

(B) lead

(C) brass

(D) iron.

21. A good magnetic material is

(A) copper

(B) iron

(C) tin

(D) brass.

22. A material *not* used in the make-up of lighting wires or cables is

(A) rubber

(B) paper

(C) lead

(D) cotton.

23. Silver is a better conductor of electricity than copper, however copper is generally used for electrical conductors. The main reason for using copper instead of silver is its
    (A) cost
    (B) weight
    (C) strength
    (D) melting point.

24. The device shown is clearly intended for use in electrical construction to
    (A) support conduit on a wall
    (B) join cable to a terminal block
    (C) ground a wire to a water pipe
    (D) attach a chain-hung lighting fixture to an outlet box.

(24)

25. The four illustrations show pairs of equal strength permanent magnets on pivots, each magnet being held in the position shown by a mechanical locking device. When they are mechanically unlocked, the magnets which are *least* likely to change their positions are pair number
    (A) 1
    (B) 2
    (C) 3
    (D) 4.

(25)

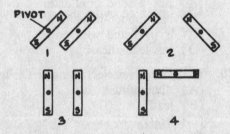

26. It is *not* correct to state that
    (A) current flowing through a resistor causes heat
    (B) rectifiers change d.c. to a.c.
    (C) the conduit of an electrical system should be grounded
    (D) ammeters are used in series in the circuit.

27. The device used to change a.c. to d.c. is a
    (A) frequency changer

(B) regulator
(C) transformer
(D) rectifier.

28. An electrical device that transmits rotation from a driving to a driven member without mechanical contact—with stepless adjustable control and with almost instantaneous response—is the
    (A) eddy current coupling
    (B) universal coupling
    (C) planetary coupling
    (D) coupling transformer.

29. Electrical contacts are opened or closed when the electrical current energizes the coils of a device called a
    (A) reactor
    (B) transtat
    (C) relay
    (D) thermostat.

30. Boxes and fittings intended for outdoor use should be of
    (A) weatherproof type
    (B) stamped steel of not less than No. 16 standard gauge
    (C) stamped steel plated with cadmium
    (D) ample strength and rigidity.

31. A Hickey is
    (A) not used in the electrical trade
    (B) only a part of a fixture
    (C) a tool used to bend small sizes of rigid conduit
    (D) used only in the plumbing trade.

32. The electrician's tapered reamer is used for
    (A) reaming the ends of rigid conduit after it is cut
    (B) reaming the threads on couplings
    (C) making holes in panel boxes
    (D) reaming the holes in bushings.

33. The device often connected across relay contacts to minimize arcing when the contacts open is a
    (A) spring
    (B) resistor
    (C) reactor
    (D) condenser.

34. Lock nuts are sometimes used in making electrical connections on studs. In these cases the purpose of the lock nuts is to
    (A) make a tighter connection
    (B) be able to connect several wires to one stud

(C) make it difficult to tamper with the connection

(D) prevent the connection from loosening under vibration.

35. When a gauge number such as "No. 4" is used in connection with a twist drill, it refers to the
(A) length
(B) hardness
(C) number of cutting edges
(D) diameter.

36. When the term "10-32" is used in connection with machine screws commonly used in lighting work, the number 32 refers to the
(A) screw length
(B) screw thickness
(C) diameter of hole
(D) threads per inch.

Answer Key

Tools and Equipment

1. A	10. B	19. B	28. A
2. A	11. C	20. D	29. C
3. C	12. B	21. B	30. A
4. A	13. A	22. B	31. C
5. C	14. B	23. A	32. A
6. C	15. C	24. A	33. D
7. D	16. A	25. C	34. D
8. C	17. C	26. B	35. D
9. C	18. C	27. D	36. D

USING TOOLS

FASTENING

1. To fasten an outlet box to a finished hollow tile wall, it is best to use
(A) wooden plugs
(B) toggle bolts
(C) through bolts and fishplates
(D) expansion bolts.

2. The fastening devices commonly used in conjunction with split lead expansion inserts to hold small outlet boxes on concrete walls are
(A) wood screws
(B) lag screws
(C) toggle bolts
(D) through bolts.

3. An outlet box should be fastened to a concrete wall by the use of
(A) expansion bolts
(B) toggle bolts
(C) wood plugs and nails
(D) porcelain inserts and screws.

4. When installing a new meter on a panel, to obtain accurate mounting
(A) drill from the back of the panel
(B) drill oversize holes
(C) use a templet
(D) use the meter to mark hole centers.

5. To fasten an outlet box to a terra cotta arch you should use

(A) wooden plug and nail
(B) expansion bolts
(C) toggle bolts
(D) ten penny nails.

6. To fasten an outlet box between the studs in a wall constructed of metal lath and plaster, you should use
(A) strong lath twine
(B) iron wire
(C) cement or plaster
(D) an approved box hanger.

7. To fasten an outlet box on a steel bulkhead you should use
(A) solder
(B) wood screws
(C) machine screws
(D) expansion bolts.

8. To fasten an outlet box to a concrete ceiling, you should use
(A) wooden plugs
(B) toggle bolts
(C) Mollys
(D) expansion bolts.

9. A small meter panel is to be fastened to a hollow tile wall. This is best done by using
(A) expansion bolts
(B) swing bolts
(C) self-threading screws
(D) toggle bolts.

10. Toggle bolts are appropriate for fastening an outlet box to a
    (A) concrete ceiling
    (B) brick wall
    (C) hollow-tile wall
    (D) wooden partition.

SOLDERING

11. When soldering two copper surfaces together they are kept clean while heating by
    (A) applying the solder quickly
    (B) frequently rubbing with emery cloth
    (C) not permitting the open flame to touch them
    (D) the use of a flux.

12. A soldering iron should not be heated to excess because this will usually
    (A) anneal the copper tip
    (B) ruin the tin on the surface of the tip
    (C) loosen the copper tip on the iron rod
    (D) burn the wooden handle.

13. Acid is not a good flux for use in soldering small electrical connections mainly because it is
    (A) non-conducting
    (B) expensive
    (C) messy to use
    (D) corrosive.

14. The flux commonly used for soldering electrical wire is
    (A) tin chloride
    (B) zinc chloride
    (C) rosin
    (D) silver amalgam.

15. Rosin is preferable to acid as a flux for soldering wire because rosin is
    (A) a nonconductor
    (B) a dry powder
    (C) a better conductor
    (D) noncorrosive,

16. In melting solder the formation of excessive dross is an indication that
    (A) the solder temperature is too low
    (B) tin content of the solder is too high
    (C) tin content of the solder is too low
    (D) too much heat is being applied.

WIRING

17. The most important reason for using friction tape over a splice is to
    (A) prevent damage to the rubber tape
    (B) increase the insulation resistance
    (C) make the splice as small as possible
    (D) prevent the wire ends from separating should the wire be pulled.

18. When moving a reel containing cable it is important to roll it in the direction indicated by the arrow marked on the reel. The reason for this is to
    (A) prevent unwinding and damaging the cable
    (B) protect the lagging from injury
    (C) make sure that the cable end is always on top
    (D) avoid reverse bends when installing the cable.

19. To cut Wiremold you would
    (A) use an approved cutter like a M.M. cutter
    (B) use a hack saw and remove the burr with a file
    (C) use a chisel
    (D) use a large pair of tin snips.

20. To cut oval duct you would
    (A) use a hack saw and remove the burr with a file
    (B) use an approved cutter like a M.M. cutter
    (C) use a cold chisel
    (D) use a pair of tin snips.

21. To cut rigid conduit you should
    (A) use a cold chisel and ream the ends
    (B) use a 3-wheel pipe cutter
    (C) use a hack saw and ream the ends
    (D) order it cut to size.

22. The length of a "Running Thread" should be not less than
    (A) a desired length
    (B) The length of a coupling plus a lock nut
    (C) twice the length of the coupling
    (D) ½ the length of the coupling.

23. When you bend a 90 degree bend in a piece of rigid conduit the radius of the inner edge shall be not less than
    (A) 1½ inches
    (B) 2½ inches
    (C) 3½ inches
    (D) 4½ inches.

24. The length of a "Panel Thread" should be not less than
    (A) the thickness of the panel box plus the thickness of the locknut and bushing

(B) not less than twice the length of the coupling
(C) the thickness of the box plus the thickness of the locknut and bushing plus ½ the length of the coupling
(D) the length of a standard pipe thread.

25. A one-inch pipe which is suitable for use as an electric conduit must be capable of withstanding, without damage, a 90-degree bend about a radius of approximately
(A) 7.5 inches
(B) 10 inches
(C) 15 inches
(D) 20 inches.

26. The one of the following that would prove *least* useful in uncoupling several pieces of conduit in a shop is a
(A) chain wrench
(B) strap wrench
(C) stillson wrench
(D) box wrench.

27. The total length of threads on a standard ¾″ conduit should be about
(A) ½ inch
(B) ¾ inch
(C) 1 inch
(D) 1½ inches.

28. To make pulling wires through conduit easier a lubricant is sometimes used. For lighting wires this lubricant is
(A) powdered pumice
(B) soap powder
(C) powdered soapstone
(D) grease.

29. When using compressed air to clean electrical equipment it is recommended that the air pressure should not exceed 50 pounds. The reason for this is that higher pressures
(A) introduce a personal hazard to the user
(B) will damage electrical connections at the terminals

(C) might blow dust on to other equipment in the vicinity
(D) may loosen insulating tapes.

30. If it is necessary to increase slightly the tension of an ordinary coiled spring in a relay, the proper procedure is to
(A) cut off one or two turns
(B) compress it slightly
(C) stretch it slightly
(D) unhook one end, twist and replace.

31. Lubrication is never used on
(A) a knife switch
(B) a die when threading conduit
(C) wires being pulled into a conduit
(D) a commutator.

32. To reverse the direction of rotation of a repulsion motor, you should
(A) move the brushes so that they cross the pole axis
(B) interchange the connection of either the main or auxiliary winding
(C) interchange the connections to the armature winding
(D) interchange the connections to the field winding.

Answer Key

(You'll learn more by writing your own answers before comparing them with these.)

Using Tools

1. B	9. D	17. A	25. B
2. A	10. C	18. A	26. D
3. A	11. D	19. B	27. B
4. C	12. B	20. A	28. C
5. C	13. D	21. C	29. D
6. D	14. C	22. B	30. A
7. C	15. D	23. C	31. D
8. D	16. D	24. C	32. A

ELECTRICIAN

MAINTENANCE AND INSTALLATION

TEST ONE

DIRECTIONS: In this test, important, common jobs are pictured. Each item shows several methods of doing the same job. Only one of the methods is entirely correct in accordance with good practice. For each item, examine the various sketches and select the one which portrays the CORRECT METHOD.

YOUR ANSWER SHEET AND OUR ANSWER KEY FOLLOW THE LAST QUESTION

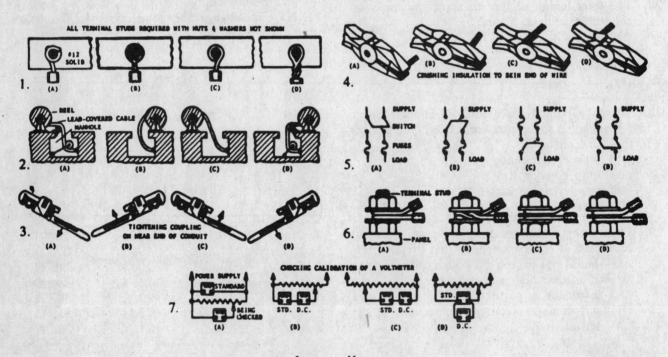

Answer Key

TEST TWO

DIRECTIONS: In this test, important, common jobs are pictured. Each item shows several methods of doing the same job. Only one of the methods is entirely correct in accordance with good practice. For each item, examine the various sketches and select the one which portrays the CORRECT METHOD.

YOUR ANSWER SHEET AND OUR ANSWER KEY FOLLOW THE LAST QUESTION

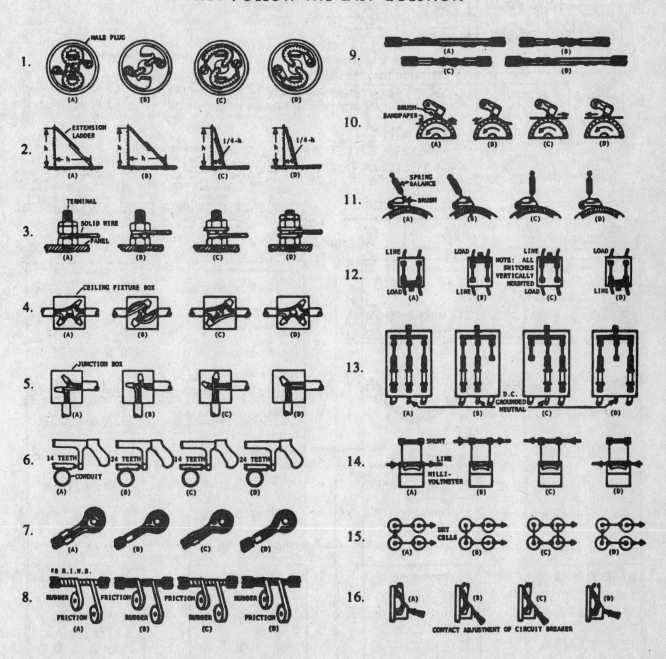

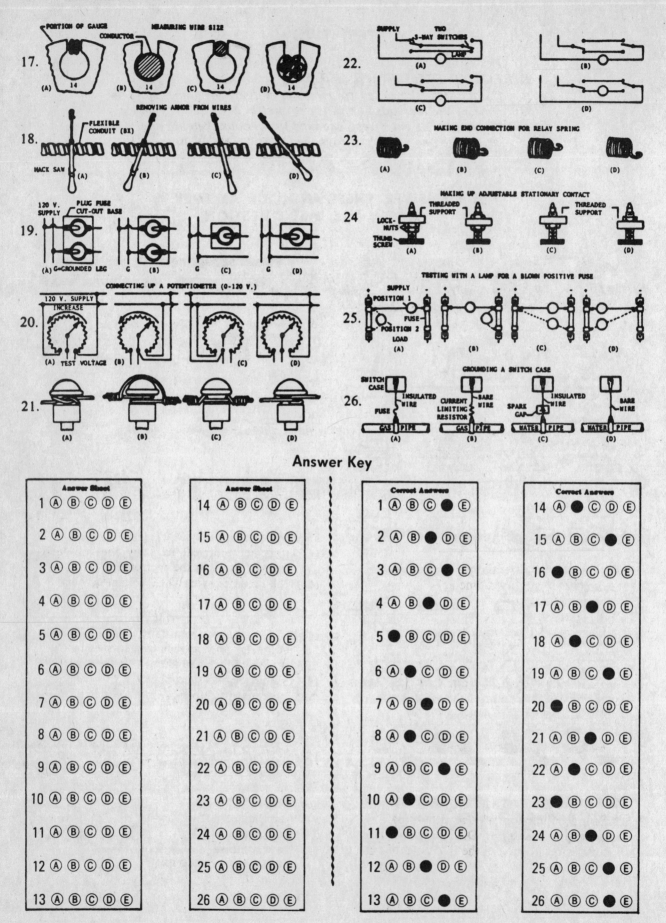

Answer Key

ELECTRICAL MEASUREMENT

If previous exams mean anything at all we can be fairly certain that these quizzes are important . . . Measurement . . . Voltage, Wattage, Amperage . . . Resistance . . . Switches, Wiring, Insulation . . . Wiring Equipment & Techniques . . . Conduits . . . Lighting . . . Special Equipment . . . Motors, Fuses, Breakers, & Bus Bars . . . Rectifiers, Rheostats, Relays, Converters, Commutators . . . Transformers . . . Generators & Batteries. All the Q & A in these quizzes have been selected from actual exams. If they appeared before, they're likely to reappear.

DIRECTIONS: For each question read all the choices carefully. Then select that answer which you consider correct or most nearly correct. Blacken the answer space corresponding to your best choice, just as you would do on the actual examination.

Measurement and measuring devices

MEASURING DEVICES

1. A D.C. wattmeter is essentially a combination of
    (A) a voltmeter and an ammeter
    (B) two ammeters
    (C) two voltmeters
    (D) a current and potential transformer.

2. Of the following meters, the one that does *not* have the zero at the center of the scale is the
    (A) control battery ammeter
    (B) main tie-line ammeter
    (C) main tie-line reactive volt-ammeter
    (D) main tie-line wattmeter.

3. A shunt in conjunction with a shunt-type ammeter is used in measuring D.C. current where
    (A) it is desired to isolate the instrument from the main circuit

(B) the current fluctuates greatly in value
(C) it is not practical to carry the full load current through the instrument
(D) the accompanying D.C. voltage is high.

4. High A.C. voltages are usually measured with a
    (A) voltmeter and current transformer
    (B) millivoltmeter and shunt
    (C) voltmeter and multiplier
    (D) potential transformer and voltmeter.

5. In the course of normal operation the instrument which will be *least* effective in indicating that a generator may overheat because it is overloaded is
    (A) an ammeter
    (B) a voltmeter
    (C) a wattmeter
    (D) a stator thermocouple.

6. Large currents in D.C. circuits are practically always measured with a
   (A) ammeter and multiplier
   (B) millivoltmeter and multiplier
   (C) ammeter and current transformer
   (D) millivoltmeter and shunt.

7. A millivoltmeter having a full scale deflection of 50 mv. is used with a 100-ampere, 50-millivolt shunt in a d.c. circuit. This combination is normally used to measure
   (A) voltage   (B) current
   (C) power   (D) resistance.

8. In the telemetering equipment the purpose of the glow tube is to provide
   (A) adequate illumination to read the meter
   (B) protection against high line voltage
   (C) rectification of the line current
   (D) a means of discharging the equipment.

9. A cycle counter is used in testing
   (A) relays
   (B) ammeters
   (C) wattmeters
   (D) voltmeters.

10. The insulation resistance of a transformer winding is readily measured with
    (A) a wattmeter
    (B) an ammeter
    (C) a megger
    (D) a Kelvin bridge.

11. To measure the voltage across a load you would
    (A) connect a voltmeter across the load
    (B) connect an ammeter across the load
    (C) connect a voltmeter in series with the load
    (D) connect an ammeter in series with the load.

12. Your foreman told you to measure the insulation resistance of some feeders. To do this you would use
    (A) a megger
    (B) a bell test
    (C) a magneto test
    (D) a service man from the Utility Company.

13. You are to check the Power Factor of a certain electrical load. You cannot get a Power Factor Meter. You would use
    (A) an ammeter, a wattmeter and a voltmeter
    (B) a voltmeter and an ammeter
    (C) a wattmeter
    (D) a Kilo-watt Hour Meter.

14. The power factor of a single phase alternating current motor may be found by using one of the following sets of AC instruments:
    (A) one voltmeter and one phase-rotation meter
    (B) one voltmeter and one ammeter
    (C) one voltmeter, one ammeter, and one wattmeter
    (D) one voltmeter, one ammeter, and one watt-hour meter.

15. The correct value of the resistance of a field coil can be measured by using
    (A) a Schering bridge
    (B) an ammeter and a voltmeter
    (C) a Kelvin double bridge
    (D) a Maxwell bridge.

16. The hot wire voltmeter
    (A) is a high precision instrument
    (B) is used only for D.C. circuits
    (C) reads equally well on D.C. and/or A.C. circuits
    (D) is used only for A.C. circuits.

17. An A.C. ammeter is calibrated to read R.M.S. values. This also means that this meter is calibrated to read the
    (A) average value   (B) peak value
    (C) effective value   (D) square value.

18. To increase the range of D.C. ammeters you would use
    (A) a current transformer
    (B) an inductance
    (C) a condenser
    (D) a shunt.

19. The electric meter *NOT* in itself capable of measuring both D.C. and A.C. voltages is the
    (A) Darsonval voltmeter
    (B) electrodynamometer voltmeter
    (C) iron vane voltmeter
    (D) inclined-coil voltmeter.

20. To increase the range of an A.C. ammeter the one of the following which is most commonly used is
    (A) a current transformer
    (B) an inductance
    (C) a condenser
    (D) a straight shunt (not U-shaped).

21. The type of meter that is suitable for direct current only is the
    (A) iron-vane type
    (B) permanent magnet type

(C) electrodynamometer type

(D) hot-wire type.

22. The open circuit test on a transformer is a test for measuring its
    (A) copper losses
    (B) iron losses
    (C) insulation resistance
    (D) the equivalent resistance of the transformer.

23. A shunt is used in parallel with a d.c. ammeter measuring large currents to
    (A) dampen the meter pointer
    (B) reduce the meter current
    (C) protect the meter against shorts
    (D) increase the sensitivity of the meter.

24. Of the following meters, the one that does *not* have the zero at the center of the scale is the
    (A) control battery ammeter
    (B) main tie-line ammeter
    (C) main tie-line reactive volt-ammeter
    (D) main tie-line wattmeter.

25. An electrician may use a megger to
    (A) measure the amount of illumination
    (B) determine the speed of an electric motor
    (C) measure the resistance of a lighting cable
    (D) test a lighting circuit for a ground.

Answer Key

(You'll learn more by writing your own answers before comparing them with these.)

Measuring Devices

1. A	6. D	11. A	16. C	21. B
2. B	7. B	12. A	17. C	22. B
3. C	8. B	13. A	18. D	23. B
4. D	9. A	14. C	19. A	24. B
5. B	10. C	15. B	20. A	25. D

USE OF MEASURING DEVICES

1. When applying a high-potential test voltage to the primary winding of a rebuilt transformer
   (A) one end of the primary winding must be grounded
   (B) the secondary winding must be short-circuited
   (C) all other parts of the transformer must be insulated from ground
   (D) the secondary winding, transformer case and core must be grounded.

2. To test and calibrate a polyphase watthour meter, using a single phase a.c. supply the best method is to connect the
   (A) voltage coils in series, current coils in parallel
   (B) current coils in series, voltage coils in parallel
   (C) current coils in parallel, voltage coils in parallel
   (D) voltage coils in series, current coils in series.

3. A certain circuit requires a maximum of 10 amperes when operating properly. If a calibrated ammeter in the circuit reads 12 amperes it is possible that
   (A) a partial short exists somewhere in the circuit
   (B) one of the branch circuits is open
   (C) the ground connection is open
   (D) a high resistance connection exists somewhere in the circuit.

4. The purpose of subjecting a newly completed lighting equipment installation to a high-potential test would be to
   (A) find the maximum voltage that the equipment will withstand
   (B) measure the insulation resistance of the wiring
   (C) check the dielectric strength of the insulation
   (D) make sure that the equipment will withstand operating voltage.

5. If a test lamp lights when placed in series with a condenser and a suitable source of d.c., it is a good indication that the condenser is
   (A) fully charged
   (B) short-circuited
   (C) fully discharged
   (D) open-circuited.

6. The insulation resistance of a cable is to be determined by the use of a voltmeter with a multiplier and a 600 volt D.C. source. The line voltage is first measured and then the insulation is connected in series with the meter and a second reading across the line is taken. If the second reading is very low compared to the first it indicates that the

(A) meter is defective
(B) cable insulation is bad
(C) cable insulation is good
(D) D.C. source has a partial short.

7. Before disconnecting an ammeter from an energized current transformer circuit, the current transformer

(A) primary should be shorted
(B) secondary should be shorted
(C) primary should be opened
(D) secondary should be opened.

8. A power factor meter is connected to a single-phase 2-wire circuit by means of

(A) 2 wires   (C) 4 wires
(B) 3 wires   (D) 5 wires

Questions 9 to 11 inclusive, refer to the diagram below.

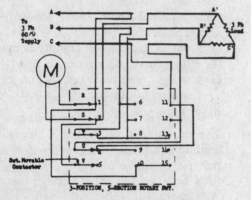

9. With switch movable contractors R, S, T, U and V in position 1, 2, 3, 4 and 5 as shown, Meter M is connected between points

(A) A-A' and load is improperly connected to supply
(B) A-A' and load is properly connected to supply
(C) C-C' and load is improperly connected to supply
(D) C-C' and load is properly connected to supply.

10. With switch movable contractors R, S, T, U and V in position 6, 7, 8, 9 and 10, the function of meter M is to measure the

(A) current in line B-B'
(B) voltage in line B-B'
(C) power drawn by the load
(D) power factor of the load.

11. With switch movable contractors R, S, T, U and V in position 11, 12, 13, 14 and 15, meter M is connected between points

(A) A-A' and load is improperly connected to supply
(B) A-A' and load is properly connected to supply
(C) C-C' and load is improperly connected to supply
(D) C-C' and load is properly connected to supply.

12. In order to properly connect a single-phase wattmeter to a circuit, you should use

(A) two current and two potential leads
(B) two current leads only
(C) two potential leads only
(D) two current leads and two power leads.

13. A d-c milliameter may be used to measure voltages

(A) when a proper shunt is used with the meter
(B) If a high external resistor is connected in series with the meter
(C) By simply connecting the meter across the line
(D) If a high external resistor is connected across the terminals of the meter.

14. To properly remove an ammeter from a high voltage bus already supplying load

(A) the load should preferably be reduced
(B) one should make sure that the switchboard is grounded
(C) the voltage at the bus should preferably be reduced when possible
(D) the case of the instrument should be grounded and the secondary winding of the current transformer short-circuited.

15. To check the full-load efficiency of a transformer its losses (core and copper) must be known. These losses

(A) cannot be obtained except by actually loading the transformer
(B) may be obtained without loading the transformer by performing a short-circuit and an open-circuit test on it

(C) may be found by measuring the input to the transformer with the secondary open

(D) May be obtained by measuring the winding resistance and calculating the I²R losses.

16. When reading a watthour meter, the hands should always be read as indicating the figure which they have last passed. If a hand is very close to a figure, whether it has actually passed this figure or not must be determined from the
(A) reading taken one hour earlier
(B) reading taken one hour later
(C) position of the hand on the next higher dial
(D) position of the hand on the next lower dial.

17. To test and calibrate a polyphase watthour meter, using a single phase a.c. supply the best method is to connect the
(A) current coils in series, voltage coils in parallel
(B) voltage coils in series, current coils in parallel
(C) current coils in series, voltage coils in series
(D) voltage coils in parallel, current coils in parallel.

18. Testing for a blown cartridge fuse by connecting a test lamp from one clip to the other of the suspected fuse will in all cases indicate a
(A) good fuse if the lamp lights up
(B) blown fuse if the lamp remains dark
(C) blown fuse if the lamp lights up
(D) good fuse if the lamp remains dark.

19. The method usually used to determine the area of the contacts actually making contact on a D.C. circuit breaker is to
(A) note the impression made on a piece of paper upon which the contacts have been closed
(B) insert a .005 feeler gauge between the closed contacts
(C) pass current through the closed contacts and measure the millivolt drop
(D) multiply the width by the length of each contact.

20. If a ground occurs on one side of a 120-volt battery control circuit, the voltage on the ground detector lamps will be
(A) 60 volts on each lamp
(B) 60 volts on one lamp and 0 volts on the other
(C) 120 volts on one lamp and 0 volts on the other
(D) 0 volts on each lamp.

21. If a ground occurs on one side of a 120-volt battery control circuit, the voltage on the ground detector lamps will be
(A) 120 volts on one lamp and 0 volts on the other
(B) 60 volts on each lamp
(C) 0 volts on each lamp
(D) 60 volts on one lamp and 0 volts on the other.

22. A generator watthour meter is read at 10:00 a.m. and again at 10:30 a.m. when the unit is taken off the line. Find the average load by subtracting the first reading from the second reading and multiplying by
(A) the meter constant
(B) the meter constant and dividing by two
(C) two and by the meter constant
(D) one thousand.

23. A 600 volt lamp cluster could *not* be used on a 600 volt circuit to test
(A) the continuity of the circuit
(B) if the circuit is energized
(C) the exact voltage of the circuit
(D) for a ground on the circuit.

Answer Key

(You'll learn more by writing your own answers before comparing them with these.)

Use of Measuring Devices

1. D	6. C	11. D	16. D	21. A
2. B	7. B	12. A	17. A	22. C
3. A	8. B-C	13. B	18. B	23. C
4. D	9. B	14. D	19. A	
5. B	10. A	15. B	20. C	

PROBLEMS IN MEASUREMENT

1. The input to a motor-generator set is 1500 watts
    and the motor and generator losses total 250
    watts. The efficiency of the set is nearest to
    (A) 88.2%   (B) 83.2%
    (C) 71.4%   (D) 16.7%

2. A kilowatthour meter with a constant of 100
    and connected to measure the power output of
    a 35000 kva unit reads 4324 at the beginning
    of a day and 1564 at the end of the day. The
    total output for the day is
    (A) 840,000 kwh   (B) 724,000 kwh
    (C) 294,400 kwh   (D) 276,000 kwh

3. If one of the two wattmeters used to measure
    the total power to a three-phase balanced delta
    connected load indicates zero the power factor
    of the load is
    (A) 100%   (B) 80%
    (C) 50%   (D) 0%

4. A voltage of about 40 volts is needed temporar-
    ily to make a particular test taking several
    hours. Someone suggests to you that a 10-ohm
    resistor and a 20-ohm resistor be connected in
    series across the 120-volt source that is avail-
    able, claiming that 40 volts will then be obtain-
    ed across the 10-ohm resistor. If these resistors
    are on hand and each is rated at 200 watts,
    you should turn down the suggestion because
    (A) the 20-ohm resistor will be overloaded
    (B) the 10-ohm resistor will be overloaded
    (C) too much power will be wasted
    (D) the combination will give too high a
        voltage.

5. On a certain voltmeter, the same scale is used
    for three ranges; these are 0-750, 0-300, and
    0-120 volts. If the scale is marked only for the
    0-120 volt range, a scale reading of 112 when
    the 750 volt range is being used corresponds
    to an actual voltage of
    (A) 622   (B) 688
    (C) 700   (D) 742

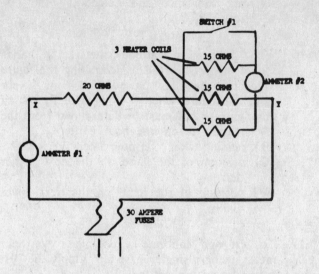

Items 6 to 11 inclusive refer to the diagram above.
Assume that the two ammeters are of negligible
resistance and that switch #1 is open unless otherwise stated.

6. The equivalent resistance of the 3 heater coils
    connected as shown is
    (A) 5 ohms   (B) 10 ohms
    (C) 15 ohms   (D) 45 ohms

7. If ammeter #2 reads 6 amperes ammeter #1
    will read
    (A) 2 amperes   (B) 6 amperes
    (C) 9 amperes   (D) 18 amperes

8. When each of the 3 heater coils carries 2 am-
    peres the power consumed by the 3 heater coils
    will total
    (A) 20 watts   (B) 180 watts
    (C) 540 watts   (D) 1350 watts

9. When switch #1 is closed the equivalent re-
    sistance of the whole circuit (points X to Y) is
    (A) 20 ohms   (B) 25 ohms
    (C) 27.5 ohms   (D) 30 ohms

10. No matter what current is flowing through the circuit, the voltage drop across the 20 ohm resistor as compared to that across the heater coils will
    (A) always be equal
    (B) always be lower
    (C) always be higher
    (D) be lower only if switch #1 is closed.

11. If the line voltage is 120 volts then the fuses will blow if
    (A) the 20 ohm resistor is shorted
    (B) the 20 ohm resistor is shorted and two heater coils are open circuited
    (C) switch #1 is closed and the 20 ohm resistor is shorted
    (D) the 20 ohm resistor develops an open circuit and switch #1 is closed.

12. The power, in watts, taken by a load connected to a three-phase circuit is generally expressed by
    (A) EI P.F. 2
    (B) EI P.F.
    (C) 3 EI P.F.
    (D) EI P.F. / 3

Questions 13 to 15 inclusive, refer to the diagram below.

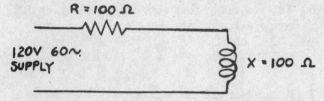

R = 100 Ω
120V 60~ SUPPLY
X = 100 Ω

13. The value of the impedance, in ohms, of the above circuit is most nearly
    (A) 200
    (B) 50
    (C) 150
    (D) 140.

14. The current, in amperes, flowing in the above circuit is most nearly
    (A) .6
    (B) 2.4
    (C) 1.2
    (D) .85.

15. The power, in watts, consumed in the above circuit is most nearly
    (A) 72
    (B) 144
    (C) 576
    (D) 36.

16. A condenser whose capacity is one microfarad is connected in parallel with a condenser whose capacity is 2 microfarads. This combination is equal to a single condenser having a capacity, in microfarads, of approximately
    (A) 2/3
    (B) 1
    (C) 3
    (D) 3/2.

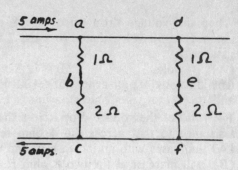

5 amps. a   d
1Ω   1Ω
b   e
2Ω   2Ω
5 amps. c   f

17. With reference to the above diagram, the current flowing through resistance ab is
    (A) 5 amperes
    (B) 4 amperes
    (C) 2½ amperes
    (D) 1½ amperes.

18. With reference to the above diagram, the voltage difference between points b and e is
    (A) 1 volt
    (B) 10 volts
    (C) 5 volts
    (D) 0 volts.

19. If the full rating of a transformer is 90 KW at 90% power factor, then the KVA rating is
    (A) 81
    (B) 90
    (C) 100
    (D) 141.

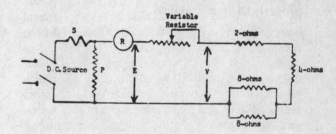

Items 20 to 27 refer to the above wiring diagram.

20. If resistance "S" (of low value) and "P" (of high value) are both associated with the same meter, the meter is
    (A) a wattmeter
    (B) a voltmeter
    (C) an ammeter
    (D) a varmeter.

21. When the d.c. voltage "E" is 100 and the current through the variable resistor is 1 ampere, the variable resistor is fixed at
    (A) 78 ohms
    (B) 86 ohms
    (C) 90 ohms
    (D) 100 ohms.

22. With the same load resistances and the same fixed value of the variable resistor as used in item 25, the d.c. voltage "E" is replaced by an a.c. voltage of 100. The current through the variable resistor is
    (A) .707 ampere
    (B) 1.00 ampere
    (C) 1.41 amperes
    (D) 1.73 amperes.

23. When the voltage drop across the 8 ohm resistances is 50 volts, that across the 2 ohm resistance is
    (A) 10 volts (B) 12.5 volts
    (C) 25 volts (D) 100 volts.

24. The *ratio* of the voltage drop across the 2 ohm resistance to that across the 4 ohm resistance
    (A) increases with an increase in line voltage
    (B) will increase if the two 8 ohm resistances are shorted
    (C) decreases as line current decreases
    (D) is independent of line current.

25. If the current through the 2 ohm resistance is 2 amperes, the total power consumed by the 2, 4, and both 8 ohm resistances is
    (A) 40 watts (B) 56 watts
    (C) 88 watts (D) 200 watts.

26. A relay "R," of negligible resistance, in series with the line as shown and set to operate at 4 amperes line current is taken out of service for repairs. The only available spare is also of negligible resistance and has a maximum current setting of 3 amperes. This spare will function properly if it is installed

    (A) in series with one of the 8 ohm resistances
    (B) in series and between the 2 and 4 ohm resistances
    (C) in parallel across the 4 ohm resistance
    (D) to directly replace the original relay.

27. With a fixed voltage "E," increasing the amount of the variable resistance put in the circuit will increase the voltage
    (A) drop across the 2 ohm resistance
    (B) "V" across the line
    (C) drop across the 8 ohm resistance
    (D) drop across the variable resistor.

Answer Key

(You'll learn more by writing your own answers before comparing them with these.)

Problems in Measurement

1. B	7. D	13. D	19. C	25. A
2. B	8. B	14. D	20. A	26. A
3. C	9. A	15. A	21. C	27. D
4. A	10. C	16. C	22. B	
5. C	11. C	17. C	23. C	
6. A	12. C	18. D	24. D	

VOLTAGE PROBLEMS

The voltage problems in this chapter touch on all phases of electrical theory and work. Many of the questions require the ability to interpret schematic wiring diagrams for generators, battery hookups and voltmeters. They have been carefully selected to approximate the type of question you may find on your exam, so if you have difficulty with these questions, don't go on to the next chapter until you have mastered them.

DIRECTIONS: For each question read all choices carefully. Then select that answer which you consider correct or most nearly correct. Write the letter preceding your best choice next to the question

1. A potential relay is connected across a 600-volt d.c. source. The resistance of the relay coil is 2400 ohms. If a resistance of 400 ohms is connected in series with the relay coil and a resistance of 1200 ohms is connected in parallel with the relay coil, the voltage across the coil will be
   (A) 200 volts   (B) 400 volts
   (C) 500 volts   (D) 550 volts.

2. If the fourth lamp in a lighted five-lamp series on a 600-volt circuit is removed from its socket, the voltage across the terminals of the empty socket is
   (A) zero   (B) 120
   (C) 480   (D) 600.

3. Two transformers with ratios of 1:2 are to be connected in parallel. To test for proper connections the circuit of figure (3) is used. The transformers may be connected in parallel by connecting lead "A" to lead "B" if the voltmeter shown reads
   (A) 120 volts   (B) 240 volts
   (C) zero volts   (D) 480 volts.

4. Three single-phase transformers having ratios of 10 to one are connected with their primaries in wye and their secondaries in delta. If the low-voltage windings are used as the primaries and the line voltage on the primary side is 208 volts then the line voltage on the secondary side is
   (A) 3600 volts   (B) 2080 volts
   (C) 1200 volts   (D) 692 volts.

5. In accordance with the voltages shown, the power supply must be
   (A) three-wire d.c.
   (B) three-phase a.c.
   (C) two-phase a.c.
   (D) single-phase a.c.

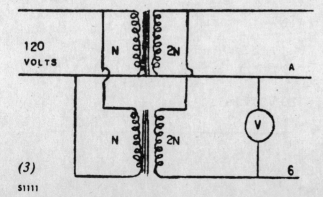

(3)

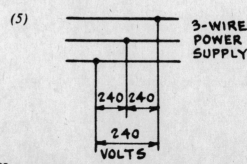

(5)

3-WIRE POWER SUPPLY

S1111

6. If the voltmeter reads 34 volts, the circuit voltage is about
   (A) 68   (B) 85
   (C) 102   (D) 119.

(6)

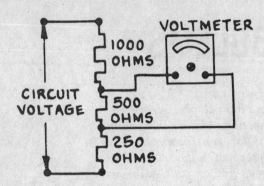

7. The range of both voltmeters shown is 0-300 volts. In this case, the a.c. meter will indicate the correct voltage and the d.c. meter will indicate
   (A) zero
   (B) a few volts too high
   (C) a few volts too low
   (D) the correct voltage.

(7)

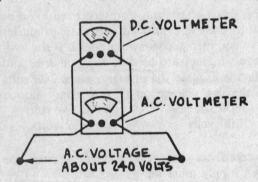

8. The reading of the voltmeter (8) should be
   (A) 50   (B) 10
   (C) 5   (D) 0

(8)

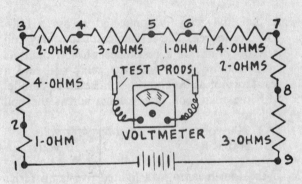

9. The reading of the voltmeter will be highest when the test prods are held on points
   (A) 1 and 4   (B) 2 and 5
   (C) 3 and 6   (D) 4 and 7.

(9)

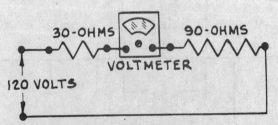

10. The reading of the voltmeter should be nearest to
    (A) 30   (B) 90
    (C) 120   (D) 240.

(10)

11 Each of the four resistors shown has a resistance of 50 ohms. If the second resistor from the left becomes open-circuited, the reading of the voltmeter will
(A) increase slightly
(B) decrease slightly
(C) fall to zero
(D) become 240 volts.

(11)

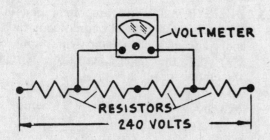

12. In electrical wiring diagrams electrical measuring devices are often abbreviated in symbolic form: of the following, the symbol commonly used to represent a direct current watt-hour meter is

(12)

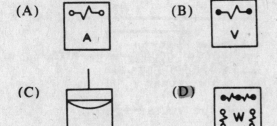

13. If the voltage of the supply is 120 volts, the readings of the voltmeters should be
(A) 60 volts on each meter
(B) 120 volts on each meter
(C) 80 volts on meter #1 and 40 volts on meter #2
(D) 80 volts on meter #2 and 40 volts on meter #1.

(13)

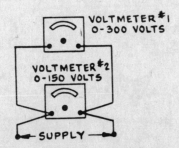

14. If the voltmeter reads 34 volts, the circuit voltage is about
(A) 68   (B) 85
(C) 102   (D) 119.

(14)

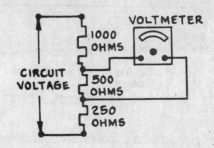

15. Meter 1 is
(A) an ammeter
(B) a frequency meter
(D) a voltmeter.
(C) a wattmeter

(15)

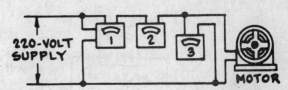

16. The reading of the voltmeter should be
(A) 600   (B) 300
(C) 120   (D) zero.

(16)

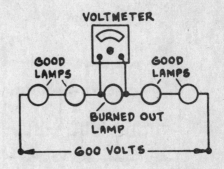

17. If the voltage of each of the dry-cells shown is 1.5 volts, the voltage between X and Y is
(A) 3   (B) 6
(C) 9   (D) 12.

(17)

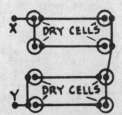

18. The reading of the voltmeter in the accompanying sketch will be
    (A) 0 volts   (B) 80 volts
    (C) 120 volts   (D) 240 volts.

(18)

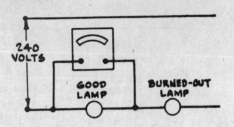

19. The two voltmeters shown are identical. If the battery voltage is 120 volts, the readings of the voltmeters should be
    (A) 120 volts on each meter
    (B) 60 volts on each meter
    (C) 120 volts on meter #1 and 240 volts on #2
    (D) 120 volts on meter #1 and zero on #2.

(19)

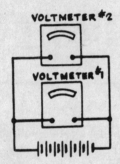

20. The voltage "X" is
    (A) 25   (B) 20
    (C) 15   (D) 5

(20)

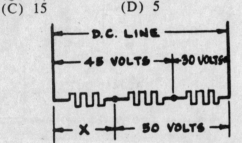

21. With the voltage drop across the four resistors as shown, the voltmeter will read
    (A) 50 volts   (B) 70 volts
    (C) 100 volts   (D) 170 volts.

(21)

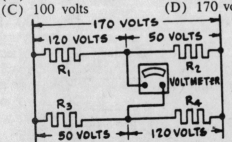

22. The voltage drop is 24 volts across resistor
    (A) #1   (B) #2
    (C) #3   (D) #4.

(22)

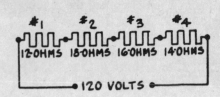

23. Five 110 volt lamps are often used in series for testing 600 volt circuits. If one bulb is removed from such a lamp bank, connected to 600 volts, the voltage across the terminals of the empty socket is
    (A) 110   (B) 490
    (C) 600   (D) zero.

24. A battery consisting of four two-volt cells in series will have a voltage of
    (A) ½ volt   (B) 2 volts
    (C) 4 volts   (D) 8 volts.

25. The voltage cross terminal 1 and terminal 2 of the transformer connected as shown is
    (A) 50 volts   (B) 100 volts
    (C) 200 volts   (D) 400 volts.

(25)

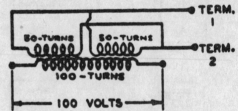

26. If 2 amperes flow through the circuit shown, the terminal voltage is
    (A) 2 volts   (B) 6 volts
    (C) 12 volts   (D) 24 volts.

(26)

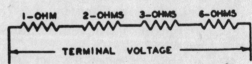

27. The voltage across the 30-ohm resistor in the circuit shown is
    (A) 4 volts   (B) 20 volts
    (C) 60 volts   (D) 120 volts.

(27)

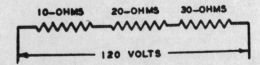

28. The terminal voltage with batteries connected as shown is
   (A) 0 volts
   (B) 1½ volts
   (C) 3 volts
   (D) 6 volts.

(28)

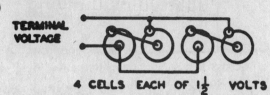

TERMINAL VOLTAGE

4 CELLS EACH OF 1½ VOLTS

29. If a ground occurs on one side of a 120-volt battery control circuit, the voltage on the ground detector lamps will be
   (A) 120 volts on one lamp and 0 volts on the other
   (B) 60 volts on each lamp
   (C) 0 volts on each lamp
   (D) 60 volts on one lamp and 0 volts on the other.

30. A 2,400 volt three-phase system with a grounded neutral has a phase to ground voltage of approximately
   (A) 800 volts
   (B) 1390 volts
   (C) 1700 volts
   (D) 7200 volts.

31. When a high potential test voltage is applied to electrical equipment, the purpose is to
   (A) break down the insulation
   (B) measure the insulation resistance
   (C) make sure the insulation will withstand operating voltage
   (D) measure dielectric strength of the insulation.

32. Current transformer secondary circuits are not usually fused because
   (A) the secondary current cannot exceed 5 amperes
   (B) the wiring is heavy enough to carry large currents safely
   (C) protection is provided by fuses in the primary circuit
   (D) excessive voltage may be developed in the secondary circuit if it is opened by a blown fuse.

33. The insulation resistance of a d.c. cable was checked by means of a high resistance d.c. voltmeter. When the cable was cold the reading obtained was 10 volts. If the test were to be repeated after the cable had been in service carrying load for several hours, you would expect the voltage reading to be
   (A) unchanged

   (B) zero volts
   (C) lower than 10 volts
   (D) higher than 10 volts.

34. An automatic voltage regulator as applied to a generator is
   (A) a transformer provided with taps for changing output voltage under load
   (B) a transformer whose secondary coils can be rotated, producing a change in secondary voltage
   (C) a booster generator, by means of which a variation of voltage can be obtained
   (D) a device commonly used to vary the voltage of a generator by changing its impedance
   (E) a device commonly used to hold the voltage of a generator or bus constant under varying load conditions.

35. If the voltage of the supply is 120 volts, the readings of the voltmeters should be
   (A) 60 volts on each meter
   (B) 120 volts on each meter
   (C) 80 volts on meter #1 and 40 volts on meter #2
   (D) 80 volts on meter #2 and 40 volts on meter #1.

(35)

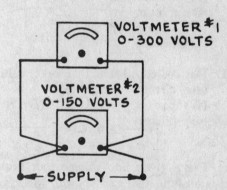

VOLTMETER #1
0-300 VOLTS

VOLTMETER #2
0-150 VOLTS

SUPPLY

36. The most practical method of determining if a 600-volt circuit is "dead" is to
   (A) examine the fuse to see if it is blown
   (B) touch it with the back of the hand
   (C) check with the nearest substation
   (D) test it with a known good bank of lamps.

37. Certain vacuum tubes have four elements inside the glass envelope; namely, a heater, a cathode, a grid, and a plate. In most vacuum tube circuits, the highest "plus" d.c. voltage is applied to the
   (A) plate
   (B) grid
   (C) cathode
   (D) heater.

38. Assume you have decided to test a sealed box having two terminals by using the hook-up shown. When you hold the test prods on the terminals, the voltmeter needle swings upscale and then quickly returns to zero. As an initial conclusion you would be correct in assuming that the box contained a
    (A) condenser   (B) choke
    (C) rectifier   (D) resistor

(38)

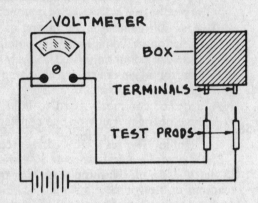

39. The rating-terms "240 volts, 10 H.P." would be properly used as part of the specifications for
    (A) transformers
    (B) motors
    (C) storage batteries
    (D) heaters

40. It is correct to state that a d.c. voltmeter can be used directly to measure
    (A) power   (B) frequency
    (C) polarity   (D) power factor

41. For a given line voltage four heater coils will consume the most power when connected
    (A) all in series
    (B) all in parallel
    (C) with two parallel pairs in series
    (D) one pair in parallel with the other two in series.

42. The factor which will have the *least* effect on the voltage at the most distant point from the source of supply for a two wire circuit is
    (A) whether the supply is 25 cycle or 60 cycle a.c.
    (B) the length of the circuit
    (C) the amount of load on the circuit
    (D) the gauge of the circuit wires.

43. If a 5-ohm, a 10-ohm, and a 15-ohm resistor are connected in series across a 120-volt circuit, the voltage across the 15-ohm resistor will be
    (A) 120 volts   (B) 60 volts
    (C) 40 volts   (D) 20 volts

44. The middle lamp burns out and is removed from a bank of five lamps connected in series across a 600 volt d.c. line. The voltage across the empty socket is
    (A) 600 and that across a good lamp 120
    (B) 120 and that across a good lamp 0
    (C) 600 and that across a good lamp 0
    (D) 120 and that across a good lamp 120.

45. When applying a high-potential test voltage to the primary winding of a rebuilt transformer
    (A) one end of the primary winding must be grounded
    (B) the secondary winding must be short-circuited
    (C) all other parts of the transformer must be insulated from ground
    (D) the secondary winding, transformer case and core must be grounded.

46. For measuring D.C. voltage, the most accurate type of meter is the
    (A) hot wire   (B) soft iron vane
    (C) induction   (D) D'Arsonval.

47. In the common 3-phase 4 wire supply system the voltage (in volts) from line to neutral is most nearly
    (A) 110   (B) 120
    (C) 208   (D) 220

48. With reference to question 47, the neutral line
    (A) does not carry current at any time
    (B) carries current at all times
    (C) has a potential difference with respect to ground of approximately zero volts
    (D) has a potential difference with respect to ground of 208 volts.

49. To transmit power economically over considerable distances, it is necessary that the voltage be high. High voltages are readily obtainable with
    (A) D.C. currents
    (B) A.C. currents
    (C) rectified currents
    (D) carrier currents.

50. With reference to question 49, the one favorable economic factor in the transmission of power by using high voltages is the
   (A) reduction of conductor cross section
   (B) decreased amount of insulation required by the line
   (C) increased I^2R loss
   (D) decreased size of generating stations.

51. In a two-phase, three-wire system, the voltage between the common wire and either of the other two wires is 200 volts. The voltage between these other two wires is then approximately
   (A) 200 volts
   (B) 283 volts
   (C) 141 volts
   (D) 100 volts.

52. In order to magnetize a steel bar, a magneto-motive force of 1000 ampere turns is necessary. The voltage that must be applied to a coil of 100 turns and 10 ohms resistance is
   (A) 1
   (B) 10
   (C) 100
   (D) 1000.

53. A single phase synchronous converter is connected on its DC side to 141.4 volt DC source of supply. The AC single phase voltage delivered by this machine is approximately
   (A) 300
   (B) 200
   (C) 150
   (D) 100.

54. The voltage induced in a loop of wire rotating in a magnetic field is
   (A) DC
   (B) pulsating DC
   (C) rectified AC
   (D) AC.

55. In a balanced three-phase wye connected load the
   (A) line to neutral voltage equals the line voltage
   (B) line to neutral voltage equals the line voltage multiplied by the square root of three
   (C) line voltage equals the line to neutral voltage divided by the square root of three
   (D) line voltage equals the line to neutral voltage multiplied by the square root of three.

56. A potential relay is connected across a 600-volt d.c. source. The resistance of the relay coil is 2,000 ohms. If a resistance of 500 ohms is connected in series with the relay coil, and a resistance of 2,000 ohms is connected in parallel with the relay coil, the voltage across the coil will be

   (A) 100 volts
   (B) 200 volts
   (C) 400 volts
   (D) 500 volts.

57. Each of the two lighting transformers in a certain transformer closet are supplied from a different phase of the same 3-phase primary feeder. The secondary voltage of each transformer is 600 volts. If a secondary terminal of one transformer is connected to a secondary terminal of the other transformer, the voltage between the two unconnected secondary terminals will be either
   (A) zero or 1200 volts
   (B) 600 or 1040 volts
   (C) zero or 1040 volts
   (D) 600 or 1200 volts.

58. A potential relay is connected across a 600-volt d.c. source. The resistance of the relay coil is 3,000 ohms. If a resistance of 500 ohms is connected in parallel with the relay coil, the voltage across the coil will be
   (A) 150 volts
   (B) 200 volts
   (C) 400 volts
   (D) 600 volts.

59. A potential of 24 volts is impressed across a potentiometer having a total resistance of 1,000 ohms. If a fixed resistance of 500 ohms is connected across one-half of the potentiometer, the voltage across the fixed resistance is
   (A) 6
   (B) 8
   (C) 12
   (D) 16.

60. If a 10-ohm, a 20-ohm, and a 30-ohm resistor are connected in series across a 120-volt circuit, the voltage across the 20-ohm resistor will be
   (A) 120 volts
   (B) 60 volts
   (C) 40 volts
   (D) 20 volts.

Answer Key

Voltage Problems

1. B	13. B	25. A	37. A	49. B
2. D	14. D	26. D	38. A	50. A
3. C	15. C	27. C	39. B	51. B
4. C	16. A	28. C	40. C	52. C
5. B	17. B	29. A	41. B	53. D
6. D	18. A	30. B	42. A	54. D
7. A	19. A	31. C	43. B	55. D
8. C	20. A	32. D	44. C	56. C
9. B	21. B	33. D	45. D	57. B
10. C	22. A	34. E	46. D	58. D
11. D	23. C	35. B	47. B	59. B
12. D	24. D	36. D	48. C	60. C

WATTAGE PROBLEMS

1. When connecting wattmeters to AC motor circuits consuming large amounts of current, it is necessary to use
   (A) current transformers
   (B) potential transformers
   (C) power shunts·
   (D) isolation transformers.

2. The wattmeters P_1 and P_2 are connected as shown to measure the power drawn by a balanced 3-phase load with a power factor of about 85 per cent. In what direction will the meters deflect?
   (A) P_1 deflects upscale and P_2 deflects down scale (reverses)
   (B) P_2 deflects upscale and P_1 deflects downscale (reverses)
   (C) Both P_1 and P_2 deflect upscale
   (D) Both P_1 and P_2 deflect downsoale (reverses).

(2)

3. The total current in a circuit which contains two 5-ohm resistances in parallel is 10 amperes. The power consumed by this circuit is
   (A) 25 watts   (B) 250 watts
   (C) 500 watts   (D) 1000 watts.

4. During a test a standard 110 volt, 5 ampere wattmeter is connected to a single phase circuit by means of a 3:1 current transformer and a 20.1 potential transformer. With a primary current of 5 amperes at 2200 volts and unity power factor the wattmeter reading, to the nearest watt, will be

(A) 60 watts   (B) 183 watts
(C) 330 watts   (D) 550 watts.

5. Four 120-watt, 120-volt heaters are connected in series on a 600-volt circuit. The total heat given off by the four heaters will be
   (A) 480 watts   (B) 600 watts
   (C) 680 watts   (D) 750 watts.

6. A megawatt is
   (A) ten watts
   (B) one hundred watts
   (C) one thousand watts
   (D) one million watts.

7. An integrating watthour meter has four dials. If, from left to right, the respective pointers are between 7 and 8, between 4 and 5, between 0 and 1, and between 3 and 4, the reading is
   (A) 7403   (B) 7413
   (C) 3047   (D) 8514.

8. In a given circuit when the power factor is unity the reactive power is
   (A) a maximum
   (B) zero
   (C) equal to I^2R
   (D) a negative quantity.

9. If a 3-phase motor connected to a 208 volt source takes 100 amperes at 90% power factor, then the input power to this motor is most nearly
   (A) 18,720 watts   (B) 20,800 watts
   (C) 32,400 watts   (D) 56,160 watts.

10. In an a.c. circuit, a low value of reactive volt amperes compared with the watts indicates
    (A) maximum current for the load
    (B) low efficiency
    (C) high power factor
    (D) unity power factor.

11. In an a.c. circuit the ratio of the power in kilowatts to the total kilovoltamperes is the

(A) load factor
(B) power factor
(C) diversity factor
(D) conversion factor.

12. The power used by the heater shown is
(A) 120 watts   (B) 720 watts
(C) 2400 watts   (D) 4320 watts.

(12)

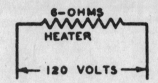

13. If the motor shown runs for one-half an hour the energy consumed is
(A) 120 watthours
(B) 1500 watthours
(C) 3000 watthours
(D) 90,000 watthours.

(13)

14. If a 100-watt tungsten lamp is compared with a 25-watt tungsten lamp of the same voltage rating, the resistance of the 100-watt lamp is
(A) higher
(B) lower
(C) the same
(D) higher with A.C., lower with D.C.

15. Two 500-watt lamps connected in series across a 110-volt line draw 2 amperes. The total power consumed is
(A) 1,000 watts   (B) 250 watts
(C) 220 watts   (D) 55 watts.

16. The number of watts of heat given off by a resistor is expressed by the formula I^2R. If 10 volts is applied to a 5-ohm resistor, the heat given off will be
(A) 500 watts   (B) 250 watts
(C) 50 watts   (D) 20 watts.

17. It is now possible to obtain a 200-watt light-bulb that is as small in all dimensions as the standard 150-watt light-bulb. The principal advantage to users resulting from this reduction in size is that
(A) maintenance electricians can carry many more light-bulbs

(B) two sizes of light-bulbs can be kept in the same storage space
(C) the higher wattage bulb can now fit into certain lighting fixtures
(D) less breakage is apt to occur in handling.

18. When the energy cost for a motor is $4.62 at 3 cents per kilowatt-hour, the energy consumed is
(A) 13.86 KWH   (B) 154 KWH
(C) 762 KWH   (D) 1386 KWH.

19. The term "60-watt" is most commonly used in identifying a
(A) fuse   (B) lamp
(C) cable   (D) switch.

20. The power factor of an a.c. circuit containing both a resistor and a condenser is
(A) 0
(B) between 0 and 1.0
(C) 1 0
(D) between 1.0 and 2.0.

21. When a 100-watt, 120-volt lamp burns continuously for 8 hours at rated voltage the energy used is
(A) 800 watt-hours
(B) 960 watt-hours
(C) 12,000 watt-hours
(D) 96,000 watt-hours.

22. Meter 1 is
(A) an ammeter
(B) a frequency meter
(C) a wattmeter
(D) a voltmeter.

(22)

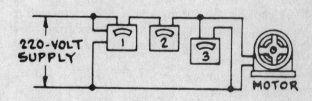

Answer Key

Wattage Problems

1. A	6. D	11. B	15. C	19. B
2. D	7. A	12. C	16. D	20. B
3. B	8. B	13. B	17. C	21. A
4. B	9. C	14. B	18. B	22. C
5. D	10. C			

ELECTRICIAN

AMPERAGE PROBLEMS

These quizzes deal with amperage in theory and practice. Although many of them are rather difficult, they do represent almost every conceivable type of question you may encounter on your exam. Take your time; don't be discouraged. Your reward will be a high score on your exam, and knowledge that will enable you to be a success on your job.

1. In an A.C. circuit delivering a constant power at a varying power factor, the current is
   (A) lowest when the power factor is leading
   (B) lowest when the power factor is lagging
   (C) constant for all power factors
   (D) lowest at 100% power factor.

2. With a reversal of power an A.C. ammeter in good condition will read
   (A) zero
   (B) the reactive current
   (C) the correct current
   (D) backwards.

3. The heating effects of 10 amperes a.c. as compared with 10 amperes d.c. are
   (A) the same
   (B) 1.41 times as great
   (C) 1.73 times as great
   (D) .707 times as great.

4. A choke coil with an iron core is connected to an alternating current source. The current flow is inversely proportional to the
   (A) reactance
   (B) impedance
   (C) resistance
   (D) inductance.

5. A milliampere is
   (A) one million amperes
   (B) 1/1,000,000 ampere
   (C) 1/1,000 ampere
   (D) one thousand amperes.

6. A relay coil with a resistance in series is connected in parallel with a contactor coil to a battery. If the current is 5 amperes in the relay coil, 5 amperes in the resistor and 3 amperes in the contactor coil, the battery current is
   (A) 13 amperes
   (B) 2 amperes
   (C) 5 amperes
   (D) 8 amperes.

7. The reading of the ammeter should be
   (A) 4.0   (B) 2.0
   (C) 1.0   (D) 0.5.

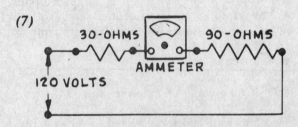

(7)

8. The instrument shown is properly connected to measure
   (A) a.c. amperes
   (B) d.c. amperes
   (C) a.c. volts
   (D) d.c. volts.

(8)

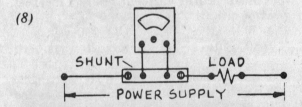

9. A coil of wire wound on an iron core draws exactly 5 amperes when connected across the terminals of a ten-volt storage battery. If this coil is now connected across the ten-volt secondary terminals of an ordinary power transformer, the current drawn will be

(A) less than 5 amperes
(B) more than 5 amperes
(C) exactly 5 amperes
(D) more or less than 5 amperes depending on the frequency.

10. The current flowing through the 6-ohm resistor in the circuit shown is
(A) 1 ampere   (B) 3 amperes
(C) 6 amperes   (D) 11 amperes.

(10)

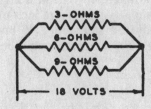

11. The current in the wire at the point indicated by the arrow is
(A) 1 ampere   (B) 2 amperes
(C) 3 amperes   (D) 4 amperes.

(11)

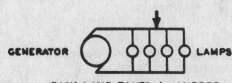

12. A copper wire with twice the diameter of another copper wire has a current carrying capacity
(A) four times as great
(B) twice as great
(C) half as great
(D) three times as great.

13. The current in the 4-ohm resistor is
(A) 5 amp.   (B) 4 amp.
(C) 3 amp.   (D) 1 amp.

(13)

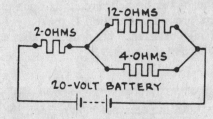

14. If fuse #1 blows in the 3-wire d.c. system shown, the current in the neutral wire will
(A) increase by 1.0 amp.
(B) increase by 0.5 amp.
(C) decrease by 1.0 amp.
(D) decrease by 0.5 amp.

(14)

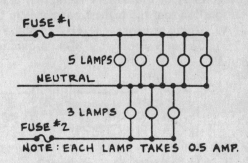

15. If the permissible current is 1,000 amperes for each square inch of cross section, the bus bar shown can carry
(A) 2250 amp.   (B) 2000 amp.
(C) 1750 amp.   (D) 1500 amp.

(15)

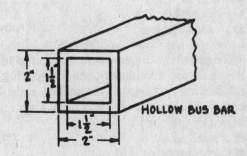

16. If the voltmeter reads 80 volts, the current in the 11-ohm resistor is
(A) 10 amp.   (B) 6.3 amp.
(C) 12 amp.   (D) 8.3 amp.

(16)

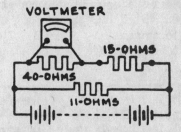

17. If ammeter #2 reads 60 amp., the reading of ammeter #1 should be about
(A) 4 amp.   (B) 15 amp.
(C) 60 amp.   (D) 900 amp.

(17)

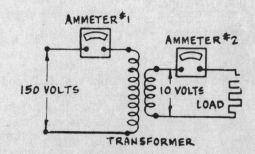

18. Regardless of the battery voltage, it is clear by inspection that the highest current is in the
    (A) 1-ohm resistor   (B) 2-ohm resistor
    (C) 3-ohm resistor   (D) 4-ohm resistor.

(18)

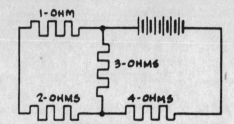

19. The term "15-ampere" is commonly used in identifying
    (A) an insulator
    (B) a fuse
    (C) a conduit
    (D) an outlet box.

20. Two dissimilar ammeters are connected in parallel, and the combination connected in series with a circuit. If one of the meters reads 4 amperes when the other meter reads 8 amperes, the current in the circuit
    (A) is 12 amperes
    (B) is 6 amperes
    (C) is 4 amperes
    (D) cannot be determined from these readings.

21. If one heater takes 10 amperes and the other heater takes 5 amperes, the current in wire 2 will be
    (A) 15 amperes   (B) 7½ amperes
    (C) 5 amperes   (D) zero.

(21)

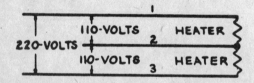

22. The maximum allowable current carrying capacity of two-conductor No. 14 rubber insulated BX cable is
    (A) 10 amperes
    (B) 12 amperes
    (C) 15 amperes
    (D) 18 amperes.

23. If the currents in resistors nos. 1, 2, and 3 are 4.8, 7.5, and 6.2 amperes respectively, then the current (in amperes) in resistor no. 4 is
    (A) 1.3   (B) 2.7
    (C) 3.5   (D) 6.1.

(23)

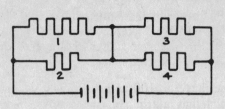

24. If the allowable current in a copper bus bar is 1,000 amperes per square inch of cross-section, the width of a standard 1/4" bus bar designed to carry 1500 amperes would be
    (A) 2"   (B) 4"
    (C) 6"   (D) 8"

25. Four heaters, each having a resistance of 30 ohms are connected in series across a 600-volt train circuit. The current taken by each heater is
    (A) 5 amperes
    (B) 17 amperes
    (C) 20 amperes
    (D) 80 amperes.

26. Reactance in a circuit decreases the current in the circuit
    (A) only when alternating current is flowing
    (B) only when direct current is flowing
    (C) only in case the circuit contains resistance
    (D) only in case the circuit contains no resistance
    (E) only in case the circuit contains capacitance.

27. A certain circuit requires a maximum of 10 amperes when operating properly. If a calibrated ammeter in the circuit reads 12 amperes it is possible that
    (A) a partial short exists somewhere in the circuit
    (B) one of the branch circuits is open
    (C) the ground connection is open
    (D) a high resistance connection exists somewhere in the circuit.

28. If the allowable current density for copper bus bars is 1000 amperes per square inch the current-carrying capacity of a circular copper bar having a diameter of two inches is approximately
    (A) 1050 amperes
    (B) 2320 amperes
    (C) 3140 amperes
    (D) 4260 amperes.

29. The current in amperes of a 220-volt, 5-H.P., d-c, motor having an efficiency of 90% is approximately
    (A) 18.8
    (B) 17
    (C) 14.3
    (D) 20.5.

30. You have a 100-ampere. 13-K.V. oil switch which has a trip coil rated up to 5 amperes. You wish the switch to open when the line current is 80 amperes. To accomplish this the trip coil should be set at
    (A) 4 amperes
    (B) 5 amperes
    (C) 3 amperes
    (D) 1 ampere.

31. Three 20-ohm resistances are connected in wye across a 208-volt, 3-phase circuit. The line current in amperes is approximately
    (A) 18
    (B) 10.4
    (C) 5.2
    (D) 6.

32. The current in amperes of a one horsepower, 120-volt, single-phase induction motor having an efficiency of 90% and operating at 0.8 power factor is approximately
    (A) 6.9
    (B) 7.8
    (C) 8.6
    (D) 6.2.

33. A standard stranded cable contains 19 strands. When measured with a micrometer the diameter of each strand is found to be 105.5 mils. If, under certain conditions, the allowable current density is 600 C.M. per ampere the allowable current-carrying capacity of this conductor is
    (A) 236 amperes
    (B) 176.3 amperes
    (C) 352.5 amperes
    (D) 705 amperes.

34. The current input per phase under rated-load conditions for a 200-H.P., 3-phase, 2300-volt, 0.8 P.F., induction motor which is 90% efficient is
    (A) 52 amperes
    (B) 90 amperes
    (C) 41.6 amperes
    (D) 46.8 amperes.

35. Referring to problem 34 the power input under rated-load conditions is approximately
    (A) 149 K.W.
    (B) 96 K.W.
    (C) 166 K.W.
    (D) 332 K.W.

36. A 600-volt d.c. circuit feeds a motor-generator set. If the generator delivers 4.8 kw, at 120 volts and the overall efficiency of the set at this load is 80 per cent, the motor line current is

    (A) 6.4 amps.
    (B) 10 amps.
    (C) 12 amps.
    (D) 30 amps.

37. An induction type overload relay has the current plug in the 10-ampere tap and is set to operate in 0.4 second at 30 amperes. This setting means that the relay will
    (A) have a minimum operating time of 0.4 second
    (B) always require 30 amperes to operate
    (C) operate in 0.2 second at 15 amperes
    (D) not operate on less than 10 amperes.

38. If a current transformer has a ratio of 100:5 and an ammeter connected to its secondary reads 1.5 amperes, the actual line current is
    (A) 7.5 amperes
    (B) 0.075 amperes
    (C) 30 amperes
    (D) 600 amperes.

(39)

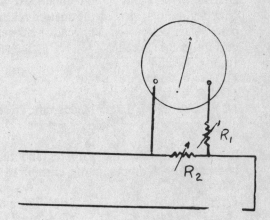

39. The above diagram represents the circuit of a D.C. ammeter. If the value of R_1 is increased while the value of R_2 remains unchanged, the
    (A) deflection of the instrument is no longer proportional to the current
    (B) range of the ammeter is decreased
    (C) range of the ammeter remains the same
    (D) range of the ammeter is increased.

40. In reference to the diagram in question 39, if the value of R_2 is decreased while the value of R_1 remains unchanged, the
    (A) range of the ammeter is increased
    (B) range of the ammeter is decreased
    (C) range of the ammeter remains the same
    (D) deflection of the instrument is no longer proportional to the current.

41. Three 30-ohm resistances are connected in delta across a 208-volt, 3-phase circuit. The line current, in amperes, is approximately
    (A) 6.93   (B) 13.86
    (C) 120   (D) 12.

42. If two 60-watt, 120-volt lamps are connected in series across a 120-volt supply, the current taken will be
    (A) less than 1/4 amp.
    (B) exactly 1/4 amp.
    (C) between 1/4 and 1/2 amp.
    (D) exactly 1/2 amp.

43. A three-wire D.C. supply system has an unbalanced load of 20 amperes in one of the outside wires and 30 amperes in the other outside wire. The current in the middle or neutral wire is
    (A) 10   (B) 25
    (C) 30   (D) 50.

44. A 100-watt, 120 volt lamp, at normal voltage, will draw about
    (A) 2/3 ampere
    (B) 5/6 ampere
    (C) 1 ampere
    (D) 1.2 amperes.

Answer Key

Amperage Problems

1. D	10. B	19. B	28. C	37. D
2. C	11. B	20. A	29. A	38. C
3. A	12. A	21. C	30. A	39. D
4. B	13. C	22. C	31. D	40. A
5. C	14. B	23. D	32. C	41. D
6. D	15. C	24. C	33. C	42. C
7. C	16. A	25. A	34. A	43. A
8. B	17. A	26. A	35. C	44 B
9. A	18. D	27. A	36. B	

ELECTRICIAN

RESISTANCE PROBLEMS

1. A field discharge resistance is connected across a generator field when the field breaker is opened. The purpose of this is to
   (A) prevent excessive voltage rise in the field when the circuit is opened
   (B) reduce the current the breaker must interrupt
   (C) prevent excessive current flow in the field when the circuit is opened
   (D) allow the generator voltage to drop very slowly.

2. One foot of a certain size of nichrome wire has a resistance of 1.63 ohms. To make a heating element for a toaster that will use 5 amperes at 110 volts, the number of feet of wire needed is approximately
   (A) 17.9   (B) 8.2
   (C) 5.5   (D) 13.5.

3. The speed of a three-phase, slip-ring, induction motor is increased with
   (A) a decrease in the secondary circuit resistance
   (B) an increase in the secondary circuit resistance
   (C) a decrease in the voltage impressed on the stator
   (D) an increase in the stator current.

4. In a 5-H.P., 220-volt, shunt motor rated at 19.2 amperes and 1500 R.P.M., the armature resistance is
   (A) smaller than that of the shunt field
   (B) larger than that of the shunt field
   (C) the same as that of the shunt field
   (D) always one-half that of the shunt field.

5. The resistance, in ohms, of a 25-ampere, 50-millivolt shunt is approximately
   (A) 2   (B) 0.2
   (C) 0.02   (D) 0.002.

(6)

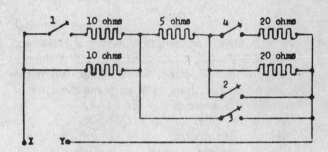

Questions 6-10 refer to diagram (6). All switches are normally open.

6. With switches No. 1 and No. 2 closed the combined resistance of the circuit in ohms is
   (A) 30   (B) 25
   (C) 10   (D) 2½

7. The switches to be closed in order to obtain a combined resistance of 5 ohms are
   (A) Nos. 1 and 3   (B) Nos. 2 and 3
   (C) Nos. 1 and 2   (D) Nos. 1 and 4.

8. If 3 amperes flow through the 5 ohm resistor with all switches open, the voltage between the terminals X and Y is
   (A) 15   (B) 60
   (C) 90   (D) 105.

9. If the line current is 10 amperes with all switches closed, the power consumed by the circuit is
   (A) 500 watts   (B) 750 watts
   (C) 1000 watts   (D) 2000 watts.

10. With only switch No. 4 closed and a line voltage of 225 volts, the drop across one of the 10 ohm resistors is
    (A) 225   (B) 90
    (C) 64.3   (D) 56.3.

11. The insulation resistance of a motor is commonly measured by the use of
    (A) an ammeter
    (B) a wattmeter
    (C) a voltmeter
    (D) a Wheatstone bridge.

12. A resistance of 20 ohms after being measured with an accurate bridge is found to be 20.05 ohms. It can be said that the percent accuracy of this resistance is
    (A) 0.25%   (B) 0.5%
    (C) 1%   (D) 1.5%.

13. A 50 millivolt meter shunt having a resistance of 0.005 ohms is to be used with a 5 milliamp. meter whose resistance is 10 ohms. When the current in this shunt is 8 amperes the current through the meter is
    (A) 4 amperes
    (B) 4 milliamperes
    (C) 2 amperes
    (D) 2 milliamperes.

14. Accurate resistances the values of which are not materially affected by changes in room temperature are usually made of an alloy commonly called
    (A) manganin
    (B) paganin
    (C) Excellin
    (D) Siemens Martin.

15. The resistor that carries the most current is the one whose resistance, in ohms, is
    (A) 4   (B) 3
    (C) 2   (D) 1.

(15)

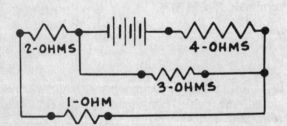

16. Compared to the total resistance of the variable resistor, the resistance between terminals 1 and 2 is
    (A) 90/330   (B) 120/330
    (C) 120/360   (D) 90/360.

(16)

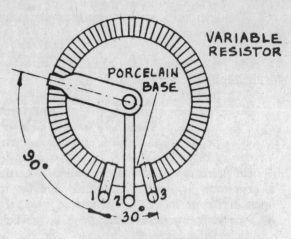

17. The device shown is one element of an iron grid-resistor. Such a large resistor would logically be used when the
    (A) resistance required is very high
    (B) voltage across it is very high
    (C) resistor is to be used outdoors
    (D) resistor must carry large currents.

(17)

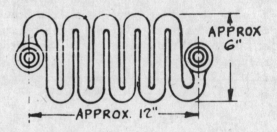

18. The resistance of 1000 feet of #10 A.W.G. wire is approximately 1 ohm. If the resistance of a coil of #10 A.W.G. wire is 1.19 ohms, the length of wire in the coil is nearest to
    (A) 1109 feet   (B) 1119 feet
    (C) 1190   (D) 1199 feet.

19. If three resistors of 175 ohms, 75 ohms, and 17 ohms respectively, are connected in parallel, the combined resistance will be
    (A) greater than 175 ohms
    (B) between 175 ohms and 75 ohms
    (C) between 75 ohms and 17 ohms
    (D) less than 17 ohms.

20. The resistance of a copper wire to the flow of electricity
    (A) increases as the diameter of the wire increases
    (B) decreases as the diameter of the wire decreases

(C) decreases as the length of the wire increases

(D) increases as the length of the wire increases.

21. The rating term "1000 ohms, 10 watts" would generally be applied to a
(A) heater   (B) relay
(C) resistor   (D) transformer.

22. The sketch shows the four resistance dials and the multiplying dial of a resistance bridge. The four resistance dials can be set to any value of resistance up to 10,000 ohms, and the multiplier can be set at any of the nine points shown. In their present positions, the five pointers indicate a reading of
(A) 13.60   (B) 136,000
(C) 130,600   (D) 13.06.

(22)

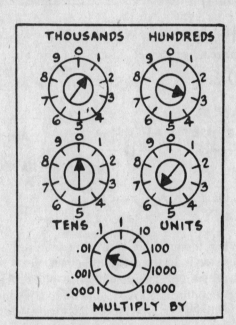

23. Regardless of the battery voltage, it is clear that the smallest current is in the resistor having a resistance of
(A) 200 ohms   (B) 300 ohms
(C) 400 ohms   (D) 500 ohms.

(23)

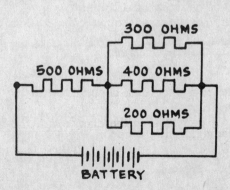

24. The total resistance in the circuit shown between terminal 1 and terminal 2 is
(A) 1½ ohms   (B) 6 ohms
(C) 9 ohms   (D) 15 ohms.

(24)

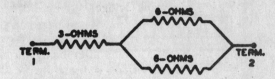

25. A high resistance connected in parallel with a potential relay across a 120-volt battery will
(A) increase the voltage across the relay
(B) make the relay inoperative
(C) have no effect on the relay
(D) increase the current through the relay.

26. A heater consists of four 15-foot lengths of wire connected in series. If the resistance of the wire is 0.14 ohms per foot, the total resistance of the heater is
(A) 0.52 ohms   (B) 2.1 ohms
(C) 6.0 ohms   (D) 8.4 ohms.

27. If a low resistance is connected in parallel with a higher resistance, the combined resistance is
(A) always less than the low resistance
(B) always more than the high resistance
(C) always between the values of the high and the low resistance
(D) higher or lower than the low resistance depending on the value of the higher resistance.

28. Comparing generally the resistance of ammeters, frequency meters and meggers, the instruments with the lowest resistances are
(A) frequency meters
(B) meggers
(C) ammeters
(D) voltmeters.

29. The resistance of a 1000-ft. length of a certain size copper wire is required to be 10.0 ohms +2%. This wire would *not* be acceptable if the resistance was
(A) 10.12 ohms   (B) 10.02 ohms
(C) 10.22 ohms   (D) 9.82 ohms.

30. If the slider connecting both resistors is 9 inches from the left-hand end of the resistors, the resistance between terminals #1 and #2 is
(A) 1125 ohms   (B) 875 ohms
(C) 750 ohms   (D) 625 ohms.

(30)

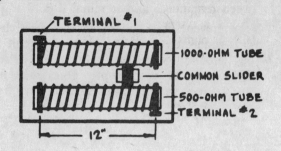

31. When a d.c. voltage of 1.50 volts is applied to a certain coil, the current in the coil is 6 amperes. The resistance of this coil is
(A) 1/4 ohm (B) 4 ohms
(C) 7½ ohms (D) 9 ohms.

32. The resistance box shown can be set to any value of resistance up to 10,000 ohms. The reading shown is
(A) 3875 (B) 5738
(C) 5783 (D) 8375.

(32)

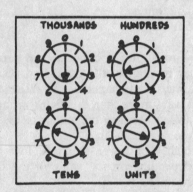

33. The total resistance in ohms between points X and Y is
(A) 0.30 (B) 3.33
(C) 15 (D) 30.

(33)

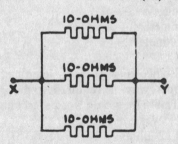

34. The resistance of a 1000-foot coil of a certain size copper wire is 10 ohms. If 300 feet is cut off, the resistance of the remainder of the coil is
(A) 7 ohms
(B) 3 ohms
(C) 0.7 ohm
(D) 0.3 ohm.

35. A wire which is three A.W.G. sizes larger than another wire has half the resistance, twice the weight, and twice the area. If a No. 10 wire has a resistance of one ohm per thousand feet, has an area of 10,000 circular mils, and weighs 32 pounds per thousand feet, the resistance of one thousand feet of No. 19 wire is
(A) 8 ohms (B) 6 ohms
(C) 1½ ohms (D) 1/8 ohm.

36. The total resistance between points 1 and 2 is
(A) more than 257 ohms
(B) between 257 and 19 ohms
(C) between 19 and 17 ohms
(D) less than 17 ohms.

(36)

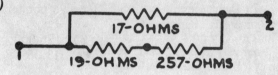

37. If the 6-volt lamp burns at normal voltage and current, resistance R must be most nearly
(A) 120 ohms (B) 60 ohms
(C) 12 ohms (D) 6 ohms.

(37)

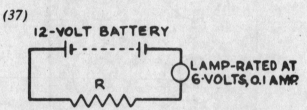

38. When the movable arm of the uniformly wound resistor is in the position shown, the resistance in ohms between terminals 2 and 3 is
(A) 2000 (B) 1800
(C) 1500 (D) 1200.

(38)

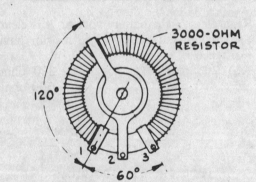

39. If the 10-ohm resistor marked X burns out, the reading of the voltmeter will become
(A) 0 (B) 20
(C) 80 (D) 100.

(39)

VOLTMETER

FIVE 10-OHM RESISTORS

—— 100 VOLTS ——

(C) connected across the field terminals, while the field current is being interrupted, to prevent high voltages in the field circuit

(D) connected between the field circuit and ground, to prevent accumulation of static

(E) connected permanently across the field, to prevent damage by armature reaction.

40. Nichrome wire having a resistance of 150 ohms per 1,000 feet is to be used for a heater requiring a total resistance of 6 ohms. The length of wire required is
(A) 4 feet (B) 9 feet
(C) 25 feet (D) 40 feet.

41. If a 220-volt heater is used on 110 volts, the amount of heat produced will be
(A) one-fourth as much
(B) one-half as much
(C) twice as much
(D) four times as much.

42. A completely short circuited heater resistance will be
(A) hotter than normal
(B) cooler than normal
(C) inoperative
(D) white hot.

43. A resistance of 5 ohms connected in series with a resistance of 10 ohms will result in a combined resistance of
(A) 2 ohms (B) 3 1/3 ohms
(C) 15 ohms (D) 7 1/2 ohms.

44. Two wires A and B have the same cross sectional area. The resistance of A is 500 ohms and that of B is 100 ohms. The number of times A is longer than B is
(A) 5 (B) 4
(C) 3 (D) 2.

45. The resistance of a circuit containing 1 ohm, 2 ohms, and 3 ohms, in parallel, is
(A) 6 ohms (B) 4.5 ohms
(C) .545 ohms (D) 5.45 ohms
(E) 5 ohms.

46. A field discharge resistance in a generator circuit is
(A) connected in series with the field, to limit field current
(B) connected across the field terminals, after the field current has been interrupted by opening the field switch, to prevent high voltages in the field circuit

47. Of the following, the copper wire or cable having the highest electrical resistance in a 100-foot length is
(A) #10 A.W.G.
(B) #12 A.W.G.
(C) 4/0 A.W.G.
(D) 250,000 C.M.

48. A rule-of-thumb is that the resistance of wire doubles (or halves) for each three A.W.G. sizes. According to this rule the resistance of a No. 18 A.W.G. wire compared to that of a No. 12 A.W.G. wire is
(A) one quarter (B) one half
(C) double (D) 4 times.

49. The resistance of a tungsten filament lamp is about 13 times as high when the lamp is on as when it is off. Accordingly, the cold resistance of a 40-watt 120-volt incandescent lamp, in ohms, is about
(A) 3 (B) 28
(C) 364 (D) 43500.

50. If two 4.8-ohm resistors are connected in parallel, the resulting resistance will be
(A) 9.6 ohms (B) 2.4 ohms
(C) 1.2 ohms (D) 0.6 ohm.

51. Essentially, the pull-out torque of a wound-rotor induction motor
(A) is independent of the rotor resistance
(B) increases rapidly as the rotor resistance is decreased
(C) decreases rapidly as the rotor resistance is decreased
(D) may rise or fall as the rotor resistance is increased, depending on the particular motor.

52. The resistance of a 3.6 kw heater when operated from a 120-volt circuit is
(A) 120 (B) 30
(C) 4 (D) 3.

53. Of the following materials, the one which has

a nearly zero temperature coefficient of resistance is
(A) copper (B) manganine
(C) carbon (D) porcelain.

54. In order to determine the insulation resistance between the frame and armature conductors of a motor, a 25,000 ohm voltmeter is connected in series with this resistance and to a 220-volt circuit. The voltmeter reads 5 volts. The insulation resistance of the motor is
(A) 25,000 ohms
(B) 125,000 ohms
(C) 1,100,000 ohms
(D) 1,075,000 ohms.

55. The resistance of each coil of a delta connected rotor of an A.C. motor is one ohm. The resistance per phase (between terminals) is
(A) 1/3 ohm (B) 3/2 ohms
(C) 2/3 ohm (D) 3 ohms.

56. The resistance of copper wire is
(A) directly proportional to its cross-sectional area
(B) directly proportional to its length
(C) inversely proportional to its length
(D) inversely proportional to its diameter.

57. If two equal resistance coils are connected in parallel, the resistance of this combination is equal to
(A) the resistance of one coil
(B) 1/2 the resistance of one coil
(C) twice the resistance of one coil
(D) 1/4 the resistance of one coil.

58. The insulation resistance of 50 ft. of #12 BS rubber covered wire, as compared to the insulation resistance of 100 ft. of this wire is
(A) 1/2 as much
(B) the same
(C) 4 times as much
(D) twice as much.

59. The resistance of a 150-scale voltmeter is 10,-000 ohms. The power, in watts, consumed by this voltmeter when it is connected across a 100-volt circuit is
(A) 10 (B) 5
(C) 2.5 (D) 1.

60. A storage battery consists of three lead cells connected in series. On open circuit the emf of the battery is 6.4 volts. When it delivers a current of 80 amperes its terminal voltage drops to 4.80 volts. Its internal resistance, in ohms, is approximately
(A) 0.01 (B) 0.02
(C) 0.03 (D) 0.04.

61. In reference to question No. 60, the terminal voltage, in volts, when the battery delivers 50 amperes is approximately
(A) 5.9 (B) 5.4
(C) 4.9 (D) 4.4.

62. Two copper conductors have the same length but the cross section of one is twice that of the other. If the resistance of the one having a cross section of twice the other is 10 ohms, the resistance of the other conductor, in ohms, is
(A) 5 (B) 10
(C) 20 (D) 30.

63. The resistance of a conductor, expressed in ohms, multiplied by the current squared; expressed in amperes, flowing in the conductor is equal to the
(A) final temperature of the conductor
(B) voltage across the conductor
(C) current loss in the conductor
(D) watts lost in heat.

64. In reference to a 130-volt, 36-watt lamp, the ratio between the cold and hot resistance of the lamp is approximately
(A) 1 to 3.5 (B) 1 to 7
(C) 1 to 12 (D) 1 to 20. 3912

65. A storage battery of 60 cells has an open circuit voltage of 120 volts. When supplying 50 amperes the voltage is 110 volts. The internal resistance of the battery is
(A) .20 ohms (B) 2.0 ohms
(C) 2.2 ohms (D) 2.4 ohms.

66. When connected across a direct current source of supply the shunt field coils of a generator take 0.1 amperes. A 450 ohm resistor is connected in series with the coils across the same source thereby reducing the current to 0.08 amperes. The resistance of the field is
(A) 81 ohms (B) 360 ohms
(C) 1800 ohms (D) 2500 ohms.

67. The equivalent resistance of a circuit having 4 parallel branches, the individual resistances of which are 1, 2, 5 and 10 ohms, is nearest to
(A) 18 ohms (B) 5.5 ohms
(C) .55 ohms (D) .18 ohms.

68. The insulation resistance of a 1000 foot piece of cable is 100 megohms between conductor and lead sheath. If three 2000 foot lengths of this cable were spliced in series to make a feeder the insulation resistance of this feeder would be nearest to
(A) 17 megohms
(B) 67 megohms
(C) 150 megohms
(D) 600 megohms.

(69)

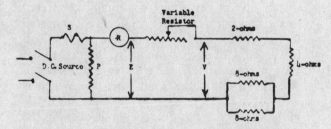

Items 69 to 76 refer to wiring diagram (69).

69. If resistances "S" (of low value) and "P" (of high value) are both associated with the same meter, the meter is
(A) a wattmeter
(B) a voltmeter
(C) an ammeter
(D) a varmeter.
2, 4, and both 8 ohm resistances is

70. When the d.c. voltage "E" is 100 and the current through the variable resistor is 1 ampere, the variable resistor is fixed at
(A) 78 ohms
(B) 86 ohms
(C) 90 ohms
(D) 100 ohms.

71. With the same load resistances and the same fixed value of the variable resistor as used in item 70, the d.c. voltage "E" is replaced by an a.c. voltage of 100. The current through the variable resistor is
(A) .707 ampere
(B) 1.00 ampere
(C) 1.41 amperes
(D) 1.73 amperes.

72. When the voltage drop across the 8 ohm resistances is 50 volts, that across the 2 ohm resistance is

(A) 10 volts
(B) 12.5 volts
(C) 25 volts
(D) 100 volts.

73. The *ratio* of the voltage drop across the 2 ohm resistance to that across the 4 ohm resistance
(A) increases with an increase in line voltage
(B) will increase if the two 8 ohm resistances are shorted
(C) decreases as line current decreases
(D) is independent of line current.

74. If the current through the 2 ohm resistance is 2 amperes, the total power consumed by the 2, 4, and both 8 ohm resistances is
(A) 40 watts
(B) 56 watts
(C) 88 watts
(D) 200 watts.

75. A relay "R", of negligible resistance, in series with the line as shown and set to operate at 4 amperes line current is taken out of service for repairs. The only available spare is also of negligible resistance and has a maximum current setting of 3 amperes. This spare will function properly if it is installed
(A) in series with one of the 8 ohm resistances
(B) in series and between the 2 and 4 ohm resistances
(C) in parallel across the 4 ohm resistance
(D) to directly replace the original relay.

76. With a fixed voltage "E", increasing the amount of the variable resistance put in the circuit will increase the voltage
(A) drop across the 2 ohm resistance
(B) "V" across the line
(C) drop across the 8 ohm resistance
(D) drop across the variable resistor.

77. If three unknown resistors are connected in series across an a.c. source of power it is certain that the
(A) power consumed by each resistor will be the same
(B) total current in the circuit is the sum of the current in each of the three resistors
(C) voltage drop across each will be the same
(D) current through each will be the same.

Answer Key

1. A	10. B	20. D	30. B	40. D	50. B	60. B	70. C
2. D	11. C	21. C	31. A	41. A	51. A	61. B	71. B
3. A	12. A	22. D	32. C	42. C	52. C	62. C	72. C
4. A	13. B	23. C	33. B	43. C	53. B	63. D	73. D
5. D	14. A	24. B	34. A	44. A	54. D	64. C	74. A
6. C	15. A	25. C	35. A	45. C	55. C	65. A	75. A
7. A	16. A	26. D	36. D	46. C	56. B	66. C	76. D
8. D	17. D	27. A	37. B	47. B	57. B	67. C	77. D
9. A	18. C	28. C	38. B	48. D	58. B	68. A	
	19. D	29. C	39. D	49. B	59. D	69. A	

SWITCHES, WIRING AND INSULATION

TYPES OF SWITCHES AND THEIR USE

1. Mercury toggle switches are sometimes used instead of regular toggle switches because they
   (A) cost less
   (B) are lighter
   (C) are easier to install
   (D) do not wear out as quickly.

2. T.P.D.T. would be used to identify a
   (A) wire   (B) conduit
   (C) fuse   (D) switch.

3. A make-and-break contact is provided in an electric bell to
   (A) keep the coil from overheating
   (B) make the armature vibrate
   (C) make the bell single stroke
   (D) prevent arcing at the push-button.

4. A make-before-break switch is used to
   (A) prevent tying two sources together
   (B) open one circuit before closing another
   (C) close one circuit before opening another
   (D) shorten the switch movement.

5. A limit switch is used on a piece of electrical apparatus to shut off the power when
   (A) the travel reaches a definite limit
   (B) the current exceeds a definite limit
   (C) the voltage is below a definite limit
   (D) frequently exceeds a definite limit.

6. The usual function of disconnect switches in a high voltage circuit is to
   (A) open or close the circuit under load
   (B) isolate from live buses equipment not in service
   (C) maintain continuity of service should the breakers fail
   (D) open the circuit in the event of overload.

7. High-voltage switches in power plants are commonly so constructed that their contacts are submerged in oil. The purpose of the oil is to
   (A) help quench arcing
   (B) lubricate the contacts
   (C) cool the switch mechanism
   (D) insulate the contacts from the switch framework.

8. In making connections to an exposed knife switch, the power supply is usually connected to the clip contacts while the load is connected to the switch blades. Connection of the load to the clips of such switches is avoided to
   (A) prevent arcing when the switch is opened
   (B) have the blades dead when the switch is open
   (C) allow changing fuses without opening the switch
   (D) prevent blowing of fuses at the time of closing the switch.

9. It is advisable to close a knife switch firmly and rapidly because then there is less
   (A) danger of shock to the operator
   (B) chance of making an error
   (C) mechanical wear of the contacts
   (D) likelihood or arcing.

10. Enclosed knife switches that require the switch to be open before the housing door can be opened, are called
    (A) service switches
    (B) air-break switches
    (C) safety switches
    (D) release switches.

11. The one of the following terms which could *not* correctly be used in describing a knife switch is
    (A) quick-break   (B) single throw
    (C) four-pole   (D) toggle.

12. The load side is usually wired to the blades of a knife switch to
    (A) prevent arcing when switch is opened
    (B) make the blades dead when switch is open
    (C) allow changing of fuses without opening switch
    (D) prevent blowing fuse when opening switch.

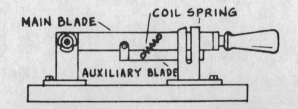

13. The purpose of the auxiliary blade on the knife switch shown is to
    (A) delay the opening of the circuit when the handle is pulled open
    (B) cut down arcing by opening the circuit quickly
    (C) retain the blades in place
    (D) increase the capacity of the switch.

14. The incoming power supply is usually wired to the "break" jaws rather than to the blades of an exposed knife switch. This practice is followed so that the
    (A) blades will be dead when the switch is open
    (B) arc will break quickly when the switch is opened
    (C) fuses can be replaced without opening the switch
    (D) switch can be closed with a minimum of arcing.

15. The operating mechanism of a Westinghouse solenoid operated oil switch has an air dashpot associated with the closing core to diminish the shock to the oil switch parts on closing. You would expect this dashpot to
    (A) speed up the closing operation
    (B) reduce the force necessary to close the switch
    (C) make the closing operation more positive
    (D) slow down the closing operation.

16. If the mercury switch is turned to the horizontal position, the mercury will flow and break the connection between the lead-in wires, thus opening the circuit. By logical reasoning, such a switch would be most useful when
    (A) the circuit must be opened quickly
    (B) there is likely to be explosive gas near the switch location
    (C) there is no restriction on noise
    (D) the switch need not be operated often.

(16)

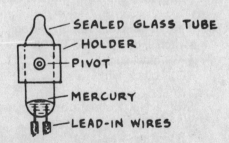

MERCURY SWITCH

17. Toggle switches of the type generally used on lighting circuits are
    (A) quick closing and quick opening
    (B) quick closing and slow opening
    (C) slow closing and slow opening
    (D) slow closing and quick opening.

18. The one of the following which could *not* be correctly used in describing a toggle switch is
    (A) single-hole mounting
    (B) slow-acting
    (C) three-way
    (D) double-pole.

Answer Key

Types and Uses

1. D	5. A	9. D	13. B	17. A
2. D	6. B	10. C	14. A	18. B
3. B	7. A	11. D	15. D	
4. C	8. B	12. B	16. B	

PROBLEMS

Items 1 to 7 inclusive in Column I are combinations of open and closed switches in diagram (1) each of which will result in one of the lamp conditions listed in Column II. For each combination in Column I, select the resulting lamp condition from Column II.

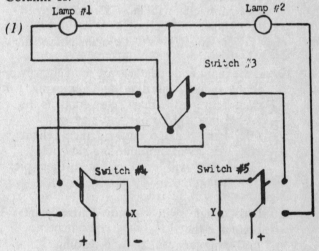

(1)

(Position of switches)
1. #3 closed to the right, #4 and #5 open
2. #3 closed to the right, #4 open, #5 closed
3. #3 closed to the right, #4 closed, #5 open
4. #3 closed to the left, #4 open, #5 closed
5. #3 closed to the left, #4 closed, #5 open
6. #3 closed to the right, #4 and #5 closed
7. #3 closed to the left, #4 and #5 closed, and jumper connected between X and Y.

COLUMN II
(A) Both lamps dark
(B) Both lamps lighted
(C) Only lamp #1 lighted
(D) Only lamp #2 lighted.

(8)

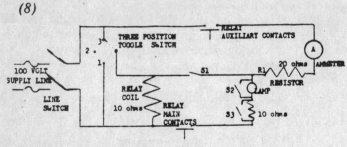

Items 8 to 15 inclusive are based on diagram (8). Switches S1 and S3 are normally closed and switch S2 is normally open. In each item assume the line switch is closed and the toggle switch remains on point #3 unless otherwise stated.

8. The above sketch is commonly known as a
   (A) parts diagram
   (B) working drawing
   (C) schematic wiring diagram
   (D) detail drawing.

9. With conditions as stated above the relay will pick up and the
   (A) lamp will be dark
   (B) ammeter will show a reading
   (C) lamp will be bright
   (D) resistor R1 will be open circuited.

10. If the main relay contacts are momentarily opened by quickly inserting, and removing, a fibre shim between the main relay contacts the
    (A) lamp will go out and stay out
    (B) lamp will go out and then relight
    (C) relay will drop out and stay out
    (D) relay will drop out and then pick up again.

11. If the toggle switch is moved from point #3 to point #2 the
    (A) ammeter will show a reading
    (B) relay will drop out
    (C) lamp will have full line voltage
    (D) resistor R1 will be open circuited.

12. If the toggle switch is moved from point #3 to point #1 the
    (A) lamp will be bright
    (B) relay will drop out
    (C) ammeter will show a high reading
    (D) line fuse will blow.

13. With the toggle switch again on point #3 if S2 is closed and S3 is opened the current in the relay coil will be
    (A) 4 amperes   (B) 5 amperes
    (C) 10 amperes   (D) 20 amperes.

14. With conditions as in Item 13 the equivalent resistance of the circuit between points #1 and #3 will be
    (A) 5 ohms   (B) 25 ohms
    (C) 20 ohms   (D) infinite.

15. With conditions as in Item 13 if S1 is opened the voltage drop across R1 is
    (A) 33 1/3 volts   (B) 50 volts
    (C) 66 2/3 volts   (D) 80 volts.

16. If an oil switch is used as a service switch in your building which is supplied with 13,500 volts, you must use between said service switch and the service wires
    (A) a removable link
    (B) nothing
    (C) a fuse
    (D) a disconnect switch.

17. You have a 100-ampere, 13 K.V. oil switch which has a trip coil rated up to 5 amperes. You have also a C.T. rated to 100 to 5 amperes. You wish the switch to open at 80 amperes line current. The setting of the trip coil to accomplish this should be
    (A) 4 amperes   (B) 5 amperes
    (C) 3 amperes   (D) 1 ampere.

(18)

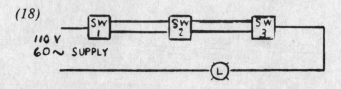

Questions 18-20 inclusive refer to diagram (18) of a lamp independently controlled from 3 points.

18. The conductor running from the supply to switch No. 1 should be the
    (A) blue wire   (B) white wire
    (C) black wire   (D) ground wire.

19. Switch No. 1 should be a
    (A) single pole switch
    (B) four way switch
    (C) two way switch
    (D) three-way switch.

20. Switch No. 2 should be a
    (A) single pole switch
    (B) two way switch
    (C) four way switch
    (D) three way switch.

Ítems 21 to 26 inclusive in Column I are combinations of closed switches in diagram (21) each of which will result in one of the lamp conditions listed in Column II. For each combination in Column I, select the resulting lamp condition from Column II.

(21)

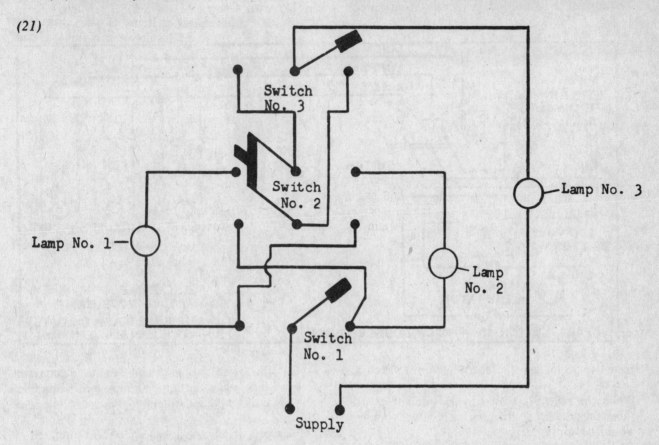

COLUMN I
(combinations of closed switches)

	switch No. 1	switch No. 2	switch No. 3
21.	left	left	right
22.	left	left	left
23.	left	right	right
24.	right	right	left
25.	right	left	right
26.	right	right	right

COLUMN II

(lamp conditions)

(A) No. 1 and No. 3 light

(B) No. 2 and No. 3 light

(C) only No. 3 lights

(D) no lights.

27. You may have to open a knife switch which may be carrying a very heavy load current. The proper way to open the switch is to
    (A) open it with a jerk so as to quickly break any arc
    (B) open it slowly so that there will not be a flashover at the contacts
    (C) open it with care, to avoid damage to the auxiliary blade by the arc
    (D) tie a 5-foot rope on the switch handle and stand clear of the switch.

28. To control a lamp independently from five different points you would use
    (A) two 3-way and three 4-way switches
    (B) four 3-way switches and one 4-way switch
    (C) three 3-way and two 4-way switches
    (D) three 4-way and two S.P.S.T. switches.

29. A lighting fixture is to be controlled independently from two different locations. The type of switch required in each of the two locations is

(A) single-pole, single-throw
(B) single-pole, double-throw
(C) double-pole, single-throw
(D) double-pole, double-throw.

30. To control a lamp independently from three

different points you would use
(A) two 3-way and one S.P.S.T. switch
(B) two 3-way and one 4-way switch
(C) two S.P.S.T. and one 3-way switch
(D) two 4-way and one S.P.S.T. switch.

(31)

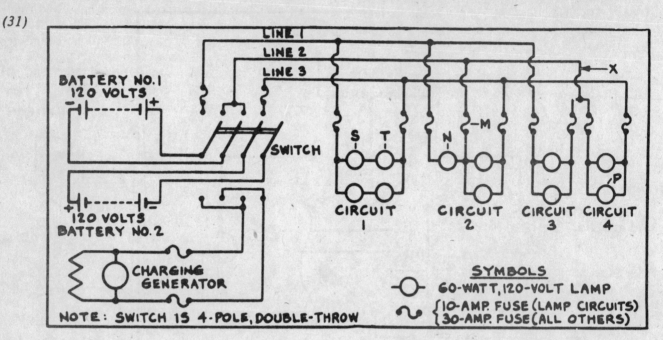

Items 31 to 38 inclusive refer to diagram (31).

31. When the switch is closed in the "down" position, the required charging generator voltage would be most nearly
(A) 240 volts   (B) 130 volts
(C) 110 volts   (D) 60 volts.

32. When the switch is closed in the "up" position, the voltage between line 1 and line 3 would be approximately
(A) 240 volts   (B) 120 volts
(C) 60 volts   (D) zero.

33. With the switch closed in the "up" position, the voltage between line 2 and line 3 would be approximately
(A) 240 volts   (B) 120 volts
(C) 60 volts   (D) zero.

34. If lamp P in circuit 4 burns out while the switch is closed in the "up" position
(A) the other lamp in circuit 4 and both lamps in circuit 3 should remain lighted
(B) all lamps in circuits 3 and 4 should become dark
(C) both lamps in circuit 3 should remain lighted and both lamps in circuit 4 should become dark

(D) the lower lamp in circuit 3 should become dark while the upper lamps in circuits 3 and 4 should remain lighted.

35. If lamp T in circuit 1 becomes short-circuited while the switch is closed in the "up" position, the most probable result will be that
(A) one of the circuit fuses will blow
(B) both of the circuit fuses will blow
(C) all other lamps in the circuit will burn brighter
(D) lamp S will burn brighter.

36. Suppose that, while the switch is closed in the "up" position, the wire breaks off at point X. The result would be that the lamps would
(A) remain lighted in circuit 3 and become dark in circuit 4
(B) become dark in circuit 3 and remain lighted in circuit 4
(C) all become dark in circuits 3 and 4
(D) all remain lighted in circuits 3 and 4.

37. If fuse M blows while the switch is closed in the "up" position
(A) all three lamps in circuit 2 will become dark
(B) all three lamps in circuit 2 will remain normally lighted

(C) lamp N will become very bright and the other two lamps very dim

(D) lamp N will become very dim and the other two lamps very bright.

38. Under normal conditions, with the switch closed in the "up" position, the current in line 2 is the current taken by one lamp multiplied by
(A) 11   (B) 7
(C) 4   (D) 1.

39. If switch "S" is closed, the ammeter readings will change as follows

(A) both will increase
(B) #1 only will increase
(C) both will decrease
(D) #2 only will increase.

(39)

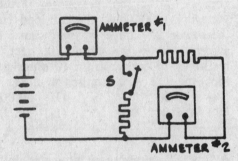

40. If a snap switch rated at 5 amperes is used for an electric heater which draws 10 amperes, the most likely result is that the
(A) circuit fuse will be blown
(B) circuit wiring will become hot
(C) heater output will be halved
(D) switch contacts will become hot.

41. The wall switch controlling a room light is usually
(A) connected across both lines
(B) a double pole type
(C) connected in one line only
(D) connected in both lines.

42. When a circuit breaker and a knife switch are connected in series in a circuit, the circuit should always be opened by
(A) tripping the circuit breaker and then opening the knife switch
(B) opening the knife switch and then tripping the circuit breaker
(C) opening the knife switch quickly, and leaving the circuit breaker closed
(D) simultaneously opening the knife switch and the breaker.

43. The two coils are wound in the directions indicated and both coils have exactly the same number of turns. When the switch is closed, the north pole of the permanent magnet will be
(A) repelled by both the left-hand and right-hand cores
(B) attracted by both the left-hand and right-hand cores
(C) attracted by the left-hand core and repelled by the right-hand core
(D) repelled by the left-hand core and attracted by the right-hand core.

(43)

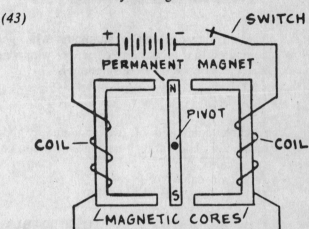

44. The double-pole double-throw switch which is properly connected as a reversing switch is
(A) 1   (B) 2
(C) 3   (D) 4.

(44)

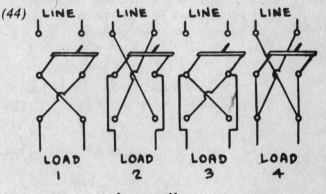

Answer Key
Problems

1. A	10. B	19. D	28. A	37. C
2. D	11. A or B	20. C	29. B	38. D
3. A	12. B	21. D	30. B	39. B
4. A	13. C	22. A	31. B	40. D
5. C	14. A	23. C	32. A	41. C
6. D	15. C	24. B	33. B	42. A
7. B	16. D	25. C	34. A	43. A
8. C	17. A	26. D	35. D	44. B
9. C	18. C	27. A	36. D	

WIRING EQUIPMENT

TYPES OF WIRE AND THEIR USES

1. The carrying capacity of aluminum wire when compared to a similar size of copper wire which has the same kind of insulation is
   (A) 84%   (B) 94%
   (C) 74%   (D) 100%.

2. A cable composed of two insulated stranded conductors laid parallel, having a common cover, is called a
   (A) twin cable
   (B) duplex cable
   (C) concentric cable
   (D) sector cable.

3. In multiple-conductor armored cable construction, a color scheme is used for identifying purpose. The color-coding of a 3-conductor cable should be which one of the following?
   (A) one white, one red and one black
   (B) two black and one white
   (C) two white and one black
   (D) one white, one black and one blue.

4. Type RL wires and cables would most likely be used for which one of the following applications?
   (A) power control switchboard
   (B) interior dry locations subject to high temperatures
   (C) interior high voltage applications
   (D) underground power distribution.

5. In panel wiring solid wire is preferred to stranded wire because it
   (A) will carry more current
   (B) has better insulation
   (C) can be "shaped" better
   (D) uses less copper.

6. Of the following, the poorest conductor of electricity is
   (A) carbon   (B) aluminum
   (C) copper   (D) silver.

7. Of the following, the best conductor of electricity is
   (A) tungsten   (B) iron
   (C) aluminum   (D) carbon.

8. The maximum voltage-drop between a d-c motor and its switchboard is not to exceed one percent of the supply voltage. If the supply voltage is 200 volts, the full-load current of the motor 100 amperes, the distance from the switchboard to the motor 100 feet, and the resistivity of copper from 10 ohms per C.M.-foot, the size wire required in C.M. is
   (A) 25,000   (B) 50,000
   (C) 100,000   (D) 200,000.

9. A type of electric wire protected by a spiral metal cover is known as
   (A) BX   (B) Romex
   (C) Ampex   (D) Conduit.

10. A stranded conductor has 37 strands each 90 mils in diameter. The area in circular mils of this conductor is most nearly
    (A) 3,300   (B) 123,200
    (C) 236,000   (D) 300,000.

11. A length of wire 1800' long is made up in a coil. If this coil has an average diameter of 6" then the number of turns in the coil is most nearly
    (A) 1,000   (B) 1,150
    (C) 1,450   (D) 7,200.

12. Laminated iron is used in a.c. magnetic circuits to
    (A) increase heat radiation
    (B) make assembly easier
    (C) reduce eddy currents
    (D) reduce permeability.

13. A copper wire one-tenth of an inch in diameter has a cross-sectional area of
    (A) 1,000 cir. mils   (B) 7,854 cir. mils
    (C) 10,000 cir. mils   (D) 31,416 cir. mils.

14. After No. 2 A.W.G., the next smaller copper wire or cable size is No.
    (A) 0
    (B) 1
    (C) 3
    (D) 4.

15. After No. 10 A.W.G., the next smaller copper wire size in common use is No.
    (A) 8
    (B) 9
    (C) 11
    (D) 12.

16. The diameter of the cable, compared to the diameter of a single conductor, is between
    (A) two and three times
    (B) three and four times
    (C) four and five times
    (D) five and six times.

(16)

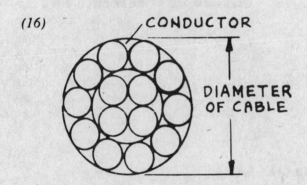

17. The conductors in a large lead-covered telephone cable are usually
    (A) stranded and rubber insulated
    (B) solid and rubber insulated
    (C) stranded and paper insulated
    (D) solid and paper insulated.

18. The sketch which correctly represents the cross-section of a standard stranded copper conductor is
    (A) 1
    (B) 2
    (C) 3
    (D) 4.

(18)

1   2   3   4

19. In measuring to determine the size of a stranded insulated conductor, the proper place to use the wire gauge is on
    (A) the insulation
    (B) the outer covering
    (C) the stranded conductor
    (D) one strand of the conductor.

20. If the following copper wire sizes were arranged in the order of increasing current carrying capacity, the correct arrangement would be
    (A) 18; 6; 0000; 500,000
    (B) 500,000; 0000; 6; 18
    (C) 0000; 18; 6; 500,000
    (D) 0000; 6; 18; 500,000.

21. Comparing No. 8 and No. 12 bare copper wire of equal lengths, the No. 8 wire will have lower
    (A) weight
    (B) cost
    (C) resistance
    (D) strength.

22. If the following bare copper wire sizes were arranged in the order of increasing weight per 1000 feet, the correct arangemnt would be
    (A) #00, #40, #8
    (C) #00, #8, #40
    (B) #40, #00, #8
    (D) #40, #8, #00.

23. The wire size most commonly used for branch circuits in residences is
    (A) #14
    (B) #16
    (C) #12
    (D) #18.

24. Standard tables are available showing the safe carrying capacity of copper wire of various sizes to avoid damage to insulation from overheating. The allowable current given is dependent on the
    (A) voltage
    (B) length of wire
    (C) type of current (a.c. or d.c.)
    (D) room temperature.

25. The sketch shows the ends of 4 bare copper wires full size with diameters as given. From left to right, the #14 wire is
    (A) first
    (B) second
    (C) third
    (D) fourth.

(25)

26. High-voltage cable which is to be installed in underground ducts is generally protected with a
    (A) steel wire armor
    (B) lead sheath
    (C) tarred jute covering
    (D) copper outer jacket.

27. "Nichrome" wire is commonly used for
    (A) transformer windings
    (B) lamp filaments
    (C) heater coils
    (D) battery connections.

28. After No. 4, the next larger American Wire Gage size is No.
(A) 2   (B) 3
(C) 5   (D) 6.

29. If one copper wire has a diameter of 0.128 inch, and another copper wire has a diameter of 0.064 inch, the resistance of 1,000 feet of the first wire compared to the same length of the second wire is
(A) one half   (B) one quarter
(C) double   (D) four times.

30. As compared with solid wire, stranded wire of the same gage size is
(A) given a higher current rating
(B) easier to skin
(C) larger in total diameter
(D) better for high voltage.

31. A stranded wire is given the same size designation as a solid wire if it has the same
(A) cross-sectional area
(B) weight per foot

(C) overall diameter
(D) strength.

32. A multi-conductor cable
(A) has a number of separate circuits
(B) is a single circuit cable composed of a number of strands
(C) is a flexible cable to carry motor current
(D) is a special car heating conductor.

Answer Key

(You'll learn more by writing your own answers before comparing them with these.)

Uses and Types of Wire

1. A	8. C	15. D	22. D	29. B
2. A	9. A	16. C	23. A	30. C
3. A	10. D	17. D	24. D	31. A
4. D	11. B	18. C	25. C	32. A
5. C	12. C	19. D	26. B	
6. A	13. C	20. A	27. C	
7. C	14. C	21. C	28. B	

WIRING SYSTEMS AND DIAGRAMS

1. The factor that determines the current carrying capacity of a two wire circuit is
(A) whether the supply is a.c. or d.c.
(B) the gage of the circuit wire
(C) the length of the circuit
(D) the number of outlets in the circuit.

2. In a balanced three phase wye-connected circuit the line voltages are equal
(A) to the voltage between any line and the neutral
(B) but the line currents are unequal
(C) and so are the line currents
(D) to the line currents.

3. Defects in wiring which permit current to jump from one wire to another before the intended path has been completed are called
(A) grounds   (B) shorts
(C) opens   (D) breaks.

4. With reference to a.c. supply circuits, the waves of voltage and current ordinarily encountered in practice are
(A) sine waves
(B) triangular waves
(C) circular waves
(D) rectangular waves.

5. If an inductive circuit carrying current is short circuited, the current in the circuit will
(A) cease to flow immediately
(B) continue to flow indefinitely
(C) continue to flow for an appreciable time after the instant of short circuit
(D) increase greatly.

6. A parallel a.c. circuit in resonance will
(A) have a high impedance
(B) act like a resistor of low value
(C) have current in each section equal to the line current
(D) have a high voltage developed across each inductive and capacitive section.

7. A certain amount of power is transmitted at a certain voltage and line loss. If the same amount of power is to be transmitted at twice the original voltage and same line loss, the effect on the weight of the transmission line is
(A) none
(B) to increase it four times
(C) to decrease it to one-fourth
(D) to decrease it to one-half.

8. The type of alternating current distribution system commonly used to supply both light and power is the

(A) 3-phase, 3-wire
(B) single-phase, 2-wire
(C) 2-phase, 3-wire
(D) 3-phase, 4-wire.

9. An input circuit has both A.C. and D.C. current flowing into it. It is desired that a coupling unit be used to transfer only A.C. The type of coupling circuit that would most effectively do this is

(9)

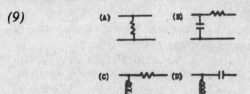

10. The letters S.P.S.T. frequently found on wiring plans refer to a type of
(A) cable   (B) switch
(C) fuse   (D) motor.

11. The letters R.I.L.C. are used in identifying
(A) transformers
(B) motors
(C) cables
(D) storage batteries.

12. An elementary wiring diagram is
(A) any single line diagram
(B) one showing all the elements of a 3 element meter
(C) one showing sequences of operation of switches and relays
(D) one showing conduit and cable runs
(E) always a single line diagram.

13. The term "exposed wiring" refers to wires that
(A) have no insulation when installed
(B) run in conduit along the outside wall of a building
(C) are not in conduit or raceway
(D) have had part of their insulation worn away.

14. In a three phase 4 wire system in which the voltage between lines is 5,500 volts, the voltage to neutral is most nearly
(A) 9,500 V.   (B) 5,500 v.
(C) 3,175 V.   (D) 1,830 V.

(15)

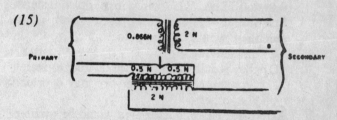

15. If the primary leads in diagram (15) are connected to a three-phase, three-wire, 208 volt system and the transformation ratios are as indicated on the diagram, the secondary leads will form a
(A) three-phase, four-wire system
(B) two-phase, four-wire system
(C) four-phase, five-wire system
(D) three-phase, three-wire system.

16. In the circuit of diagram (15) the voltage between the secondary leads "A" and "B" is
(A) 208 volts   (B) 120 volts
(C) 416 volts   (D) 240 volts.

Answer Key

(You'll learn more by writing your own answers before comparing them with these.)

Systems and Diagrams

1. B	5. C	8. D	11. C	14. C
2. C	6. A	9. D	12. C	15. B
3. B	7. C	10. B	13. B or C	16. C
4. A				

CORRECT WIRING TECHNIQUES

1. A certain lighting circuit requires the installation of No. 10 A.W.G. wire. If No. 10 wire is not available, it would be poor practice to use two No. 12 A.W.G. wires in parallel instead, because
   (A) they would take up too much room in the conduit
   (B) they would require twice as long to install
   (C) an open circuit in one wire may overload the other
   (D) the total conductor area would be smaller.

2. When applying rubber tape to a wire splice it should be applied with
   (A) no tension, to avoid stretching
   (B) just enough tension to hold it in place
   (C) as much tension as possible short of tearing the tape
   (D) sufficient tension to pull it to approximately half its original width.

3. The function of a spiking test on a power cable is to
   (A) determine if the sheath has deteriorated
   (B) determine if the cable is alive
   (C) find weak spots in the copper
   (D) test for compound leakage.

4. The one of the following which is *NOT* a common splicing rule is
   (A) wires of the same size should be spliced together in line
   (B) a joint, or splice, must be as mechanically strong as the wire itself
   (C) a splice must provide a path for the electric current that will be as good as another wire
   (D) all splices must be mechanically and electrically secured by means of solder.

5. Two-phase power may be converted to 3-phase power by
   (A) means of transformers connected in open-V
   (B) means of Scott connected transformers
   (C) means of an auto-transformer
   (D) none of the above methods.

6. The most valid objection for not fusing the middle wire of a 3-wire system with a grounded neutral is that
   (A) it will increase the replacement cost of the fuses
   (B) shutdown will be increased due to the blowing of the neutral fuse
   (C) blowing of the neutral fuse may unbalance the voltages on the two sides of the system with possible burnout of some of the lamps
   (D) the size of the neutral wire must be made twice as large as the ungrounded line wires.

7. The size of the mandrel to be pulled through a duct before the cable is pulled shall be approximately
   (A) one inch smaller than the duct
   (B) one-half inch smaller than the duct
   (C) one-quarter inch smaller than the duct
   (D) the same size as the duct.

8. When removing wooden lagging from a reel of cable or wire, which is about to be installed, it is good practice to place the lagging in a neat pile away from the reel mainly to avoid
   (A) interference with the pulling of the cable
   (B) damage to the lagging
   (C) losing the lagging
   (D) criticism for untidiness.

9. When wiring a 600 volt d.c. series circuit, the first positive connection must be to the center contact of the socket. The most likely reason for this requirement is to
   (A) lessen the voltage drop in the circuit
   (B) make the wiring uniform
   (C) reduce the amount of wire required to make the connections
   (D) lessen the hazards of a shock when screwing a bulb into its socket.

(10)

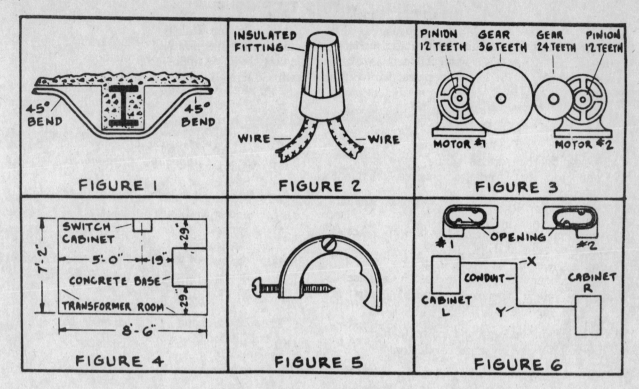

FIGURE 1   FIGURE 2   FIGURE 3

FIGURE 4   FIGURE 5   FIGURE 6

Items 10 to 15¹ inclusive refer to diagram (10). Each item gives the proper figure to use with that item.

10. When a wire is pulled into the conduit shown in Figure 1, it must go around bends amounting to a total of
(A) 0°   (B) 90°
(C) 180°   (D) 360°.

11. Wires are often spliced by the use of a fitting like the one shown in Figure 2. The use of this fitting does away with the need for
(A) skinning   (B) cleaning
(C) twisting   (D) soldering.

12. The two identical motors in Figure 3 are connected to the same power supply and are wired so that they normally tend to turn in the same direction. When the power is turned on
(A) the motors will stall
(B) both motors will turn at normal speed in the same direction
(C) motor #1 will turn in its normal direction driving motor #2 backwards
(D) motor #2 will turn in its normal direction driving motor #1 backwards.

13. The dimensions of the concrete base shown in Figure 4 are

(A) 14″ x 28″   (B) 23″ x 28″
(C) 23″ x 29″   (D) 14″ x 29″

14. The device shown in Figure 5 is a
(A) C-clamp
(B) test clip
(C) battery connector
(D) ground clamp.

15. Figure 6 shows two types of conduit fitting (#1 and #2) used as pull boxes at sharp bends in conduit runs. The figure also shows the layout of a conduit run on the wall between cabinets L and R. If wire is to be pulled into the conduit starting at cabinet L, and the wire is to be continuous without a splice from cabinet L to cabinet R, the best choice of fittings is to have a
(A) #1 at corner X and a #2 at corner Y
(B) #2 at both corners X and Y
(C) #1 at both corners X and Y
(D) #2 at corner X and a #1 at corner Y.

16. When removing the insulation from a wire before making a splice, care should be taken to avoid nicking the wire mainly because the
(A) current carrying capacity will be reduced
(B) resistance will be increased
(C) wire tinning will be injured
(D) wire is more likely to break.

Items 17 to 26 inclusive in Column I are common
uses for insulated wires or cables. Column II lists
and describes a variety of insulated wires and cables.
For each item in Column I, select the most appropriate wire or cable from Column II.

COLUMN I
(uses)

17. Six-volt doorbell circuit wiring
18. Conductors in large lead-covered telephone cables
19. Portable lamp leads
20. Branch circuits in residences
21. Coil of a telephone receiver
22. Branch circuit conductors for a 10-h.p., 250-volt motor
23. Conductors in lighting fixtures
24. Test leads for use with a portable 150-volt voltmeter
25. High-tension underground power cables
26. 120-volt service entrance conductors

COLUMN II
(wire or cable)

	Size	Conductor	Insulation
(A)	#4/0	stranded	oil-saturated paper
(B)	#6	stranded	rubber
(C)	#14	solid	rubber
(D)	#18	solid	wax-treated cotton
(E)	#18	stranded	rubber
(H)	#19	solid	dry paper
(J)	#20	solid	enamel
(K)	#40	solid	enamel

*DIRECTIONS: For each question read all choices carefully.
Then select that answer which you consider correct or most
nearly correct. Write the letter preceding your best choice next to
the question*

27. When applying rubber tape to a lighting circuit splice, it is necessary to
    (A) have the cambric backing against the conductors
    (B) heat the tape properly before applying
    (C) use rubber cement on the conductors
    (D) stretch the tape properly during application.

28. The best of the following tools to use for cutting off a piece of single-conductor #6 rubber insulated lead covered cable is a
    (A) pair of electrician's pliers
    (B) hacksaw
    (C) hammer and cold chisel
    (D) lead knife.

29. Of the following, it would be most difficult to solder a copper wire to a metal plate made of
    (A) copper   (B) brass
    (C) iron   (D) tin.

30. To make a good soldered connection between two stranded wires, it is *least* important to
    (A) twist the wires together before soldering

    (B) use enough heat to make the solder flow freely
    (C) clean the wires carefully
    (D) apply solder to each strand before twisting the two wires together.

31. It is good practice to connect the ground wire for a building electrical system to a
    (A) gas pipe
    (B) cold water pipe
    (C) vent pipe
    (D) steam pipe.

32. Of the following, the least undesirable practice if a specified wire size is not available for part of a circuit is to
    (A) use two wires of 1/2 capacity in parallel as a substitute
    (B) use the next larger size wire
    (C) use a smaller size wire if the length is short
    (D) reduce the size of the fuse and use smaller wire.

33. To straighten a long length of wire, which has been tightly coiled, before pulling it into a conduit run, a good method is to
    (A) roll the wire into a coil in the opposite direction
    (B) fasten one end to the floor and whip it against the floor from the other end
    (C) draw it over a convenient edge
    (D) hold the wire at one end and twist it with the pliers from the other end.

34. The *least* important action in making soldered connection between two wires is to
    (A) use the proper flux
    (B) clean the wires well
    (C) use plenty of solder
    (D) use sufficient heat.

35. When tightening a terminal screw connection, the end of the wire should pass around the screw in the same direction as the screw is turned so that
    (A) the wire will act as a locknut
    (B) the screw can be removed more easily
    (C) any pull on the wire will tighten the screw
    (D) the wire will not turn off.

36. The most practical way to determine in the field if a large coil of #14 wire has the required length for a given job is to
    (A) weigh the coil and compare with a new 1000-foot coil
    (B) measure the electrical resistance and compare with a 1000-foot coil
    (C) measure the length of one turn and multiply by the number of turns
    (D) unwind the coil and lay the wire alongside the conduit before pulling it in.

37. To determine which wire of a two-wire 120-volt a.c. line is the grounded wire, one correct procedure is to
    (A) connect a center-zero voltmeter across the line and note the direction of movement of the pointer
    (B) quickly touch each line wire in turn to a cold-water pipe
    (C) connect one lead of a test lamp to the conduit, and test each side of the line with the other lead
    (D) thrust the two line wires about an inch apart into a slice of raw potato and watch for discoloration.

38. The wires in the right-hand junction box are to be spliced so that the switch will control both lighting fixtures and the fixtures will be connected in parallel. The wires to be spliced, in accordance with good wiring practice, are
    (A) 1 to 4, 2 to 6, 3 to both 5 and 7
    (B) 1 to 6, 2 to 5, 3 to both 4 and 7
    (C) 1 to 7, 2 to both 5 and 6, 3 to 4
    (D) 1 to 5, 2 to both 6 and 7, 3 to 4.

(38)
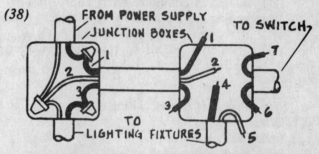

39. Wire splices in modern home and business building wiring systems are made both mechanically firm and of low resistance by means of
    (A) mechanical connectors (C) brazing
    (B) spot welding   (D) plastic tape.

Answer Key

(You'll learn more by writing your own answers before comparing them with these.)

Correct Wiring Techniques

1. C	9. D	17. D	25. A	33. B
2. D	10. C	18. H	26. B	34. C
3. D	11. D	19. E	27. D	35. D
4. D	12. A	20. C	28. B	36. C
5. B	13. B	21. K	29. C	37. C
6. C	14. D	22. B	30. D	38. B
7. C	15. D	23. E	31. B	39. A
8. A	16. D	24. E	32. B	

ELECTRICIAN

CONDUITS

DIRECTIONS: For each question read all choices carefully. Then select that answer which you consider correct or most nearly correct. Write the letter preceding your best choice next to the question

1. With respect to pulling wires into a conduit, it is usually specified that a certain percentage of the conduit area must be left unoccupied. The purpose of this requirement is to permit
   (A) pulling in the wires without undue strain or abrasion
   (B) pulling in additional wires later if needed
   (C) pulling out the wires for replacement even if the insulation has swelled
   (D) circulation of air so that the insulation will not be damaged by heat.

2. When installing electric wiring it is essential that all conduits be
   (A) concealed
   (B) rigidly supported
   (C) left exposed
   (D) given identifying markers.

3. The internal diameter of 1/2-inch electrical conduit is approximately
   (A) 0.422 inch　　(B) 0.5 inch
   (C) 0.552 inch　　(D) 0.622 inch.

4. The most important reason for using a condulet-type fitting in preference to making a bend in a one-inch conduit run is to
   (A) obtain a neater job
   (B) cut down length of conduit needed
   (C) avoid possible flattening of conduit when bending
   (D) make wire pulling easier.

5. Electrical wires are run through conduit in order to
   (A) increase the current carrying capacity of the wires
   (B) protect the wires from damage
   (C) decrease the cost of initial installation
   (D) increase the break-down voltage of the wires.

6. When a conduit enters a knock-out in an outlet box, it should be provided with a
   (A) locknut on the inside and a bushing on the outside
   (B) bushing on the inside and a locknut on the outside
   (C) bushing and a locknut on the outside
   (D) bushing and a locknut on the inside.

7. The main reason for grounding conduit installations is to
   (A) reduce leakage between wires
   (B) prevent short circuits
   (C) save wiring
   (D) prevent conduit from becoming alive to ground.

8. The inside edge on the end of conduit is reamed after cutting mainly to
   (A) aid in screwing on the bushing
   (B) prevent injury to the wire
   (C) make pulling the wire easier
   (D) finish the end of the thread.

9. A conduit is to be run diagonally across a 6 foot by 8 foot room. If the ends of the conduit are to be one foot from the room corners, the conduit should be cut to
   (A) 8 feet　　(B) 9 feet
   (C) 10 feet　　(D) 12 feet.

DIRECTIONS: *The sketches in Column I are of* WIRING DE-VICES *suitable for the* DOTTED LOCATIONS *on one of the four sketches in Column II. For each* DEVICE *in Column I, select the suitable* LOCATION *from Column II.*

COLUMN I- WIRING DEVICES

COLUMN II- DOTTED LOCATIONS

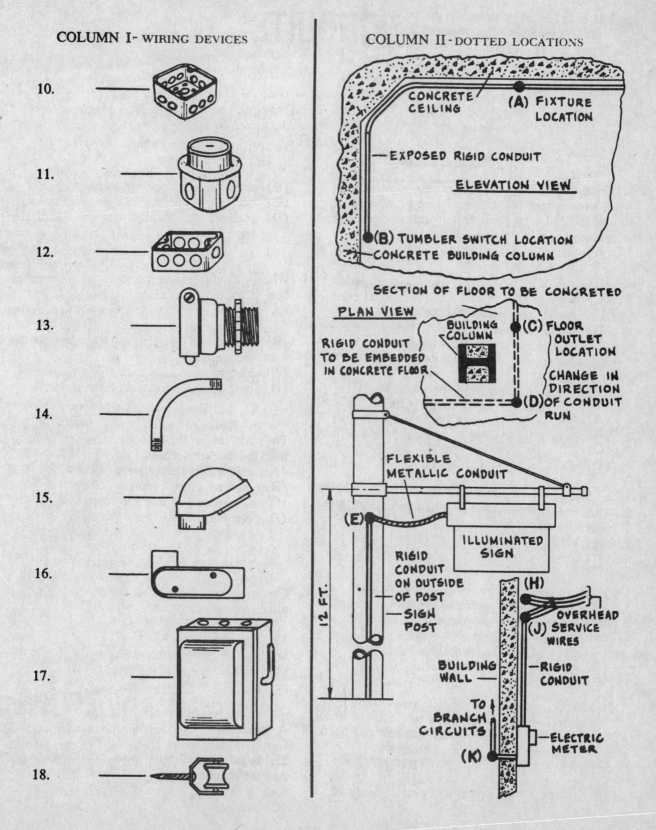

19. To support conduit on a hollow tile wall, use
    (A) through-bolts
    (B) lag screws
    (C) machine screws
    (D) toggle bolts.

20. If each circuit originates at the switchboard, the total amount of wire required for the conduit runs shown (neglecting connections) is

    (A) 5300 ft.   (B) 2650 ft.
    (C) 2400 ft.   (D) 1600 ft.

(20)

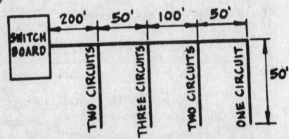

NOTE: TWO WIRES PER CIRCUIT

21. According to the national electrical code, a run of conduit between two outlet boxes should not contain more than four quarter-bends. The most likely reason for this limitation is that more bends will
    (A) result in cracking the conduit
    (B) make the pulling of the wire too difficult
    (C) increase the wire length unnecessarily
    (D) not be possible in one standard length of conduit.

22. Standard iron conduit comes in 10-foot lengths. The number of such lengths required for a run of 23 yards is
    (A) 3   (B) 4
    (C) 6   (D) 7.

23. Rigid conduit is generally secured to sheet metal outlet boxes by means of
    (A) threadless couplings
    (B) box connectors
    (C) locknuts and bushings
    (D) conduit clamps.

24. Checking a piece of rigid electrical conduit with a steel scale, you measure the inside diameter as 1 1/16″ and the outside diameter as 1 5/16″ The nominal size of this conduit is
    (A) 3/4″   (B) 1″
    (C) 1 1/4″   (D) 1 1/2″.

(25)

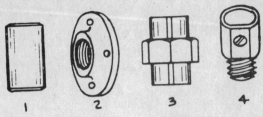

25. The standard coupling for rigid electrical conduit is
    (A) 1   (B) 2
    (C) 3   (D) 4.

26. Where galvanized steel conduit is used, the primary purpose of the galvanizing is to
    (A) increase mechanical strength
    (B) retard rusting
    (C) provide a good surface for painting
    (D) provide good electrical contact for grounding.

27. When a number of rubber insulated wires are being pulled into a run of conduit having several sharp bends between the two pull boxes, the pulling is likely to be hard and the wires are subjected to considerable strain. For these reasons it is advisable in such a case to
    (A) push the wires into the feed end of the conduit at the same time that pulling is being done
    (B) pull in only one wire at a time
    (C) use extra heavy grease
    (D) pull the wires back a few inches after each forward pull to gain momentum.

28. The six wires shown are to be properly connected so that the lighting fixture can be controlled by a single-pole on-off switch. The correct connections in accordance with established good practice are
    (A) 1 to 3 and 5; 2 to 4 and 6
    (B) 1 to 5; 2 to 3; 4 to 6
    (C) 1 to 3 and 6; 2 to 4 and 5
    (D) 1 to 3; 4 to 5; 2 to 6.

(28)

CONDUIT TO POWER SUPPLY
JUNCTION BOX
CONDUIT TO LIGHTING FIXTURE
CONDUIT TO SWITCH

29. Rigid conduit must be so installed as to prevent the collection of water in it between outlets.

In order to meet this requirement, the conduit should *not* have a

(A) low point between successive outlets

(B) high point between successive outlets

(C) low point at an outlet

(D) high point at an outlet.

30. One advantage of cutting 1″ rigid conduit with a hacksaw rather than with a 3-wheel pipe cutter is that

(A) the cut can be made with less exertion

(B) the pipe is not squeezed out of round

(C) less reaming is required after the cut

(D) no vise is needed.

31. When a long thread is used on one of two pieces of conduit joined by a coupling secured with a lock nut as indicated in the sketch, the probable reason for the use of this long thread is that

(A) one piece of conduit has been cut too short

(B) expansion or contraction of conduit due to temperature changes has to be compensated for

(C) neither conduit was free to turn when the coupling was made

(D) the joint has to be firmly anchored in a concrete wall.

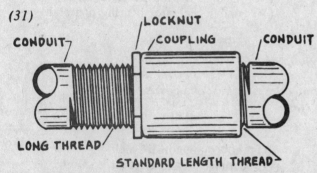

32. If each of the four 90° conduit elbows has the dimensions shown, the distance S is

(A) 20″   (B) 22″

(C) 24″   (D) 26″

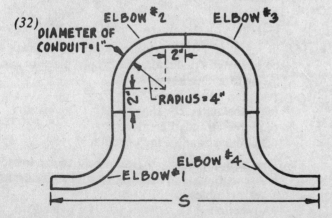

33. The sketch shows four standard rigid electrical conduit sizes in cross-section. The one which is nominal 1/2-inch conduit is No.

(A) 1   (B) 2

(C) 3   (D) 4.

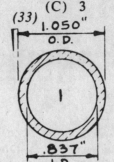

34. The National Electrical Code requires that conduit must be continuous from outlet to outlet, must be mechanically and electrically connected to all fittings, and must be suitably grounded. The reason for having the conduit electrically continuous and grounded is to

(A) provide a metallic return conductor

(B) shield the wires inside the conduit from external magnetic fields

(C) make it easy to test wiring connections

(D) prevent electrical shock which might otherwise result from contact with the conduit.

35. A conduit coupling is sometimes tightened by using a strap wrench rather than by using a Stillson wrench. The strap wrench is used when it is important to avoid

(A) crushing the conduit

(B) stripping the pipe threads

(C) bending the conduit

(D) damaging the outside finish.

36. A standard pipe thread differs from a standard screw thread in that the pipe thread

(A) is tapered

(B) is deeper

(C) requires no lubrication when cutting

(D) has the same pitch for any diameter of pipe.

Answer Key
Conduits

1. A	9. A	16. E	23. C	30. C
2. B	10. A	17. K	24. B	31. C
3. D	11. C	18. H	25. A	32. D
4. D	12. B	19. D	26. B	33. B
5. B	13. E	20. A	27. A	34. D
6. B	14. D	21. B	28. D	35. D
7. B	15. J	22. D	29. A	36. A
8. D				

INSULATION

DIRECTIONS: Column I lists ELECTRICAL INSULATING MATERIALS, *each of which is commonly employed for one of the* USES *listed in Column II. Select the most common use and record the corresponding letter in Column I.*

COLUMN I - INSULATING MATERIALS

1. slate
2. asbestos
3. impregnated paper
4. varnish
5. wood
6. soft rubber
7. enamel
8. mica
9. fibre
10. porcelain

COLUMN II - USES

(A) in lamp cord
(B) between commutator bars
(C) on small magnet wire
(D) for large switchboard panels
(E) on transformer laminations
(H) in heater cords
(K) for high tension bus insulators
(L) storage battery plate separators
(M) in high tension power cable
(P) under generator bearing pedestal.

DIRECTIONS: For each question read all choices carefully. Then select that answer which you consider correct or most nearly correct. Write the letter preceding your best choice next to the question

11. A good electrical insulator which will resist a very high temperature is
(A) bakelite   (C) transformer oil
(B) enamel   (D) mica.

12. When skinning a small wire, the insulation should be "penciled down" rather than cut square to
(A) prevent the braid from fraying
(B) save time in making the splice
(C) decrease danger of nicking the wire
(D) allow more insulation in the splice.

13. Asbestos is commonly used as the covering of electric wires in locations where there is likely to be high
(A) voltage   (B) temperature
(C) humidity   (D) current.

14. Overloading insulated wire or cable for long periods of time is considered poor practice because it usually causes
(A) over expansion of the conductor

(B) the conductor to melt
(C) damage to the duct or conduit
(D) the insulation to deteriorate.

15. Rubber insulation on an electrical conductor would most quickly be damaged by continuous contact with
(A) acid   (B) water
(C) oil   (D) alkali.

16. In measuring to determine the size of a stranded insulated conductor, the proper place to use the wire gauge is on
(A) the insulation
(B) the outer covering
(C) the stranded conductor
(D) one strand of the conductor.

17. The material which is *least* likely to be found in use as the outer covering of rubber insulated wires or cables is
(A) cotton   (C) lead
(B) varnished cambric   (D) neoprene.

18. If each of the 19 strands of the conductor shown has a diameter of 0.024″, and the thickness of the insulation is 0.047″, the diameter over the insulation is
(A) 0.107″   (B) 0.167″
(C) 0.214″   (D) 0.238″

(18)

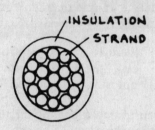

19. Assuming that the same kind of insulating material is used on each of the four copper conductors shown, the one intended for the highest voltage service is number
(A) 1   (B) 2
(C) 3   (D) 4.

(19)

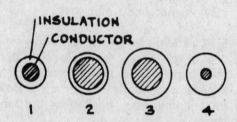

20. Circulating shaft currents through the bearings of a turbo-generator will cause pitting and deterioration of the bearing surface, these circulating currents are stopped by

(A) having an insulating pad under one generator pedestal
(B) the insulating property of the lubricating oil
(C) insulating the shaft from the machine frame
(D) having an insulating section in the shaft.

21. The life of insulation used in electrical installations is directly affected by heat. Of the following, the electrical insulation which can *least* withstand heat is
(A) enamel
(B) rubber
(C) fiberglass
(D) mica.

22. One advantage of rubber insulation is that it
(A) does not deteriorate with age
(B) is able to withstand high temperatures
(C) does not absorb much moisture
(D) is not damaged by oil.

Answer Key

(You'll learn more by writing your own answers before comparing them with these.)

Insulation

1. D	6. A	11. D	15. C	19. D
2. H	7. C	12. C	16. D	20. A
3. M	8. B	13. B	17. B	21. B
4. E	9. P	14. D	18. C	22. C
5. L	10. K			

LIGHTING AND WIRING

1. After a new series lighting circuit has been completely installed, but before any lamps are in place, a standard lamp bank is connected across the fuse clips with the fuse out, and the circuit switch is closed. Lamps are then screwed into the sockets of one series, one lamp at a time, starting at the ground end. If there is a ground on any series wire, the lamp bank will light when the
   (A) first lamp is screwed in
   (B) lamp on the low side of the ground is screwed in
   (C) lamp on the high side of the ground is screwed in
   (D) last lamp is screwed in.

2. The grounded leg of a lighting circuit is always connected to the shells of the lighting sockets to
   (A) ground the circuit
   (B) reduce the possibility of accidental shock
   (C) simplify the wiring
   (D) avoid burning out lamps.

3. Light fixtures suspended from chains should be wired so that the
   (A) wires do not support the fixture
   (B) wires help support the fixture
   (C) chains have an insulated link
   (D) chain is not grounded to prevent short-circuits.

4. Portable lamp cord is likely to have
   (A) steel armor
   (B) stranded wires
   (C) paper insulation
   (D) number 8 wire.

5. A test lamp using an ordinary lamp bulb is commonly used to test
   (A) for polarity of a d.c. power supply
   (B) whether a power supply is a.c. or d.c.
   (C) whether a circuit is overloaded
   (D) for grounds on 120-volt circuits.

6. One advantage of D.C. lighting is
   (A) the ease of locating a burnt out lamp
   (B) the possibility of using five lamp clusters where necessary

(C) there is no necessity of providing a special lighting transformer
(D) one side of the circuit is grounded.

7. When testing a lighting circuit for grounds, the device which would be least useful is
   (A) a lamp bank   (B) a megger
   (C) an ammeter   (D) a voltmeter.

8. One advantage of using series circuits for street lighting is
   (A) lower voltage circuit
   (B) decreased copper requirement
   (C) longer lamp life
   (D) higher lamp efficiency.

9. Five 120 volt lamps are placed in series across a 600 volt circuit and light normally. One of the lamps is then removed and replaced with a good plug fuse. Under these conditions the total illumination supplied by the remaining 4 lamps will be
   (A) greater than for the 5 lamps
   (B) less than for the 5 lamps
   (C) approximately the same as for the 5 lamps
   (D) zero because the lamps will burn out almost immediately.

10. In the accompanying diagram the lamps that are lighted with normal brightness are
    (A) 1 and 4 only
    (B) 1 and 3 only
    (C) 1 and 2 only
    (D) only No. 1.

(10)

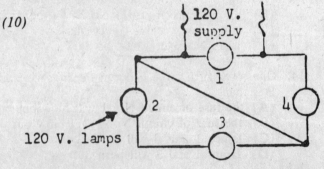

11. Your helper suggests that, in order to increase the amount of light on the job you are doing,

you should substitute two 100-watt lamps for two of the 36-watt lamps in the lamp bank you are using. If you follow this suggestion the result will be that

(A) all 5 lamps will burn at normal brightness
(B) all 5 lamps will be very dim
(C) the two 100-watt lamps will be dim, and the other 3 will be very bright
(D) the two 100-watt lamps will be very bright, and the other 3 will be dim.

12. Two 120-volt lamps are connected in series across a 120-volt battery which is ungrounded. The common connection of the lamps is grounded. If the lamp which is connected directly to the negative side of the battery should have a broken filament, a ground fault on the negative side of the battery would be indicated by

(A) both lamps being dark
(B) the good lamp being lit at full brilliancy
(C) the good lamp being short circuited
(D) the good lamp being lit at approximately half brilliancy.

(13)

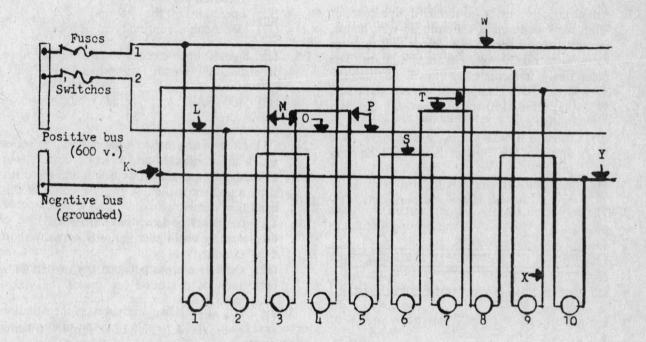

Items 13 to 18 inclusive are based on diagram (13) of portions of two series lighting circuits carried in a single conduit. Refer to this sketch in answering these items.

13. One indication of a cross between the two wires at M is that
(A) the 5 lamps of circuit No. 1 will be dark
(B) the 5 lamps of circuit No. 2 will be dark
(C) lamp No. 2 only will be dark
(D) lamp No. 3 only will be dark.

14. One result of a cross between the two wires at P is that
(A) the fuse of circuit No. 1 will blow out
(B) the fuse of circuit No. 2 will blow out
(C) lamps 1 and 3 will be dark
(D) lamps 1 and 3 will burn out.

15. Of the lamps shown, the fewest will become dark if there is an open circuit at
(A) K   (B) L
(C) S   (D) W.

16. Of the lamps shown, the greatest number will be affected by a ground at
(A) K   (B) L
(C) X   (D) Y.

17. If the two wires at T become crossed
(A) lamps 8 and 10 will become very dim
(B) lamp 9 will become very dim
(C) the fuse for circuit 2 will burn out
(D) the fuse for circuit 1 will burn out.

18. If each lamp takes a current of 0.35 amp., the current in the wire from X to K, due only to the lamps shown, is
(A) zero   (B) 0.35 amp.
(C) 1.75 amps.   (D) 3.50 amps.

19. A bank of 5 similar 120 volt lamps in series was to be used across a 600 volt line to furnish illumination. When connected across the 600 volt source the first lamp remained dark and the other lamps lit up extra brilliant for a few moments and then went dark. The probable cause of this action was that
    (A) the line voltage was too low to light all lamps
    (B) socket of the first lamp had an open circuit
    (C) all lamps were defective
    (D) socket of the first lamp was shorted.

20. An electrician, using a standard five-in-series lamp bank containing 130-volt, 36-watt lamps, removes two of the 36-watt lamps and replaces them with two 30-volt, 1.6-ampere lamps. The most likely immediate result will be that the
    (A) two 30-volt lamps will remain dark and the three 130-volt lamps will be very bright
    (B) three 130-volt lamps will remain dark and the two 30-volt lamps will be very bright
    (C) two 30-volt lamps will burn out
    (D) three 130-volt lamps will burn out.

(21)

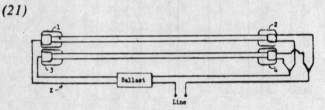

Items 21 to 25 inclusive refer to a standard lighting fixture in diagram (21) using two 72-inch, T-12, "slimline" fluorescent lamps which are fed from a 120-volt, 60-cycle, a.c. line, and are connected as shown in the above sketch. Under normal operating conditions, each lamp takes a current of 425 ma. and draws 55 watts, while the ballast loss is 34 watts.

21. The "high voltage" sockets are
    (A) 1 and 2   (B) 1 and 3
    (C) 2 and 4   (D) 3 and 4.

22. The actual line current taken by the fixture in normal operation is about 1.6 amperes, while the current calculated from the given voltage and wattage is about 1.2 amperes. This difference indicates that the
    (A) ballast must require considerable leakage current
    (B) line voltage is usually more than 120 volts
    (C) power factor of the equipment is less than 1.0

    (D) information given is only a rough approximation.

23. If a 0-5 amp. a.c. ammeter were connected in series with line X, the reading of the meter with the lamps operating would be
    (A) 0.43   (B) 0.85
    (C) 1.6   (D) 4.25.

24. Two wires are connected to each of sockets 2 and 4 in order to provide for
    (A) heating of the lamp filaments
    (B) breaking the circuit when the lamps are removed
    (C) operation of the starters
    (D) dependable continuity of service.

25. The highest open-circuit voltage in the type of installation shown is approximately
    (A) 200 volts   (B) 400 volts
    (C) 600 volts   (D) 800 volts.

26. Of the ten lamps in two adjacent 5-lamp series which are connected to the same circuit, four of the lamps are uniformly bright and the other six are uniformly dim. A possible cause of this condition is that
    (A) two sizes of lamp have been used
    (B) one socket in each series is partially short circuited
    (C) there is a cross between the two series
    (D) there is a ground on one of the series.

Items 27 to 32 inclusive are based on the situation described below. Refer to this situation in answering these items.

SITUATION: One of your jobs is the installation and connection of 20 single-lamp incandescent lighting fixtures as indicated in diagram (27). The outlet boxes supporting the fixtures are to be fastened to the flanges of the roof cross beams. The job requires only a single conduit between outlet boxes, but alternate fixtures must be connected to each of two lighting circuits which will come off the lighting panel shown. It is also specified that a separate negative return wire must be used for each circuit, and that all lamps must be connected in 5-lamp series. The braid covering of the wires is required to be black for positive, white for negative and red for series.

(27)

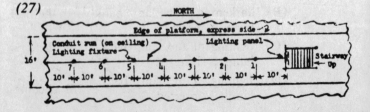

Note: The lighting panel is 300 feet from the southernmost lighting fixture.

27. With respect to the amount of wire needed, it is correct to say that the
    (A) white and black are about equal
    (B) red is about half the white
    (C) black is about double the red
    (D) white is about as much as the other two together.

28. The total number of wires in the conduit between fixtures 3 and 4 will be
    (A) 2   (B) 4
    (C) 5   (D) 6.

29. The total number of wires in the conduit between fixtures 17 and 18 (not shown in the sketch) will be
    (A) 2   (B) 4
    (C) 5   (D) 6.

30. Inspecting the wires connected to a fixture socket, you would know that an error had been made if you found that the colors of the two wires were
    (A) white and black   (B) white and red
    (C) black and red   (D) red and red.

31. The instrument that would prove *least* useful in testing for opens, grounds, and crosses after the wiring has been completed is the
    (A) ammeter   (B) voltmeter
    (C) ohmmeter   (D) megger.

32. To test one of the completed circuits before lamps have been placed in any socket and before the circuit switch is closed, a 5-lamp bank has been connected between the positive bus and the circuit positive wire at the lighting panel. If now the lamps of one series are placed in their sockets one at a time, starting with the one connected to the positive wire, a ground would positively be indicated by
    (A) darkening of the lamp bank when the first lamp is inserted
    (B) darkening of the lamp bank when the fifth lamp is inserted
    (C) lighting of the lamp bank when the first lamp is inserted
    (D) lighting of the lamp bank when the fifth lamp is inserted.

33. In order to use fluorescent lighting in a building which has only a 110 volt DC supply, it is necessary to use
    (A) fluorescent lamps designed for DC
    (B) fluorescent fixtures with an approved DC auxiliary or inductance unit and a series resistance of the correct value
    (C) fluorescent fixtures ordinarily used on AC
    (D) fluorescent fixtures ordinarily used on AC but equipped with a rectifier.

(34)

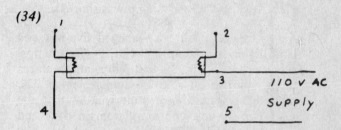

The glow type starter used to operate a fluorescent lamp is designed to act as a time switch which will connect the two filament type electrodes in each end of the lamp in series with the ballast during the short preheating period when the lamp is first turned on. The starter will then open the circuit to establish the arc.

The following questions, numbered 34 and 35, are to be answered in keeping with the above statement and diagram (34) which is an incomplete diagram of the connections of a fluorescent lamp. The ballast and starter are not shown.

34. From the above statement, the competent electrician's helper should know that the starter should be shown connected between points
    (A) 4 and 3   (B) 1 and 2
    (C) 4 and 5   (D) 3 and 5.

35. From the above statement, the competent electrician's helper should know that the choke of the ballast should be shown connected between points
    (A) 4 and 3   (B) 1 and 2
    (C) 4 and 5   (D) 3 and 5.

Items 36 to 41 inclusive refer to diagram (36) and symbols for an incandescent lighting system installation. Refer to the sketch and symbols in answering these items. Assume a spacing of 10 feet between lighting fixtures, a distance of 75 feet from the lighting panel to the first fixture in each group, and that each circuit will be completely independent.

(36)

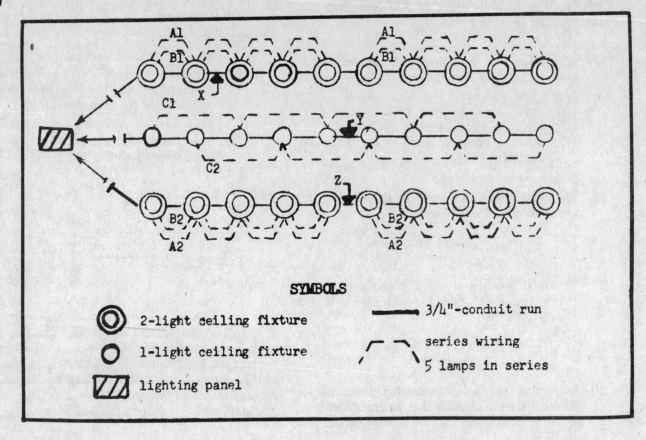

SYMBOLS

◎ 2-light ceiling fixture   ——— 3/4"-conduit run

○ 1-light ceiling fixture   ⌐⌐ series wiring
                                                 5 lamps in series

▨ lighting panel

36. The number of standard lengths of conduit required for this job is about
  (A) 24   (B) 27
  (C) 51   (D) 78.

37. When the extension is in operation, a ground on a negative wire at **X** will
  (A) blow one circuit fuse
  (B) blow two circuit fuses
  (C) cause the series farthest from the panel to be dark
  (D) have no appreciable effect on the performance of the installation.

38. The number of wires in the conduit at **Z** will be
  (A) 3   (B) 4
  (C) 5   (D) 6.

39. The number of switches used to control the extension of the lighting system will be
  (A) 3   (B) 4
  (C) 5   (D) 6.

40. When the extension is in operation, a ground on the series wire of circuit C1 at **Y** will
  (A) darken two lamps and cause three to be abnormally bright
  (B) darken three lamps and cause two to be abnormally bright
  (C) blow the circuit fuse
  (D) have no appreciable effect on the performance of the installation.

41. The length of red wire needed for this job is about
  (A) 350 feet   (B) 500 feet
  (C) 1200 feet   (D) 1750 feet.

42. An unbalanced load of incandescent lamps is connected on a 3-wire D.C. circuit. If the neutral wire should become opened at the service
  (A) all the lamps will be extinguished
  (B) nothing will happen and the lamps will continue to burn at the same brilliancy before the neutral became opened
  (C) the lamps on the less loaded side will burn with greater brilliancy and possibly burn out
  (D) the lamps on the more loaded side will burn with greater brilliancy than originally.

43. An electric light bulb operated at *more* than its rated voltage will result in a
    (A) longer life and dimmer light
    (B) longer life and brighter light
    (C) shorter life and brighter light
    (D) shorter life and dimmer light.

44. In a bowling alley, the lighting is satisfactory under normal conditions but when the electric heaters are turned on during cold weather the lights become dimmer and the lighting is insufficient. The factor which probably contributes most to this effect is the
    (A) distance from the source of power
    (B) size of the circuit fuses
    (C) current taken by the lamps
    (D) size of the circuit conductor.

45. A certain lighting circuit is now wired with No. 14 AWG wire. Additional lamps to be added to the circuit will increase the current beyond the capacity of this size wire. The wire of equal length and the same material required to replace the No. 14 wire will have
    (A) greater weight and lower resistance
    (B) less weight and lower resistance
    (C) greater weight and higher resistance
    (D) less weight and higher resistance.

46. A certain five-lamp series cluster has 36-watt lamps installed. If these lamps are replaced with five 100-watt lamps, the result will be that the
    (A) fuse for the circuit will blow
    (B) lamps will burn out very quickly
    (C) amount of light will be increased
    (D) lamps will be very dim.

47. The five lamps shown are each rated at 120-volts 60-watts. If all are good lamps, lamp No. 5 will be
    (A) much brighter than normal
    (B) about its normal brightness
    (C) much dimmer than normal
    (D) completely dark.

(47)

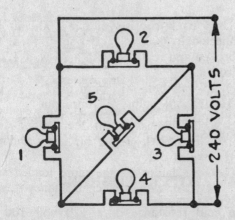

48. A group of 5 lamps is connected in series and each lamp is rated at 130 volts. For full voltage burning of the lamps, the voltage of the supply which feeds these circuits must be
    (A) 650 volts   (B) 260 volts
    (C) 130 volts   (D) 26 volts.

49. On an ungrounded circuit, lamps connected as shown would normally be used to
    (A) provide a grounded neutral
    (B) indicate an accidental ground on either line
    (C) show whether the line is alive
    (D) indicate which line fuse is blown.

(49)

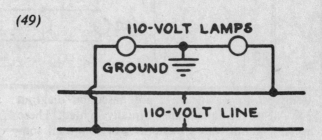

50. 22 lamps are all connected in a single series circuit which is fed at 600 volts. The voltage rating of each individual lamp in the series must be approximately
    (A) 600 volts   (B) 120 volts
    (C) 30 volts   (D) 22 volts.

51. The most satisfactory temporary replacement for a 40-watt, 120-volt incandescent lamp, if an identical replacement is not available, is a lamp rated at
    (A) 100 watts, 240 volts
    (B) 60 watts, 130 volts
    (C) 40 watts, 32 volts
    (D) 15 watts, 120 volts.

52. If the applied voltage on an incandescent lamp is increased 10%, the lamp will
    (A) have a longer life
    (B) consume less power
    (C) burn more brightly
    (D) fail by insulation breakdown.

(53)

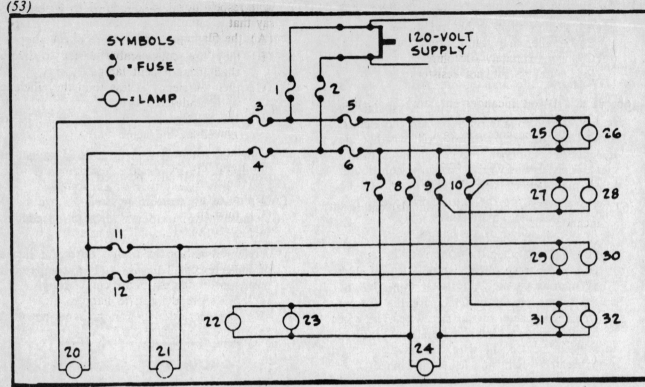

Items 53 to 61 inclusive are based on diagram (53). All of the lamps are normally lighted. These items in Column I are descriptions of abnormal conditions each of which is caused by one of the faults listed in Column II. For each item in Column I, select the most likely fault from Column II.

COLUMN I
(abnormal conditions)

53. Lamp Nos. 24, 27, 28, 31, and 32 dark
54. Lamp Nos. 27, 28, 31, and 32 dark
55. Lamp Nos. 21, 29, and 30 dark
56. Lamp Nos. 22 and 23 dark
57. Only lamp No. 24 dark
58. Lamp Nos. 20, 21, 29, and 30 dark
59. Lamp Nos. 22, 23, and 24 dark
60. Lamp Nos. 22, 23, 24, 25, 26, 27, 28, 31, and 32 dark
61. Only lamp No. 20 dark

COLUMN II
(faults)

(A) Either fuse No. 11 or fuse No. 12 blown
(B) Fuse No. 9 blown
(C) Fuse No. 10 blown
(D) Lamp burned out
(E) Either fuse No. 9 or fuse No. 10 blown
(H) Either fuse No. 5 or fuse No. 6 blown
(J) Fuse No. 8 blown
(K) Fuse No. 7 blown
(L) Either fuse No. 3 or fuse No. 4 blown
(M) Either fuse No. 1 or fuse No. 2 blown.

62. To test whether a 110-volt lighting circuit is alive,
    (A) touch each wire in turn to ground
    (B) touch the ends of the wires together
    (C) use a voltmeter across the line
    (D) use an ammeter across the line.

63. If two identical lamps normally connected in parallel to a 110 volt line are reconnected to be in series across the same line, they will
    (A) give more light
    (B) give less light
    (C) consume more power
    (D) consume the same power.

64. A lamp bank consists of five 100-watt bulbs connected to 600 volts. If one of these bulbs is broken and replaced with a 25-watt 120-volt bulb, the
    (A) 25-watt bulb will burn out
    (B) 100-watt bulbs will burn out
    (C) 100-watt bulbs will be brighter
    (D) 25-watt bulb will be very dimly lighted.

TYPES OF LIGHTING

65. The cold resistance of a 120 volt 100 watt

Tungsten incandescent lamp is
(A) greater than its hot resistance
(B) smaller than the hot resistance
(C) approximately 100 ohms
(D) equal to the hot resistance.

66. If a 110-volt incandescent lamp is burned at 130 volts the result will be
(A) less than normal light
(B) shorter lamp life
(C) a blown circuit fuse
(D) decreased lamp efficiency.

67. The resistance of the tungsten filament in any incandescent lamp is
(A) highest when the lamp is off
(B) highest when the lamp is on
(C) lowest when the lamp is on
(D) approximately the same at all times.

68. With respect to common electric light bulbs, it is correct to state that the
(A) circuit voltage has no effect on the life of the bulb
(B) filament is made of carbon
(C) base has a left hand thread
(D) lower wattage bulb has the higher resistance.

69. When an incandescent lamp to be used for general lighting has a mogul base it is a positive indication that it is rated at over
(A) 200 watts   (B) 300 watts
(C) 500 watts   (D) 750 watts.

70. The efficiency in lumens per watt of a 10 watt fluorescent lamp
(A) is less than that of a 40 watt incandescent lamp
(B) is the same as that of a 40 watt incandescent lamp
(C) is greater than that of a 40 watt incandescent lamp
(D) may be greater or less than that of a 40 watt incandescent lamp, depending on the manufacture.

71. The average life of a 100 watt incandescent light bulb is approximately
(A) 100 hrs.   (B) 400 hrs.
(C) 1000 hrs.   (D) 10,000 hrs.

72. The filament of a regular incandescent electric lamp is usually made of
(A) tungsten   (B) carbon
(C) nickel   (D) iron.

73. With respect to fluorescent lamps it is correct to say that
(A) the filaments seldom burn out
(B) they are considerably easier to handle than incandescent lamps
(C) their efficiency is less than the efficiency of incandescent lamps
(D) the starters and the lamps must be replaced at the same time.

74. A method which is sometimes used to increase the useful life of incandescent lamps is to
(A) burn at less than rated voltage
(B) burn at more than rated voltage
(C) turn the lamps off when not needed
(D) prohibit the use of shades.

75. One disadvantage in using fluorescent instead of incandescent lighting is that, compared to incandescent lamps, fluorescent lamps
(A) are more difficult to handle
(B) provide less light for the same power
(C) give more glare
(D) have shorter lives.

76. Fluorescent lamps compared to incandescent lamps
(A) emit more lumens per watt
(B) are more adversely affected by vibratory conditions
(C) are less critical to voltage dips or variations
(D) cannot be adapted to D.C. operation.

77. The inert gas present in an incandescent lamp is primarily intended to
(A) increase the luminous output
(B) decrease filament evaporation
(C) activate the surface of the filament
(D) reduce the hazards when the glass is shattered.

Answer Key

1. D	17. A	33. B	49. B	65. B
2. B	18. B	34. B	50. C	66. B
3. A	19. D	35. C	51. B	67. B
4. B	20. A	36. C	52. C	68. D
5. D	21. B	37. D	53. B	69. B
6. C	22. C	38. B	54. C	70. C
7. C	23. A	39. D	55. A	71. C
8. B	24. B	40. A	56. K	72. A
9. A	25. C	41. B	57. D	73. A
10. A	26. C	42. C	58. L	74. A
11. C	27. C	43. C	59. J	75. A
12. B	28. D	44. D	60. H	76. A
13. D	29. B	45. A	61. D	77. B
14. C	30. A	46. C	62. C	
15. D	31. A	47. D	63. B	
16. B	32. C	48. A	64. A	

WIRING SPECIAL SYSTEMS

1. An interior telephone system in which each party or station may call any other station but on which there may be only one conversation without interference is called
   (A) selective ringing, selective talking
   (B) selective ringing, common talking
   (C) code ringing, common talking
   (D) no name as it does not exist.

2. The following equipment must be used on a "2-line, Return Call" signal system
   (A) 2 bells, 2 metallic lines, 2 ordinary push buttons and 2 sets of batteries
   (B) 2 bells, 2 metallic lines, 2 return call push buttons and 2 sets of batteries
   (C) 2 bells, 2 metallic lines, 2 return call push buttons and 1 set of batteries
   (D) 2 bells, 2 metallic lines, 2 ordinary push buttons and 1 set of batteries.

3. The function of the "Retard" or Impedance Coil in a Selective Ringing-Common Talking interior telephone system is
   (A) to prevent talking current from passing through the transmitter
   (B) to prevent the shunting of voice currents through the battery
   (C) to decrease the distance over which you may speak
   (D) to prevent the ringing current from passing through the receiver.

4. When the thermostat calls for heat
   (A) relay A is energized bringing in the motor only
   (B) relay A is energized bringing in the ignition only
   (C) relay A is energized bringing in the motor and ignition
   (D) relay B is first energized.

5. Momentary power failure while burner is in operation causes
   (A) both relays to drop out
   (B) relay A to drop out only
   (C) relay B to drop out only
   (D) the relay to go out on safety.

6. An interior fire-alarm system best suited to the needs of such buildings as hospitals, public schools, institutions, etc., would be an
   (A) open-circuit, noncode, nonsupervised system
   (B) closed-circuit, noncode, supervised system
   (C) closed-circuit, box code, supervised system
   (D) closed-circuit, box code, presignal, supervised system.

7. Interior Fire Alarm Systems may be divided into
   (A) two basic groups—Pre-Signal and Dual
   (B) 1 group only—open circuit
   (C) 1 group only—closed circuit
   (D) two basic groups—open circuit and closed circuit.

8. An open circuit type of Interior Fire Alarm System consists of
   (A) vibrating gongs and break glass stations
   (B) single stroke gongs and break glass stations
   (C) vibrating gongs and coded stations
   (D) electrically supervised gongs and boxes.

(4)

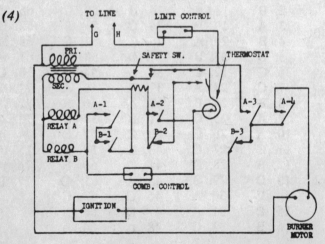

DIAGRAM OF PROTECTOR RELAY FOR OIL BURNER

S1111

9. Modern approved Closed Circuit Fire Alarm Systems should have the following trouble indicators
   (A) trouble light only
   (B) milli-ammeter only
   (C) trouble bell only
   (D) milli-ammeter, time limit device and trouble bell and light.

10. An approved Closed Circuit Type of Interior Fire Alarm should consist of
    (A) mechanical gongs and coded stations
    (B) vibrating gongs and coded stations
    (C) electrically supervised gongs and stations and may be coded or not
    (D) single stroke gongs and strap key.

11. The electric energy required to raise the temperature of the water in a pool is 1000 kwh. The heat losses are 25 per cent. The total heating energy required is
    (A) 1000 kwh   (B) 1250 kwh
    (C) 1333 kwh   (D) 1500 kwh.

12. A 6000 watt 3-phase heater composed of three resistance units in delta is connected to a 3-phase 208 volt supply. The resistance, in ohms, of each resistance unit is most nearly
    (A) 20.8   (B) 41.6
    (C) 83.2   (D) 208.

13. Based upon the data given in question 12, if the 3 heater resistance units are now connected in star (or wye) to a 3-phase 208 volt supply, the power, in watts, consumed by this heater is most nearly

(A) 10,400   (B) 6,000
(C) 3,500   (D) 2,000.

14. A resistor is connected across a supply of "E" volts. The heat produced in this resistor is proportional to I^2R. If R is reduced in value, the heat produced in this resistor now
    (A) increases
    (B) decreases
    (C) remains the same
    (D) is indeterminate.

15. An A.C. current of one ampere R.M.S. flowing through a resistance of 10 ohms has the same heating value as a D.C. current of
    (A) one ampere flowing through a 10 ohm resistance
    (B) one ampere flowing through a 5 ohm resistance
    (C) two amperes flowing through a 10 ohm resistance
    (D) five amperes flowing through a 1 ohm resistance.

Answer Key

(You'll learn more by writing your own answers before comparing them with these.)

Wiring Special Systems

1. B	4. C	7. D	10. C	13. D
2. B	5. A	8. A	11. C	14. A
3. B	6. D	9. D	12. A	15. A

ELECTRIC MOTORS

Types

GENERAL QUESTIONS

1. The most common type of motor that can be used with both A-C and D-C sources is
   (A) the repulsion motor
   (B) the series motor
   (C) the rotary converter
   (D) the shunt motor.

2. One type of electric motor tends to "run away" if it is not always connected to its load. This motor is the
   (A) d.c. series
   (B) d.c. shunt
   (C) a.c. induction
   (D) a.c. synchronous.

3. A motor which will not operate on d.c. is the
   (A) series motor
   (B) shunt motor
   (C) induction motor
   (D) compound motor.

Items 4 to 8 inclusive in Column I are various kinds of electrical machines each with a d.c. field which is made *variable* for one of the specific purposes given in Column II. For each item in Column I, select the specific purpose for which the field is made variable from Column II.

COLUMN I
(machines with variable d.c. fields)
4. D.C. motor   7. A.C. generator
5. Rotary converter   8. D.C. generator
6. Synchronous motor

COLUMN II
(specific purposes)
   (A) to change the voltage
   (B) to change the speed
   (C) to change the power factor
   (D) to change the frequency.

9. The type of motor that does *not* have a commutator is the
   (A) synchronous   (B) shunt
   (C) squirrel cage   (D) series.

DC, SERIES AND SHUNT MOTORS

10. The torque of a shunt motor varies as
    (A) the armature current
    (B) the square of the armature current
    (C) the cube of the armature current
    (D) the cube of the field current.

11. If the field of a shunt motor while running under no lead opens, the motor will
    (A) stop running immediately
    (B) continue to run at a very slow speed
    (C) run away
    (D) gradually slow down until it stops.

12. In a 5 H.P., 220-volt shunt motor rated at 19.2 amperes and 1500 r.p.m., the armature resistance is
    (A) smaller than that of the shunt field
    (B) larger than that of the shunt field
    (C) the same as that of the shunt field
    (D) always ½ as large as that of the shunt field.

13. Comparing the shunt field winding with the series field winding of a compound d.c. motor, it would be correct to say that the shunt field winding has
    (A) more turns but the lower resistance
    (B) more turns and the higher resistance
    (C) fewer turns and the lower resistance
    (D) fewer turns but the higher resistance.

14. In selecting a starting box for a d.c. shunt motor it would be necessary to know the motor
    (A) shunt field resistance and field current
    (B) armature resistance and full load current
    (C) full load current and speed
    (D) field current, full load current and speed.

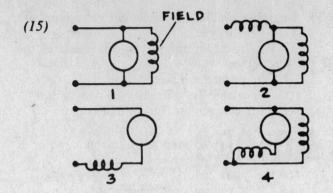

(15)

15. Each of the four sketches shows the proper schematic connections for one kind of d.c. motor. The one showing the connections for a shunt motor is number
    (A) 1
    (B) 2
    (C) 3
    (D) 4.

16. It is desired to run a d.c. shunt motor at a speed lower than its rated speed. The most practical way to accomplish this would be to connect a suitable resistance in
    (A) series with the field
    (B) series with the armature
    (C) parallel with the field
    (D) parallel with the armature.

17. If the two line leads of a D.C. series motor are reversed the motor will
    (A) not run
    (B) run backwards
    (C) run the same as before
    (D) become a generator.

18. In the selection of a direct current motor
    (A) a series motor should be chosen where the motor is operated at very light loads
    (B) a series motor should be used where the required starting torque is low
    (C) a series motor should be used where the required starting torque is high
    (D) a shunt motor should be used where the starting torque required is high and it starts under loaded conditions.

19. In the case of a compound wound D.C. motor operating at constant voltage, with a very light load, increasing the resistance which is in series with the shunt field will
    (A) have no effect on the motor speed
    (B) cause the motor to slow down
    (C) cause the motor to either speed up or slow down depending on the type of load
    (D) cause the motor to speed up.

20. To change the direction of rotation of a cumulative wound D.C. motor you must
    (A) reverse the connections to the armature
    (B) reverse the connections to the shunt field
    (C) reverse the connections to the series field
    (D) do nothing as it cannot be done.

21. Series type motors for electrically driven rheostats or governors have a split series field
    (A) for better speed control
    (B) to change the direction of rotation
    (C) to produce a greater starting torque
    (D) for more accurate voltage regulation.

22. To start a 7½ H.P., 220-volt, D.C. motor you should use
    (A) a compensator
    (B) an across the line starter
    (C) a suitable starting box
    (D) a "Start-Run" switch.

23. In the D.C. series motor when the load torque is decreased, the
    (A) armature rotates at a lower speed
    (B) armature rotates at a higher speed
    (C) current through the field is increased
    (D) current through the armature is increased.

24. Series type motors for electrically driven rheostats or governors have a split series field to
    (A) obtain low motor speed
    (B) decrease the current consumption
    (C) change the direction of rotation
    (D) produce greater starting torque.

25. In the D.C. series motor, the field
    (A) has comparatively few turns of wire
    (B) has comparatively many turns of wire
    (C) is connected across the armature
    (D) current is less than the line current.

26. To properly start a 15 hp. D.C. compound motor, you should use a
    (A) transformer
    (B) 4-point starting Rheostat
    (C) compensator
    (D) diverter.

27. The ordinary direct current series motor does not operate satisfactorily with alternating current. One of the main reasons for this is
    (A) excessive heating due to eddy currents in the solid parts of the field structure
    (B) that the armature current and field current are out of phase with each other

(C) that the field flux lags 120° in time phase with respect to the line voltage

(D) excessive heating due to the low voltage drop in the series field.

28. A d.c. elevator motor, on a gearless traction machine, has a series field for compounding during the acceleration period. This field is cut out when the motor has reached full speed, for the purpose of
(A) preventing excessive speed
(B) reducing the line current
(C) providing constant speed over a wide range of load conditions
(D) saving the cost of losses in the series field
(E) providing the same speed in the up and down directions.

29. The temperature of the shunt field of a d.c. motor increases from 20°C to 60°C after 3 hours operation. This increase in temperature of the field coils
(A) will have no effect on the operation of the motor
(B) will tend to slow down the motor due to an increase in the resistance of the field coils
(C) will tend to speed up the motor due to an increase in resistance of the field coils
(D) will tend to slow down the motor due to a decrease in resistance of the field coils.

30. A d.c. series motor
(A) cannot be used for driving loads that require high starting torque
(B) is a constant speed motor
(C) should be directly connected to its load
(D) may run away if its field becomes opened.

31. The total developed torque of a d.c. motor is dependent upon
(A) the armature current and the flux per pole
(B) the speed of the motor
(C) the type of armature winding
(D) none of the above.

32. Of the following statements, the one which is most accurate concerning D.C. motors is
(A) a lap-wound motor has two brushes regardless of the number of poles
(B) a series-wound motor has as many brushes as there are poles
(C) a lap-wound motor has as many brushes as there are poles
(D) regardless of the type of armature winding the number of parallel paths is always two.

33. Interpole windings in direct current motors are used primarily
(A) as a means for varying the speed of the motor
(B) to reduce armature reaction
(C) increase the efficiency of the motor
(D) to compensate for field leakage.

34. The best way to start a large shunt motor is with
(A) a weak field
(B) full voltage on the armature
(C) a compensator
(D) a strong field.

INDUCTION AND POLYPHASE MOTORS

35. If two of the three line leads to a three-phase squirrel-cage induction motor are interchanged the motor will
(A) reverse its direction of rotation
(B) be shorted
(C) not run
(D) run above synchronous speed.

36. One identifying feature of a squirrel-cage induction motor is that it has no
(A) windings on the stationary part
(B) commutator or slip rings
(C) air gap
(D) iron core in the rotating part.

37. Large squirrel cage induction motors are usually started at a voltage considerably lower than line voltage to
(A) avoid excessive starting current
(B) obtain a low starting speed
(C) permit starting under full load
(D) allow the rotor current to build up gradually.

38. To reverse the direction of rotation of a 3-phase motor, it is necessary to
(A) increase the resistance of the rotor circuit
(B) interchange all three line connections
(C) interchange any two of the three line connections
(D) reverse the polarity of the rotor circuit.

39. To reverse the direction of rotation of a Split-Phase motor you would
(A) do nothing as it cannot be done
(B) reverse the main lines
(C) reverse the polarity of all windings
(D) reverse the polarity of the starting or **auxiliary winding.**

40. Speed control by a method that requires two wound rotor induction motors with their rotors rigidly connected together is called speed control by
(A) change of poles
(B) field control
(C) concatenation
(D) voltage control.

41. To properly start a 15 hp. 3-phase induction motor, you should use a
(A) shunt
(B) 4-point starting Rheostat
(C) compensator
(D) diverter.

42. To reverse the direction of rotation of a re-pulsion-induction motor you should
(A) loosen the set screw and move rocker arm to proper place
(B) interchange the terminal connections
(C) increase the line voltage
(D) do nothing as it cannot be done

(43)

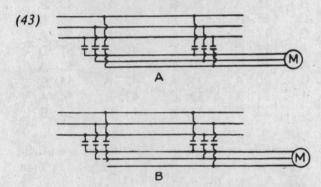

43. Two possible connections, one incorrect, for reversing a wound motor 3-phase induction motor are shown above. The contactors are inter-locked mechanically. The correct circuit and the proper interlock is given by which of the following items?
(A) circuit A and both close together
(B) circuit A and one closed, other open
(C) circuit B and both close together
(D) circuit B and one closed, other open.

OTHER TYPES OF MOTORS

44. A certain machine is driven by a 1750-r.p.m., d.c., shunt motor. If the power supply is to be changed to three-phase, 60 cycles, a.c., the most suitable replacement motor would be a
(A) series motor
(B) repulsion motor
(C) squirrel-cage induction motor
(D) capacitor motor.

45. The two small a.c. motors are identical, but pinion #2 has twice the diameter of pinion #1. The motors are connected to the same power supply and are wired so that they nor-mally tend to turn in *opposite* directions. When the power is first turned on
(A) the motors will stall
(B) both motors will turn at near normal speed in the same direction
(C) motor #2 will turn in its normal direc-tion driving motor #1 backwards
(D) motor #1 will turn in its normal direc-tion driving motor #2 backwards.

(45)

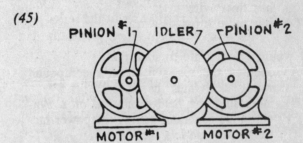

46. The correct method of measuring the power taken by an a.c. electric motor is to use a
(A) wattmeter
(B) voltmeter and an ammeter
(C) power factor meter
(D) tachometer.

47. To start a 7½ H.P., 3-Phase, 208-volt A.C. motor you should use
(A) a "4 point" starting box
(B) a "3 point" starting box
(C) a M-G set
(D) an across-the-line starter.

48. A repulsion motor is equipped with
(A) slip rings
(B) a commutator
(C) neither a commutator nor slip rings
(D) both a commutator and slip rings.

49. The synchronous speed of a 25 cycle 10 pole motor is
(A) 250 R.P.M.   (B) 600 R.P.M.
(C) 150 R.P.M.   (D) 300 R.P.M.

50. Increasing the field excitation of a synchronous motor above its normal value when the load remains constant will
(A) result in a leading power factor
(B) result in a lagging power factor
(C) result in either a leading or lagging power factor depending on the kind of load
(D) have no effect on the power factor.

51. An advantage of a synchronous motor over a wound-rotor induction motor is that
    (A) its speed may be more readily controlled
    (B) its speed does not depend on the frequency of the supply
    (C) it has no brushes to contend with
    (D) the power factor of the motor may be varied.

52. In a compound motor, the series field as compared with the shunt field
    (A) carries more current
    (B) has higher resistance
    (C) has finer wire
    (D) has more turns of wire.

53. It would be accurate to state that
    (A) opening the series field of a compound motor accelerates the motor
    (B) increasing the field excitation of a synchronous generator causes the power factor to become less lagging
    (C) opening the shunt field of a shunt motor accelerates the motor
    (D) decreasing the field excitation of a synchronous motor causes the power factor to become less lagging.

54. If you tried to start a compound motor in which the series field was open circuited, the motor

    (A) would not start
    (B) would blow the fuse
    (C) would "Run Away"
    (D) would reverse.

55. The proper way to reverse the direction of rotation of a compound motor is to
    (A) interchange the line leads
    (B) interchange the armature connections
    (C) interchange the shunt field connections
    (D) interchange the series field connections.

Answer Key

(You'll learn more by writing your own answers before comparing them with these.)

Types of Motors

1. B	12. A	23. B	34. D	45. D
2. A	13. B	24. C	35. A	46. A
3. C	14. B	25. A	36. B	47. B
4. B	15. A	26. B	37. A	48. B
5. C	16. B	27. A	38. C	49. D
6. C	17. C	28. C	39. D	50. A
7. A	18. C	29. C	40. C	51. D
8. A	19. D	30. C	41. C	52. A
9. C	20. A	31. A	42. A	53. C
10. A	21. B	32. C	43. B	54. A
11. C	22. C	33. B	44. C	55. B

MOTOR OPERATION

PARTS, WIRING AND PROTECTIVE DEVICES

1. The gears most commonly used to connect two shafts which intersect are usually a form of
   (A) Spur gears
   (B) Bevel gears
   (C) Spiral gears
   (D) Herring bone gears.

2. Assume that the field leads of a large, completely disconnected d.c. motor are not tagged or otherwise marked. You could readily tell the shunt field leads from the series field leads by the
   (A) length of the leads
   (B) size of wire
   (C) thickness of insulation
   (D) type of insulation.

(3)

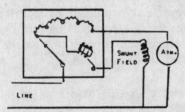

3. The circuit of figure (3) shows a d.c. motor starter. One of the features of this starting box is
   (A) an overload release
   (B) a no-field release
   (C) a reverse-current release
   (D) an underload release.

4. On motors with brakes, the brake magnet coil is
   (A) de-energized when current is fed to motor
   (B) energized when current is fed to motor
   (C) energized after motor reaches normal speed
   (D) de-energized after motor reaches low speed.

5. The commutator bars of a motor are made of
   (A) mica   (C) copper
   (B) carbon   (D) phosphor bronze.

(6)

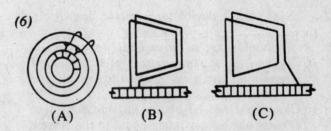

(A)   (B)   (C)

6. The three windings shown above belong respectively to the
   (A) ring, lap, and wave types of closed-coil windings
   (B) ring, lap and wave types of open-coil windings
   (C) ring, lap, and wave types of reverse-coil windings
   (D) ring, lap, and wave types of cumulative-coil windings.

7. Simplex lap windings have as many armature circuits as there are
   (A) commutator bars
   (B) number of coils
   (C) number of active conductors
   (D) poles.

8. Pigtails are used on carbon brushes to
   (A) hold the brush in the holder
   (B) supply the proper pressure
   (C) make a good electrical connection
   (D) compensate for wear.

9. When thermal overload relays are used for the protection of polyphase induction motors their primary purpose is to protect the motors in case of
   (A) reversal of phases in the supply
   (B) low line voltage
   (C) short circuit between phases
   (D) sustained overload.

10. The one of the following devices which is commonly used to prevent damage in case of reversal of leads in reconnecting the wiring of three phase motors is a
    (A reverse current relay
    (B) reverse power relay
    (C) reverse phase relay
    (D) reverse power factor relay.

11. Motor frames are usually positively grounded by a special connection in order to
    (A) remove static
    (B) protect against lightning
    (C) provide a neutral
    (D) protect against shock.

12. The protective device for a motor branch circuit
    (A) should have a rating equal to or greater than the starting current of the motor
    (B) should have a rating equal to the full load current of the motor
    (C) should not be of the instantaneous type
    (D) should have a rating equal to the current capacity of the circuit conductors.

13. When both fuses and thermal cutouts are used in a motor circuit, the
    (A) ratings of the fuses should be the same as those of the thermal cuts
    (B) fuses are used to protect against continuous, but not large overloads
    (C) thermal cutouts are used to protect against continuous overloading
    (D) thermal cutouts are used to protect against short-circuits in the motor and branch circuit.

14. An induction motor circuit would *never* be protected by
    (A) a fuse
    (B) a thermal cut-out
    (C) an overload relay
    (D) a reverse power relay.

15. Most motor starters are provided with either an undervoltage protective device or an undervoltage release device. A starter with an
    (A) undervoltage protective device would be used to open a supply circuit upon failure or reduction of voltage and keep it open until manually closed
    (B) undervoltage protective device would be used to open a supply circuit upon failure or reduction of voltage and automatically reclose it upon return of normal voltage

    (C) undervoltage protective device controls the motor voltage and keeps it at a safe value
    (D) undervoltage release device would be used to prevent opening a supply circuit when voltage fluctuations occur in the power system.

16. A polyphase motor may be protected against reversal of rotation by using a
    (A) reverse speed relay
    (B) reverse power relay
    (C) reverse phase relay
    (D) reverse current relay.

OPERATION AND MAINTENANCE

17. A newly installed three phase induction motor which is to drive a pump is found to be rotating in the wrong direction. This can be corrected by
    (A) connecting the motor to the other end of the pump
    (B) interchanging all three leads
    (C) interchanging any two motor leads
    (D) a quick opening and reclosing of the main line switch.

18. To change the direction of rotation of a cumulative compound-wound, d.c. motor and maintain its characteristics you must
    (A) reverse the connections to the armature
    (B) reverse the connections to the shunt field
    (C) reverse the connections to the series field
    (D) reverse the connections to the armature and the series field.

19. In normal operation, one type of fault that is *not* likely to develop in the armatures of motors and generators is
    (A) short circuit
    (B) open circuit
    (C) ground
    (D) reversed coils.

20. If you attempted to start a d.c. compound motor in which the series field was open-circuited, the motor
    (A) would not start
    (B) would blow the fuse
    (C) would run away
    (D) would start in the reverse direction.

21. To temporarily change the direction of rotation of a single-phase, shaded-pole, induction motor you would

(A) do nothing since it cannot be done
(B) reverse the connections to the starting winding
(C) shift the brushes to the opposite neutral
(D) reverse the line leads.

22. For maximum safety the magnetic contactors used for reversing the direction of rotation of a motor should be
(A) electrically interlocked
(B) electrically and mechanically interlocked
(C) mechanically interlocked
(D) operated from independent sources.

23. Silver electrical contactors are tarnished most readily by
(A) oxygen   (B) hydrogen
(C) nitrogen   (D) sulphur.

24. The lubricant used for sleeve bearings on motors is usually
(A) vaseline   (B) oil
(C) graphite   (D) grease.

25. The correct method of measuring the power taken by an a.c. electric motor is to use a
(A) wattmeter
(B) voltmeter and an ammeter
(C) power factor meter
(D) tachometer.

26. To measure the power taken by a d.c. electric motor with only a single instrument you should use
(A) voltmeter
(B) an ammeter
(C) a wattmeter
(D) a power factor meter.

27. The speed of a d.c. shunt motor is generally regulated by means of a
(A) switch for reversal of the armature supply
(B) source of variable supply voltage
(C) variable resistance in the armature circuit
(D) rheostat in the field circuit.

28. A carbon brush in a d.c. motor should exert a pressure of about 1½ lbs. per square inch on the commutator. A much lighter pressure would be most likely to result in
(A) sparking at the commutator
(B) vibration of the armature
(C) the brush getting out of line
(D) excessive wear of the brush holder.

29. New brushes for a motor should be fitted to the commutator by using a
(A) round file
(B) half-round file
(C) strip of sandpaper
(D) strip of emery cloth.

30. One sure sign that there has been sparking at the brushes of a stopped d.c. motor would be
(A) the odor of hot rubber insulation
(B) hot bearings
(C) grooves worn around the commutator
(D) pits on the commutator surface.

31. A common way of reducing the chances of uneven commutator wear is to
(A) use brushes of different hardness
(B) allow some end play in the motor bearings
(C) anneal the commutator after assembly
(D) turn the commutator down frequently.

32. If an unusual amount of dust is found around the base of a motor which is being inspected, the proper procedure to follow is to
(A) take no action but report the motor for further inspection
(B) remove the dust
(C) inspect the bearings for signs of excessive wear
(D) lubricate the motor.

33. If one bearing housing of a running motor feels exceptionally hot but there is no unusual vibration, the most logical conclusion is that the
(A) motor is being overloaded
(B) bearing needs lubrication
(C) shaft has become worn
(D) motor has been running a long time.

34. While a certain d.c. shunt motor is driving a light load, part of the field winding becomes short circuited. The motor will most likely
(A) increase its speed
(B) decrease its speed
(C) remain at the same speed
(D) come to a stop.

35. To measure the voltage and current supplied to a D.C. motor, connect the
(A) voltmeter across the line and ammeter in series with the motor
(B) ammeter across the line and voltmeter in series with the motor
(C) voltmeter and ammeter in series with the motor
(D) voltmeter and ammeter across the line.

36. A practical method of checking the magnetic polarity of the field poles of a direct current motor is by the use of
    (A) an iron or steel tool
    (B) iron filings
    (C) a magnetic compass
    (D) a megger.

37. The reason for using oil rings in bearings is to
    (A) increase the bearing surface
    (B) maintain proper oil level
    (C) prevent oil leaks
    (D) lubricate the bearing.

38. A condition which will *not* cause a brush on the collector ring to carry less than its share of the current is
    (A) low brush pressure
    (B) low resistance of the brush
    (C) an insulating glaze on the brush face
    (D) a loose shunt or pigtail.

39. A good practical test to determine whether a wetted down motor has been sufficiently dried out is
    (A) an insulation test
    (B) an armature resistance test
    (C) a high-voltage break down test
    (D) a flash over test

DIRECTIONS: *Column I lists various* COMBINATIONS OF CLOSED SWITCHES *in the diagram below. Each of these combinations will result in one of the* MOTOR OPERATING CONDITIONS *listed in Column II. Match up Columns I & II. Next to each combination in Column I write the letter of the resulting operating condition from Column II.*

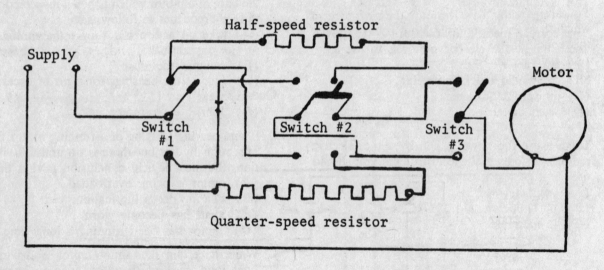

COLUMN I

COMBINATIONS OF CLOSED SWITCHES

	switch #1	switch #2	switch #3
40.	up	up	up
41.	up	up	down
42.	up	down	down
43.	down	down	down
44.	down	down	up
45.	down	up	down

COLUMN II

MOTOR OPERATING CONDITIONS

(A) run full speed

(B) run half speed

(C) run quarter speed

(D) not running.

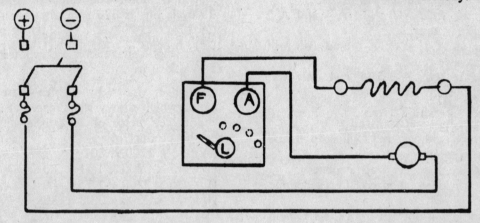

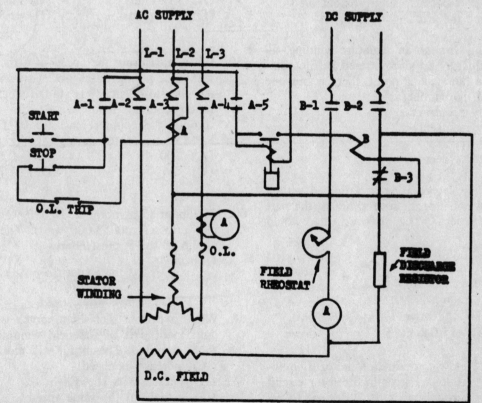

46. To stop a 7½ H.P. motor you should

(A) overload the motor until you stall it

(B) open the line or disconnect switch

(C) remove the fuses

(D) push the belt off the pulley.

You were sent to see why a D.C. motor does not run. The motor was connected as indicated in diagram (47).

(47)

47. After examining the job and the diagram you came to the conclusion that

(A) the motor will not run, the field circuit is connected incorrectly

(B) the motor will run if the fuses are good since the job is wired correctly

(C) the motor will not run, armature circuit is connected incorrectly

(D) the motor will not run, the starting box is connected incorrectly.

48. You are running a D.C. motor the armature of which has an open coil. You could identify this condition by

(A) increase in motor speed

(B) decrease in motor speed

(C) the coil getting excessively hot

(D) seeing and hearing a pronounced electric arc under the brushes as the defective coil passed.

Questions (49) to (52) refer to diagram 49.

(49)

49. The above sketch represents a starter diagram of a
    (A) synchronous motor
    (B) DC series motor
    (C) wound rotor induction motor
    (D) squirrel cage induction motor.

50. When start P.B. is pressed
    (A) Contactor A-1, A-2, A-3, A-4, A-5, B-1 and B-2 will close at once
    (B) Contactor A-1, A-2, A-3, A-4 and A-5 will close at once
    (C) Contactor A-2, A-3, A-4 and B-3 will close at once
    (D) Contactor A-2, A-3 and A-4 only will close at once.

51. After the start button is pressed
    (A) the motor will run but will stop unless field is energized
    (B) the DC field is energized at once
    (C) the DC field is energized after a definite time
    (D) the motor will not run until the DC field is energized.

52. The field discharge resistor acts to
    (A) steady the DC field during start period
    (B) improve the power factor
    (C) dissipate the energy stored in the field after the DC field supply is cut off
    (D) quench the arc.

53. If, in tracing through an armature winding, all of the conductors are encountered before coming back to the starting point, there is but one closure and the winding is
    (A) doubly reentrant
    (B) singly reentrent
    (C) triply reentrant
    (D) quintuply reentrant.

54. If a main unit is operating at full load with a leading power factor for several hours, the part you would expect to become overheated would be the
    (A) brushes and rings
    (B) field rheostat
    (C) armature winding
    (D) field winding.

PROBLEMS

55. A certain wound rotor induction motor is equipped with a variable resistor in the rotor circuit for starting purposes only. It is desired to replace this resistor with one that can be used also for motor speed control. Compared with the original resistor, the new resistor should have
    (A) higher total resistance
    (B) lower total resistance
    (C) higher current carrying capacity
    (D) lower current carrying capacity.

56. If the no-load speed of a squirrel cage type induction motor connected to a three phase 25 cycle line is 373 rpm, the motor has
    (A) 2 poles   (B) 4 poles
    (C) 6 poles   (D) 8 poles.

57. The power drawn by a three-phase induction motor which draws 15 amperes at 2200 volts and power factor of 80% is given, in watts, by the product of
    (A) 15 x 2200 x .80
    (B) 15 x 2200 x 1.41 x .80
    (C) 15 x 2200 x 1.73 x .80
    (D) 15 x 2200 x 3.00 x .80.

58. It is desired to limit the starting current to the armature of a D.C. motor taking current from a 120 volt source to 10 amperes. If the armature resistance is 0.2 ohms, the resistance in the armature circuit should be
    (A) 118 ohms   (B) 11.8 ohms
    (C) 120 ohms   (D) 20 ohms.

59. When measuring the speed of a d.c. motor by means of a stop-watch and a revolution counter, the stop watch was started when the revolution counter read 50. At the end of 80 seconds the counter read 1,650. The average RPM of the motor during this period was
    (A) 200   (B) 1,200
    (C) 1,600   (D) 1,700.

60. The input to a motor is 16,000 watts and the motor losses total 3,000 watts. The efficiency of the motor is most nearly
    (A) 68.4%   (B) 81.25%
    (C) 84.21%   (D) 87.5%.

61. While a certain d.c. shunt motor is driving a light load, part of the field winding becomes short circuited. The motor will most likely
    (A) increase its speed
    (B) decrease its speed
    (C) remain at the same speed
    (D) come to a stop.

62. When a certain motor is started up, the incandescent lights fed from the same circuit dim down somewhat and then return to approximately normal brightness as the motor comes up to speed. This definitely shows that the
    (A) starting current of the motor is larger than the running current
    (B) insulation of the circuit wiring is worn
    (C) circuit fuse is not making good contact
    (D) incandescent lamps are too large for the circuit.

63. If a single-phase induction motor draws 10 amperes at 240 volts, the power taken by the motor
    (A) will be 2400 watts
    (B) will be more than 2400 watts
    (C) will be less than 2400 watts
    (D) may be more or less than 2400 watts depending on the power factor.

(64)

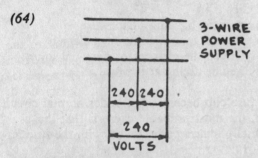

64. In accordance with the voltages shown, the power supply must be

(A) three-wire d.c.
(B) three-phase a.c.
(C) two-phase a.c.
(D) single-phase a.c.

65. A coil of wire wound on an iron core draws exactly 5 amperes when connected across the terminals of a ten-volt storage battery. If this coil is now connected across the ten-volt secondary terminals of an ordinary power transformer, the current drawn will be
    (A) less than 5 amperes
    (B) more than 5 amperes
    (C) exactly 5 amperes
    (D) more or less than 5 amperes depending on the frequency.

66. If the speed of a synchronous motor connected to a 60-cycle power line is 1200 rpm, the number of poles it must have is
    (A) 2
    (B) 4
    (C) 6
    (D) 8.

67. Under load, the current in the armature conductors of a DC dynamo give rise to an independent excitation which alters both the magnitude and distribution of the flux produced by the field alone. This magnetizing action of the armature is called
    (A) armature reaction
    (B) dynamic breaking
    (C) field reaction
    (D) radial excitation.

Answer Key

(Please make every effort to answer the questions on your own before looking at these answers. You'll make faster progress by following this rule.)

1. B	10. C	19. D	27. D	35. A	43. D	51. C	59. B
2. B	11. D	20. A	28. A	36. C	44. C	52. C	60. B
3. B	12. C	21. A	29. C	37. D	45. A	53. B	61. A
4. B	13. C	22. B	30. D	38. B	46. B	54. C	62. A
5. C	14. D	23. D	31. B	39. A	47. C	55. C	63. C
6. A	15. A	24. B	32. B	40. B	48. D	56. D	64. B
7. D	16. C	25. A	33. B	41. D	49. A	57. C	65. A
8. C	17. C	26. C	34. A	42. A	50. B	58. B	66. C
9. D	18. A						67. A

ELECTRICIAN

FUSES

FUSES - THEORY AND PRACTICE

1. The part of a circuit which melts when the current abnormally exceeds the allowable carrying capacity of the conductor is called
   (A) circuit breaker
   (B) thermo cutout
   (C) overload trip
   (D) fuse.

2. If a fuse becomes hot under normal load, a probable cause is
   (A) rating of the fuse is too high
   (B) rating of the fuse is too low
   (C) insufficient pressure at the fuse clips
   (D) excessive tension in the fuse clips.

3. If it were necessary to replace a 50-ampere cartridge fuse with a 65-ampere cartridge fuse of the same voltage rating, it would always be necessary to replace
   (A) all wiring in the protected circuit
   (B) the renewable link in the fuse
   (C) the fuse only
   (D) the cut-out and the fuse.

4. Good practice requires that cartridge fuses be removed from their clips by using a fuse puller rather than by using the bare hand. The reason for using the fuse puller is that the
   (A) fuse clips may be damaged by pulling at the wrong angle
   (B) fuse is less likely to break
   (C) bare hand may be burned or otherwise injured
   (D) use of the bare hand slows down removal of fuse and causes arcing.

5. The one of the following statements about a plug fuse that is most valid is that it should
   (A) always be screwed in lightly to assure easy removal
   (B) never be used to hold a coin in the fuse socket
   (C) never be replaced by someone unfamiliar with the circuit

   (D) always be replaced by a larger size if it burns out frequently.

6. A fuse puller is used in replacing
   (A) plug fuses
   (B) link fuses
   (C) ribbon fuses
   (D) cartridge fuses.

7. The most important reason for using a fuse-puller when removing a cartridge fuse from the fuse clips is to
   (A) prevent blowing of the fuse
   (B) prevent injury to the fuse element
   (C) reduce the chances of personal injury
   (D) reduce arcing at the fuse clips.

8. If a fuse clip becomes hot under normal circuit load, the most probable cause is that the
   (A) clip makes poor contact with the fuse ferrule
   (B) circuit wires are too small
   (C) current rating of the fuse is too high
   (D) voltage rating of the fuse is too low.

9. Before pulling or inserting fuses, it is good practice where possible to
   (A) always make sure that the fuses are blown
   (B) jumper the supply leads
   (C) remove the power from the circuit by opening the switcn
   (D) ground all leads on both sides of the fuses.

10. The main reason why a blown fuse should not be bridged temporarily by a copper wire is because
    (A) the wire may disrupt violently when a short circuit occurs
    (B) the circuit may not be protected adequately against overload
    (C) the wire will maintain an arc when it blows
    (D) there is danger of electric shock by coming in contact with the wire.

11. The action of a common plug fuse depends on the principle that the

(A) current develops heat
(B) voltage breaks down a thin mica disk
(C) current expands and bends a link
(D) voltage develops heat.

12. Consumers are warned never to use a coin instead of a spare fuse. The reason for this warning is that
(A) the protection of the fuse will be lost
(B) additional resistance will be placed in the circuit
(C) mutilating coins is illegal
(D) shock hazard is increased.

Items 13 to 19 inclusive are based on the fuse information given below. Read this information carefully before answering these items.

FUSE INFORMATION

Badly bent or distorted fuse clips cannot be permitted. Sometimes the distortion or bending is so slight that it escapes notice, yet it may be the cause for fuse failures through the heat that is developed by the poor contact. Occasionally the proper spring tension of the fuse clips has been destroyed by overheating from loose wire connections to the clips. Proper contact surfaces must be maintained to avoid faulty operation of the fuse. Electricians should remove oxides that form on the copper and brass contacts, check the clip pressure, and make sure that contact surfaces are not deformed or bent in any way. When removing oxides, use a well-worn file and remove only the oxide film. Do not use sandpaper or emery cloth as hard particles may come off and become embedded in the contact surfaces. All wire connections to the fuse holders should be carefully inspected to see that they are tight.

13. Fuse failure because of poor clip contact or loose connections is due to the resulting
(A) excessive voltage
(B) increased current
(C) lowered resistance
(D) heating effect.

14. Oxides should be removed from fuse contacts by using
(A) a dull file
(B) emery cloth
(C) fine sandpaper
(D) a sharp file.

15. One result of loose wire connections at the terminal of a fuse clip is stated in the above paragraph to be
(A) loss of tension in the wire
(B) welding of the fuse to the clip

(C) distortion of the clip
(D) loss of tension of the clip.

16. Simple reasoning will show that the oxide film referred to is undesirable chiefly because it
(A) looks dull
(B) makes removal of the fuse difficult
(C) weakens the clips
(D) introduces undesirable resistance.

17. Fuse clips that are bent very slightly
(A) should be replaced with new clips
(B) should be carefully filed
(C) may result in blowing of the fuse
(D) may prevent the fuse from blowing.

18. From the fuse information paragraph it would be reasonable to conclude that fuse clips
(A) are difficult to maintain
(B) must be given proper maintenance
(C) require more attention than other electrical equipment
(D) are unreliable.

19. A safe practical way of checking the tightness of the wire connection to the fuse clip of a live 120-volt lighting circuit is to
(A) feel the connection with your hand to see if it is warm
(B) try tightening with an insulated screwdriver or socket wrench
(C) see if the circuit works
(D) measure the resistance with an ohmeter.

20. If a cartridge fuse is hot to the touch when you remove it to do some maintenance on the circuit, this most probably indicates that the
(A) voltage of the circuit is too high
(B) fuse clips do not make good contact
(C) equipment on the circuit starts and stops frequently
(D) fuse is oversized for the circuitfl

21. If one end of a cartridge fuse becomes unusually warm, the first action on the part of the electrician should be to
(A) tighten the fuse clips
(B) replace the fuse with a larger one
(C) transfer some load to another circuit
(D) notify his foreman.

22. The length of a standard cartridge fuse depends on the circuit
(A) power
(B) amperage

(C) voltage

(D) type of current (a.c. or d.c.).

23. If a fuse of higher than the required current rating is used in an electrical circuit
   (A) better protection will be afforded
   (B) the fuse will blow more often since it carries more current
   (C) serious damage may result to the circuit from overload
   (D) maintenance of the large fuse will be higher.

24. When fuses and thermal cutouts are both used in a motor circuit
   (A) the fuses protect the motor against light overloads
   (B) the fuses protect the motor and circuit against shorts

(C) the thermal cut-outs protect the motor and circuit against shorts

(D) the thermal cut-outs protect the motor against overheating.

Answer Key

Theory and Practice

1. D	6. D	11. A	16. D	21. A
2. C	7. C	12. A	17. C	22. C
3. D	8. A	13. D	18. B	23. C
4. C	9. C	14. A	19. B	24. B
5. B	10. B	15. D	20. B	

FUSES-TYPES AND RATINGS

1. In ordering standard cartridge fuses it is necessary to specify only
   (A) the current capacity
   (B) the voltage of the circuit
   (C) the current capacity and the voltage of the circuit
   (D) the power to be dissipated.

2. The largest size regular plug fuse used is rated at
   (A) 15 amperes   (B) 20 amperes
   (C) 30 amperes   (D) 40 amperes.

3. The range of sizes of cartridge fuses with ferrule ends is from
   (A) 0 to 60 amperes
   (B) 0 to 30 amperes
   (C) 31 to 50 amperes
   (D) 61 to 100 amperes.

4. A 600-volt cartridge fuse is most readily distinguished from a 250-volt cartridge fuse of the same ampere rating by comparing the
   (A) insulating materials used
   (B) shape of the ends
   (C) diameters
   (D) lengths.

5. Renewable fuses differ from ordinary fuses in that
   (A) burned out fuse elements can be replaced readily
   (B) they can carry higher overloads
   (C) burned out fuses can be located more easily
   (D) they can be used on higher voltages.

6. A 10 ampere cartridge fuse provided with a navy blue label has a voltage rating, in volts, of
   (A) 220   (B) 250
   (C) 550   (D) 600.

7. Knife blade ends on a cartridge fuse are a positive indication that the fuse is rated at over
   (A) 600 volts   (B) 250 volts
   (C) 100 amperes   (D) 60 amperes.

8. In general, the principal factor that determines the current rating of the fuse that should be installed in a lighting circuit is the
   (A) wattage of the individual lamps
   (B) capacity of the smallest wire in the circuit
   (C) voltage of the circuit
   (D) capacity of the largest wire in the circuit.

Answer Key

Types and Ratings

1. C	3. A	5. A	7. D
2. C	4. D	6. B	8. B

PROBLEMS

1. Testing for a blown cartridge fuse by connecting a lamp from one clip to the other of the suspected fuse will in all cases indicate a
   (A) blown fuse if the lamp remains dark
   (B) good fuse if the lamp lights up
   (C) blown fuse if the lamp lights up
   (D) good fuse if the lamp remains dark.

2. A blown "one-time" fuse is replaced with a good fuse of the same rating. When the switch is closed the new fuse also blows. In this case
   (A) a fuse of higher current rating should be used
   (B) a fuse having a greater time lag should be tried
   (C) some of the load should be transferred to another circuit
   (D) the circuit should be checked before trying another fuse.

3. One of the two plug-fuses in a 120-volt circuit blows because of a short circuit. If a 120-volt lamp is screwed into the fuse socket while the circuit is still shorted, the lamp will
   (A) burn dimly
   (B) remain dark
   (C) burn out
   (D) burn normally.

4. Before removing a "blown" 600 volt fuse it is always desirable to
   (A) open the circuit at another point on the line side
   (B) shut down the station
   (C) jumper the fuse
   (D) ground the circuit.

5. If the 30 ampere fuse is blown frequently on a house lighting circuit
   (A) check the load and condition of equipment
   (B) insert a fuse of higher current rating
   (C) insert a fuse of higher voltage rating
   (D) check the line voltage.

6. A 120-volt lighting circuit feeding 10 single-lamp 120-volt fixtures is protected by a 15-ampere fuse. If the same size lamp is used in all 10 fixtures the largest lamp that can be used without blowing the fuse is
   (A) 100 watts   (B) 150 watts
   (C) 200 watts   (D) 250 watts.

Questions 7 and 8 refer to the diagram below.

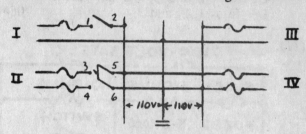

7. Circuit No. I in the above diagram
   (A) is not properly fused as it should have one fuse in each leg
   (B) supplies 220 volts to the load
   (C) is grounded if a pair of test lamps light when placed between point 2 and ground
   (D) supplies 110 volts to the load at the board.

8. Circuit No. II in the above diagram
   (A) is not properly fused as it should have only one fuse in the hot leg
   (B) supplies 110 volts to the load at the board
   (C) is grounded if a pair of test lamps light up when placed between points 5 and 6
   (D) is grounded if, with the switch in the open position, test lamps light up when placed between points 3 and 5.

9. The maximum size of fuse for protecting a 10 HP, 3-phase, 220 Volt motor should be
   (A) 20 amperes   (B) 35 amperes
   (C) 60 amperes   (D) 75 amperes
   (E) 90 amperes.

10. A 115/230 volt three wire lighting circuit sub-main, supplies fused branch circuits. It has a grounded neutral and consists of 3 no. 8 rubber covered wires. It should be protected at the distribution panel by
    (A) fuses of not over 35 amperes in all three lines
    (B) fuses of not over 15 amperes in all three lines
    (C) fuses of not over 35 amperes in the ungrounded lines, with the neutral unfused
    (D) fuses of not over 15 amperes in the ungrounded lines, with the neutral unfused
    (E) three single pole 35 ampere switches.

11. When the switch is closed, it is reasonable to expect the blowing of
 (A) fuse 2, but not fuses 1 and 3
 (B) fuses 1 and 2, but not fuse 3
 (C) fuses 2 and 3, but not fuse 1
 (D) fuses 1, 2, and 3.   0841

(12)

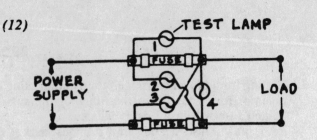

(11)

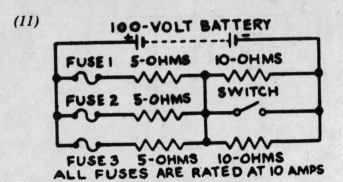

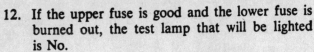

12. If the upper fuse is good and the lower fuse is burned out, the test lamp that will be lighted is No.
 (A) 1   (B) 2
 (C) 3   (D) 4.

Answer Key

(You'll learn more by writing your own answers before comparing them with these.)

Problems

1. C	4. A	7. D	9. B	11. D
2. D	5. A	8. D	10. C	12. C
3. D	6. B			

ELECTRICIAN

BREAKERS AND BUS BARS

1. A piece of electrical equipment that serves the same purpose as a fuse is a
   (A) transformer
   (B) generator
   (C) switch
   (D) circuit breaker.

2. A d.c. panel type circuit breaker is adjusted so that the
   (A) arcing tip will open before the main contact
   (B) main contact will close before the arcing tip
   (C) main contact will open before the arcing tip
   (D) arcing tip and main contact will open at the same time.

3. Arcing tips are used on air circuit breakers to
   (A) increase the contact
   (B) protect the main contacts
   (C) decrease the arcing time
   (D) limit the short circuit current.

4. The reason modern circuit breakers are constructed to be "trip free" is that such breakers
   (A) cannot be held closed when there is an overload
   (B) can be closed with less effort
   (C) cannot be opened accidentally
   (D) can be opened with less arcing.

5. The push buttons used in the control circuits of some remote-controlled lighting switches are required only to make, not break, the control circuit. In such cases, the breaking of the control circuit is generally accomplished by
   (A) a relay on the control panel
   (B) an auxiliary contact on the lighting switch
   (C) a blow-out coil on the main contacts of the lighting switch
   (D) an auxiliary toggle switch on the control panel.

6. A breaker is said to be trip free if
   (A) the closing and tripping operatons are independent
   (B) it will trip on any value of reverse current
   (C) the tripping devices operate easily
   (D) it is not latched in position when closed.

7. A Trip Free Circuit Breaker is one
   (A) that is found only in large generating stations
   (B) that cannot be re-closed once it opens
   (C) that rings an alarm when it opens
   (D) that cannot be closed by hand while the abnormal condition which caused it to open exists.

8. The trip-coil of a circuit breaker is connected into a line through a current transformer rated at 200:5 amperes. If normal line current is 120 amperes and the circuit breaker should open at 125% normal line current, the trip mechanism should be set to operate when the trip-coil current is
   (A) 6.25 amperes   (B) 3.75 amperes
   (C) 1.94 amperes   (D) 14.1 amperes.

9. To work on a high voltage bus with remote controlled switches, after isolating the bus, the safest procedure before working on the bus is
   (A) short circuit and ground the bus
   (B) tag the control switches on the control board
   (C) notify the shift operator on the control board
   (D) use rubber gloves and mats
   (E) notify the power company supplying the power.

10. A copper bus bar an inch in diameter has a cross sectional area of
    (A) 3,141,600 C.M.   (B) 1,000,000 C.M.
    (C) 785,400 C.M.   (D) 100,000 C.M.

11. Figure A below is the electric circuit and B a simplified drawing of the magnetic circuit of the trip mechanism of a D.C. circuit breaker which opens if the armature drops to the position shown. The circuit breaker remains closed if the load current is zero and the line voltage is normal. It will open if
   (A) both the line voltage and load current are reversed
   (B) the load current is reversed and line voltage is normal
   (C) the load current is excessive and line voltage is normal
   (D) the line voltage is excessive and load current is normal.

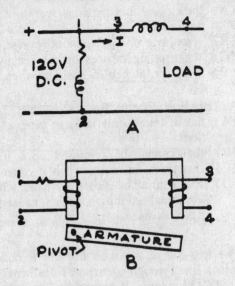

12. In order that a circuit breaker may be remotely opened it must be equipped with which one of the following tripping devices?

(A) shunt trip
(B) time-delay trip
(C) trip-free mechanism
(D) inverse-time trip.

13. The reason modern circuit breakers are constructed to be "quick breaking" is that such breakers
   (A) can be operated at more than 100% rating
   (B) cannot be held closed when there is an overload
   (C) can be opened with less arcing
   (D) cannot be closed accidentally.

14. The "Normal Current Density" of copper bus is 100 amperes per square inch. The number of amperes which a 2 1/2 x 1/4 inch copper bus may carry under these conditions is
   (A) 625 amperes   (B) 1000 amperes
   (C) 1250 amperes   (D) 500 amperes.

15. The weight of a 10 foot section of a 2" x 1/8" copper bus bar, which is made of copper having a density of 0.32 lbs. per cu. in., is most nearly
   (A) 0.82 lbs.   (B) 7.7 lbs.
   (C) 9.6 lbs.   (D) 30.0 lbs.

Answer Key

Breakers and Bus Bars

1. D	4. A	7. D	10. B	13. C
2. C	5. B	8. B	11. B	14. A
3. B	6. A	9. A	12. A	15. C

ELECTRICIAN

RECTIFIERS

1. A bake-out is generally considered necessary for a rectifier if
   (A) it has been subjected to a heavy overload
   (B) it has been operating at light load for a long period
   (C) more than three months have elapsed since previous bake-out
   (D) it has been open to atmosphere for a long period.

2. The possibility of an arc back in a rectifier is increased by
   (A) operating the rectifier at less than rated capacity
   (B) the presence of mercury vapor in the rectifier tank
   (C) the absence of non-condensible gases in the rectifier tank
   (D) operating the rectifier at more than rated capacity.

3. The material that is least suitable for rectifier vacuum seals is
   (A) mercury   (B) aluminum
   (C) mycalex   (D) rubber.

4. A commonly used method of controlling the d.c. voltage of a rectifier is by
   (A) inserting a rheostat in the main positive lead
   (B) varying the tank pressure
   (C) controlling the potential of the anode grids
   (D) increasing or decreasing the interphase transformer ratio.

5. In order to furnish DC for the operation of relays and control circuits, where only a source of AC is available and the use of batteries is not convenient, gas and vacuum tubes are used extensively as rectifiers. The schematic diagram shown below represents a typical
   (A) full wave rectifier
   (B) push pull rectifier
   (C) bridge rectifier
   (D) half wave rectifier.

(5)

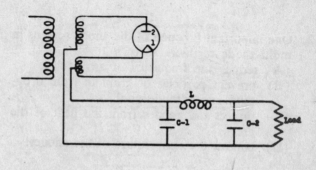

6. In reference to sketch in question 5, tube element 1 represents the
   (A) filament   (B) plate
   (C) suppressor   (D) grid.

7. In reference to sketch in question No. 5, tube element 2 represents the
   (A) suppressor   (B) filament
   (C) grid   (D) plate.

8. In reference to sketch in question No. 5, the circuit element marked L together with C-1 and C-2 act to
   (A) smooth the voltage across the load
   (B) change the frequency across the load
   (C) rectify the incoming AC
   (D) maintain the factor cos ∅ intact

9. A copper oxide rectifier consisting of four units arranged in a full-wave bridge circuit is to be used to charge a 6-volt storage battery. The rectifier may be considered as having a linear volt-ampere characteristic yielding 6 amperes when the voltage drop across each unit is 3-volts. The average charging current when the peak value of the applied alternating voltage is 20 is approximately
   (A) 6.7   (B) 14
   (C) 8.1   (D) 10.

10. In a multi-anode rectifier, anode grids are provided to
    (A) give mechanical support to the anode tips
    (B) permit convenient access to the anodes
    (C) increase the heat radiating surface of the anodes
    (D) control the rectifier arc.

11. The surge eliminator for a rectifier is connected
    (A) across a secondary winding of the power transformer
    (B) across a primary winding of the power transformer
    (C) from the tank to the cathode
    (D) from the cathode to the negative bus.

12. One important function of the anode screens in multi-anode rectifiers is to
    (A) reduce the frequency of arc backs
    (B) prevent particles of graphite from dropping into cathode pool
    (C) protect the anodes from the heat of the arc
    (D) control the temperature of the anodes.

13. Most of the large mercury are rectifiers in com-single-phase or 3-phase rectifiers. One of the principal reasons for this is that

    (A) a smoother, more even d.c. voltage is obtained
    (B) the cathode is required to carry a smaller current
    (C) less routine maintenance work is required
    (D) an even number of phases is essential for good operation.

Answer Key

(You'll learn more by writing your own answers before comparing them with these.)

Rectifiers

1. D	4. C	7. D	10. D	13. A
2. D	5. D	8. A	11. A	
3. D	6. A	9. A	12. A	

Rheostats—Relays

1. Burnt or pitted contact studs on a synchronous generator field rheostat should be
   (A) dressed with a file
   (B) smoothed with emery cloth
   (C) restored with a burnishing tool
   (D) resurfaced by brazing.

2. If an open circuit is discovered in an exciter shunt field rheostat between two contact points, the exciter
   (A) must be left out of service until the open coil or grid is replaced
   (B) can be operated if the open coil or grid is short-circuited
   (C) must be operated at low loads with reduced field
   (D) can be operated without the field rheostat by exciting the field from the exciter bus.

3. Series type motors for electrically driven rheostats or governors have a split series field to
   (A) obtain low motor speed
   (B) decrease the current consumption
   (C) change the direction of rotation
   (D) produce greater starting torque.

4. A relay coil with a resistance in series is connected in parallel with a contactor coil to a battery. If the current is 5 amperes in the relay coil, 5 amperes in the resistor and 3 amperes in the contactor coil, the battery current is
   (A) 13 amperes   (B) 2 amperes
   (C) 5 amperes   (D) 8 amperes.

5. The electrical device occasionally connected across relay contacts to minimize arcing when the contacts open is
   (A) a condenser
   (B) a resistor
   (C) an inductance coil
   (D) a carbon tip.

6. An induction type overcurrent relay usually
   (A) operates instantaneously
   (B) has a constant time delay for all settings
   (C) has increased time delay with an increase in current
   (D) has decreased time delay with an increase in current.

7. An electrical helper notices that a certain relay does not pick up promptly when its control circuit is closed. Of the following faults, the only one that could be the cause of this delayed operation is a
   (A) control wire broken off one of the relay terminals
   (B) burned out fuse
   (C) burned out relay coil
   (D) fuse making poor contact.

8. Differential relays are installed to protect against
   (A) overcurrents
   (B) reverse currents
   (C) internal faults
   (D) no voltage
   (E) reverse power.

9. A hesitating relay is
   (A) to allow for momentary impulse type closing control
   (B) to provide a definite time for tripping an overload
   (C) one that stops half way unless interlock circuits are clear
   (D) an a.c. relay with insufficient shading
   (E) used for remote control of field rheostat motors.

10. An induction type overcurrent relay
    (A) operates quicker with large currents than with small ones
    (B) operates quicker with small currents than with large ones
    (C) operates in the same time with any overload current
    (D) operates eventually even on currents less than the trip-setting value
    (E) always operates instantaneously.

11. An induction overcurrent relay has its time setting adjusted by means of an index lever which is moved over a scale with graduations numbered 1 to 10. Moving the lever from 10 towards 1
    (A) increases the time of operation on large overloads, only when the maximum current connection is used
    (B) decreases the time of operation on large overloads, only when the maximum current connection is used

(C) increases the time of operation on large overloads, only when the minimum current connection is used

(D) decreases the time of operation on large overloads, only when the minimum current connection is used

(E) decreases the time of operation on large overloads, when any current connection is used.

12. In relay testing, a cycle counter is used
    (A) to measure the frequency of the system voltage
    (B) to determine the number of operations of a relay in a 24 hour period
    (C) to check the current required to operate a relay
    (D) to check the time of operation of a relay
    (E) to determine the operating frequency of an under-frequency relay.

13. Series type motors for electrically driven rheostats have a split series field to
    (A) change the direction of rotation
    (B) decrease the current consumption
    (C) obtain low motor speed
    (D) produce greater starting torque.

14. A photoelectric relay system could not be used for which one of the following applications?
    (A) controlling the temperature of a furnace
    (B) amplifying audio frequencies
    (C) sorting objects of different sizes
    (D) counting moving objects without physical contact.

(15)
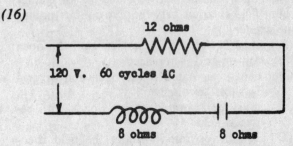

15. A relay circuit is connected to a 120 volt 60 cycle AC supply as shown above. The current flowing in the circuit is
    (A) 20 amperes   (B) 15 amperes
    (C) 12 amperes   (D) 8.57 amperes.

(16)

```
            12 ohms
     ┌──────WWWW──────────┐
   ↑ │                    │
120 V.  60 cycles AC      │
   ↓ │                    │
     └──oooo────────┤├────┘
        8 ohms      8 ohms
```

16. In the above AV circuit, the capacitative reactance is equal to the inductive reactance. Under these conditions the current is
    (A) a minimum   (B) 10 amperes
    (C) 6 amperes   (D) 4 amperes.

Answer Key

Rheostats—Relays

1. A	5. A	8. C	11. E	14. B
2. B	6. D	9. A	12. D	15. C
3. C	7. D	10. A	13. A	16. B
4. D				

Rotary converters—Commutators

1. The speed of a rotary converter in normal operation is governed by the frequency of the a.c. supply and the
   (A) d.c. load
   (B) number of poles
   (C) a.c. voltage
   (D) shunt field current.

2. When a rotary converter is started on reduced a.c. voltage (from the a.c. side), if the d.c. polarity of the rotary is reversed the operator should
   (A) shut the machine down and re-start
   (B) close the field switch "down" until correct polarity is indicated then close it in the "up" position
   (C) close the field switch "down" and leave it in that position
   (D) open the oil switch momentarily and then reclose it.

3. The power factor of a synchronous converter in normal operation will change from lag to lead if the
   (A) load increases to a high value
   (B) load drops to a low value
   (C) field current is reduced to a low value
   (D) d.c. bus voltage drops suddenly.

4. The overspeed device on a rotary converter is usually arranged so that when it operates it will open the rotary
   (A) positive breaker or switch
   (B) oil switch
   (C) negative breaker or switch
   (D) oil switch and positive breaker or switch.

5. One purpose for having dampers or amortisseur windings on rotary converter pole faces is to
   (A) equalize the field strength
   (B) provide a compound field
   (C) minimize hunting
   (D) improve admission of cooling air.

6. When an induction motor is mounted on the shaft of a rotary converter for starting purposes, the motor usually has two less poles than the rotary. It is constructed this way
   (A) to simplify the stator winding
   (B) so that its synchronous speed is higher than the speed of the rotary
   (C) because it is smaller than the rotary
   (D) to keep the starting current at a low value.

7. The most likely cause for overspeed on a rotary in service is
   (A) loss of A.C. power
   (B) loss of D.C. power
   (C) low A.C. frequency
   (D) loss of field.

8. When rotary brushes are properly adjusted, the contact pressure of the brushes on the commutator will be
   (A) greatest at the top brushes
   (B) the same for all brushes
   (C) smallest at the side brushes
   (D) smallest at the bottom brushes.

9. Weakening the field of a rotary operating in parallel with other rotaries will cause the
   (A) brushes to spark
   (B) D.C. output to increase
   (C) speed to decrease
   (D) D.C. output of this rotary to decrease.

10. In case of a short circuit in the windings of a rotary converter, the device which limits the duration of the excessive A.C. current is the
    (A) overload relay
    (B) overspeed device
    (C) transformer
    (D) reverse current relay.

11. The simplest way to check the bearing of a rotary for excessive heating is by
    (A) a thermometer
    (B) feeling the housing
    (C) noting discoloration of the housing
    (D) detecting odors.

12. The purpose of having the armature of a rotary converter oscillate is so that the
    (A) brushes will wear evenly
    (B) area of contact between brushes and commutator will be increased
    (C) armature will be better ventilated
    (D) commutator will wear evenly.

13. The interpole (commutating) field winding of a rotary converter is usually connected
    (A) in series with the armature on the negative side
    (B) in series with the armature on the positive side
    (C) in parallel with the armature
    (D) in parallel with the shunt field.

14. A 3000 kw. rotary converter operating at full load with a d.c. voltage of 625 volts would deliver a direct current of
    (A) 1875 amps
    (B) 2083 amps
    (C) 3625 amps
    (D) 4800 amps.

15. A piece of No. 1/9 emery cloth should be used to grind the commutator of a d-c motor
    (A) whenever there is sparking at the brushes
    (B) under no condition
    (C) when the commutator is rough or worn
    (D) when the brushes do not make good contact.

16. A simple method of checking a commutator for tightness is to
    (A) feel the surface for uneven spots
    (B) check one of the V-ring bolts with a wrench
    (C) tap it lightly with a small hammer
    (D) measure the diameter at several points.

17. If high mica develops on a commutator, it is corrected by
    (A) undercutting
    (B) stoning
    (C) shimming the copper
    (D) smoothing with sandpaper.

18. Mica is commonly used in electrical construction for
    (A) commutator bar separators
    (B) switchboard panels
    (C) strain insulators
    (D) heater cord insulation.

Answer Key

(You'll learn more by writing your own answers before comparing them with these.)

Rotary Converters—Commutators

1. B	5. C	9. D	13. A	17. A
2. B	6. B	10. A	14. D	18. A
3. B	7. A	11. B	15. B	
4. A	8. B	12. D	16. C	

Condensers—Exciters
Reactors—Alternators

1. It is suspected that a condenser is short-circuited. In order to test the condenser, it is put in series with a 120-volt test lamp across 120 volts d.c. If the condenser is short-circuited, the lamp should
(A) flash on and then become and remain dark
(B) flash on and off intermittently
(C) give off normal light
(D) remain dark.

2. A one-microfarad condenser is connected in series with a one-half microfarad condenser. The resulting capacity of the combination is
(A) one-half microfarad
(B) one-third microfarad
(C) one and one-half microfarad
(D) one-microfarad.

3. The reason for connecting a condenser across relay contacts which make and break frequently is to
(A) make the relay slow acting
(B) make the relay quick acting
(C) reduce pitting of the contacts
(D) raise the power factor of the circuit.

4. An alternator in parallel with other alternators, all having automatic voltage regulators, is to be taken off the bus. The usual procedure before opening the alternator switch is to
(A) do nothing
(B) reduce the power feed to the prime mover
(C) reduce the alternator field
(D) increase the alternator field
(E) increase the power feed to the prime mover.

5. Two alternators operating in parallel are driven by governor regulated turbines. They supply a unity power factor load and each has been individually adjusted to unity power factor. Increasing the field current of one
(A) increases its load
(B) increases the frequency
(C) causes its power factor to become leading
(D) causes its current to decrease
(E) causes its power factor to become lagging.

6. An alternator is supplying load in parallel with one or more machines of considerably larger rating. In order to increase its load
(A) field current is increased
(B) power factor is increased
(C) field current is decreased
(D) speed is decreased
(E) prime mover power input is increased.

7. The rating of an alternator, as given on its nameplate, is 800 kw., 0.8 power factor. The significance of this rating is that the alternator
(A) always operates at 0.8 power factor
(B) can supply an 800 kw., 0.8 lagging power factor load at rated voltage
(C) can supply a 1000 kv.-a. load, any power factor, at rated voltage
(D) is fully loaded at 800 kw., any power factor
(E) efficiency is highest with an 800 kw., 0.8 power factor load.

8. You have just wired up two 3-phase alternators. You have checked the frequency and voltage of each. They are the same. Before you would connect these alternators in parallel you would
(A) check the steam pressure
(B) check the speed of the turbine
(C) check the phase rotation
(D) lubricate everything.

9. When exciter brushes are properly adjusted, the contact pressure of the brushes on the commutator will be
(A) greatest at the top brushes
(B) smallest at the side brushes
(C) smallest at the bottom brushes
(D) the same for all brushes.

Answer Key

Condensers—Exciters

1. C	3. C	5. E	7. B	9. D
2. B	4. B	6. E	8. C	

TRANSFORMERS

Theory, Use, Parts and Wiring

1. The primary and secondary coils of a transformer always have
   (A) the same size of wire
   (B) a common magnetic circuit
   (C) separate magnetic circuits
   (D) different number of turns.

2. The maximum load a power transformer can carry is limited by its
   (A) temperature rise
   (B) insulation resistance
   (C) oil's dielectric strength
   (D) voltage ratio.

3. The transformer is based on the principle that energy may be effectively transferred by induction from one set of coils to another by a varying magnetic flux, provided both sets of coils
   (A) are not on a common magnetic circuit
   (B) have the same number of turns
   (C) are on a common magnetic circuit
   (D) do not have the same number of turns.

4. In a transformer the induced emf per turn in the secondary winding is
   (A) equal to the induced emf per turn in the primary winding
   (B) not equal to the induced emf per turn in the primary winding
   (C) equal to the induced emf per turn in the primary winding multiplied by the ratio N-1/N-2
   (D) equal to the induced emf per turn in the primary winding divided by the ratio N-1/N-2.

5. Transformer cores can be composed of laminated sheet metal rather than solid metal and as a result
   (A) eddy currents are reduced
   (B) less insulation is needed on the windings
   (C) oil penetrates the core more easily
   (D) the voltage ratio is higher than the turn ratio.

6. Compared to the secondary of a loaded step-down transformer, the primary has
   (A) higher voltage and lower current
   (B) lower voltage and higher current
   (C) lower voltage and current
   (D) higher voltage and current.

7. Current transformers for meters and relays usually have
   (A) five ampere secondaries
   (B) ten ampere secondaries
   (C) a ten to one ratio
   (D) a hundred to one ratio
   (E) a one to one ratio.

8. An auto-transformer is used in preference to a two winding transformer
   (A) where it is desired to isolate two circuits
   (B) where the ratio of transformation is low
   (C) where neither the primary or secondary is over 250 Volts
   (D) because the auto-transformer is safer to operate
   (E) where a large number of taps are needed.

9. When a step-up transformer is used, it increases the
   (A) voltage   (B) current
   (C) power   (D) frequency.

10. For a given 3-phase transformer the connection giving the highest secondary voltage is
    (A) Wye primary, Delta secondary
    (B) Delta primary, Delta secondary
    (C) Wye primary, Wye secondary
    (D) Delta primary, Wye secondary.

11. The purpose of laminating the core of a power transformer is to keep the
    (A) hysteresis loss at a minimum
    (B) eddy current loss at a minimum
    (C) copper losses at a minimum
    (D) friction losses at a minimum.

S1111

12. An insulating transformer is used in the rectifier control circuit to
    (A) prevent the possibility of high voltage being impressed on the low voltage a.c. supply
    (B) obtain full wave rectification
    (C) lower the voltage
    (D) obtain single phase power from the three phase supply.

13. A booster transformer is a transformer connected
    (A) in such a manner as to increase the load on the line by a fixed percentage
    (B) as a delta-connected bank
    (C) as an auto-transformer to raise the line voltage by a fixed percentage
    (D) in such a manner as to raise the frequency by a fixed percentage.

14. The interphase transformer used with a multi-anode rectifier
    (A) causes the anodes to overlap in firing
    (B) permits only one anode to fire at a time

    (C) causes each anode to fire over a shorter period of time
    (D) acts as an insulating transformer between power transformer and anodes.

15. The primary and secondary coils of a transformer always have
    (A) the same size of wire
    (B) a common magnetic circuit
    (C) separate magnetic circuits
    (D) different number of turns.

Answer Key

Theory, Use, Parts and Wiring

1. B	4. A	7. A	10. D	13. C
2. A	5. A	8. B	11. B	14. A
3. C	6. A	9. A	12. A	15. B

Operation and maintenance: transformers

1. In the operation of dry-type transformers the accumulation of dust on the windings and core is objectionable mainly because it
   (A) may short circuit the windings
   (B) tends to corrode the metal
   (C) absorbs oil and grease
   (D) reduces the dissipation of heat.

2. The terminals of the secondary winding of a current transformer in whose primary winding current is flowing and whose secondary winding is open circuited, must never be
   (A) connected to the current coil of a watt-meter
   (B) short circuited
   (C) connected to an ammeter
   (D) touched with your hands.

3. The relative polarity of the windings of a transformer is determined by
   (A) open circuit test
   (B) phasing out
   (C) short circuit test
   (D) polarimeter test.

4. The secondary of a single-phase transformer consists of two similar coils and it is required to place them in parallels. A common procedure is to connect any two terminals together and impress not more than the normal voltage upon either coil. With a voltmeter, measure the voltage across the other two terminals. The coils are correctly connected in parallel if the voltmeter reads
   (A) twice the impressed voltage
   (B) zero
   (C) one-half the impressed voltage
   (D) a fraction of the impressed voltage.

5. Connecting up power transformer windings requires
   (A) knowledge of the frequency
   (B) an open circuit test
   (C) a short circuit test
   (D) phasing out of the leads.

6. A synchronous motor driven d.c. shunt generator has been properly connected to a bus supplied from other parallel generators, and is carrying no load. A decrease of its shunt field current will

   (A) cause it to supply power to the bus
   (B) cause it to operate as a motor at the same speed and in the same direction of rotation
   (C) cause it to operate as a motor, reversing its direction of rotation
   (D) cause it to operate as a motor, at a higher speed and in the same direction of rotation
   (E) cause no change.

7. The common cause of contamination by water of oil in transformers located indoors is
   (A) electrolytic action of high voltage on air
   (B) condensation of moisture from air in the upper part of the tank
   (C) decomposition of organic matter in the oil
   (D) the use of filter blotters that have absorbed moisture from the air
   (E) leaky bushings.

8. The secondary of a current transformer whose primary is connected in a high voltage line and whose primary current is normal, should never be
   (A) subjected to too high a secondary current overload
   (B) short circuited
   (C) grounded
   (D) open circuited
   (E) connected at any point with the secondary of a similar transformer whose primary is another high voltage line.

9. If three single phase transformers are connected delta to delta, and the secondary of one develops short circuits between coils, the load may be partially carried by
   (A) disconnecting the damaged secondary, leaving the primaries all connected in delta
   (B) short circuiting the damaged section
   (C) removing the damaged transformer from the circuit entirely
   (D) no method with the two remaining transformers
   (E) disconnecting the primary of the damaged transformer, leaving the secondaries all connected in delta.

10. From your knowledge of electrical equipment you know that the part of a transformer which is most subject to damage from high temperature is the
    (A) iron core
    (B) copper winding
    (C) winding insulation
    (D) frame or case.

11. Before disconnecting an ammeter or relay from an energized current transformer circuit, the
    (A) circuit should be opened
    (B) fuse should be removed
    (C) current transformer secondary should be shorted
    (D) current transformer primary circuit should be shorted. 1301

12. In general, the most important point to watch in the operation of transformers is the
    (A) primary voltage
    (B) exciting current
    (C) core loss
    (D) temperature.

13. A common use for auto-transformers in electrical power work is as
    (A) starting compensators for induction motors
    (B) current limiting reactors
    (C) instrument current transformers
    (D) insulating transformers.

14. A single-phase a.c. potential of 60 volts is required for test purposes. A 440-volt a.c. source and two identical transformers with 440-volt primary windings and 120-volt secondary windings are available. For this purpose the transformers should be connected with
    (A) primaries in parallel, secondaries in parallel
    (B) primaries in series, secondaries in series
    (C) primaries in parallel, secondaries in series
    (D) primaries in series, secondaries in parallel.

15. The secondary of a current transformer in whose primary winding current is flowing should
    (A) always be short-circuited
    (B) not be connected to the current coil of a wattmeter

(C) not be open-circuited
(D) not be short-circuited.

16. Oil is used in many large transformers to
    (A) lubricate the core
    (B) lubricate the coils
    (C) insulate the coils
    (D) insulate the core.

17. Almost all transformers used to supply rotary converters have primary winding taps. Changing tap connections on these transformers would have the direct effect of changing the
    (A) rotary d.c. voltage
    (B) rotary speed
    (C) setting of the rotary overload relays
    (D) load capacity of the rotary.

18. A rotary converter is supplied through a bank of three single-phase air-blast transformers. During operation one of the transformers is found to be considerably hotter than normal while the other two transformers are at normal temperature. A probable cause for this condition would be
    (A) low air pressure
    (B) overload on rotary
    (C) dampers not opened on the one transformer
    (D) rotary operated at low power factor.

Answer Key

(You'll learn more by writing your own answers before comparing them with these.)

Operation and Maintenance

1. D	5. D	9. C	13. A	16. C
2. D	6. B	10. C	14. D	17. A
3. B	7. B	11. C	15. C	18. C
4. B	8. D	12. D		

ELECTRICIAN

TRANSFORMER PROBLEMS

1. A 10 to 1 step down transformer has 44,000 volts on the primary and 4,400 on the secondary. If the taps are changed to reduce the number of turns in the primary by 2.5% then the secondary voltage will be most nearly
   (A) 4,290 v.　　　　(B) 4,390 v.
   (C) 4,410 v.　　　　(D) 4,510 v.

2. If the input to a 10 to 1 step-down transformer is 15 amperes at 2400 volts, the secondary output would be nearest to
   (A) 1.5 amperes at 24,000 volts
   (B) 150 amperes at 240 volts
   (C) 1.5 amperes at 240 volts
   (D) 150 amperes at 24,000 volts.

3. If the input to a 10 to 1 step-down transformer is 25 amperes at 1200 volts, the secondary output would be nearest to
   (A) 2.5 amperes at 12,000 volts
   (B) 250 amperes at 120 volts
   (C) 2.5 amperes at 120 volts
   (D) 250 amperes at 12,000 volts.

4. When the input to a 6-to-1 step-up transformer is 12 amperes at 120 volts, the output is approximately
   (A) 72 amperes at 20 volts
   (B) 2 amperes at 20 volts
   (C) 2 amperes at 720 volts
   (D) 72 amperes at 720 volts.

5. If the input to a 5 to 1 step-down transformer is 100 amperes at 2200 volts, the output will be nearly
   (A) 100 amperes at 440 volts
   (B) 500 amperes at 440 volts
   (C) 20 amperes at 11,000 volts
   (D) 500 amperes at 2200 volts.

6. Three single-phase transformers are connected in delta on both the primary and secondary sides. If one of the transformers burn out the

system can continue to operate but its capacity, in terms of the capacity of the original arrangement, is reduced to
(A) 66 2 3%　　　　(B) 57.8%
(C) 115%　　　　　(D) 100%.

(7)

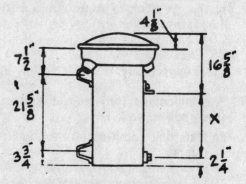

7. On the transformer the dimension marked "X" is
(A) 9 7/8"　　　　(B) 14"
(C) 18 1/8"　　　　(D) 19 1/8 .

0831

8. If the secondary of a 10 to 1 step-up transformer is connected to the primary of a 2 to 1 step-up transformer, the total step-up of both transformers combined is
(A) 20 to 1　　　　(B) 12 to 1
(C) 8 to 1　　　　　(D) 5 to 1.

(9)

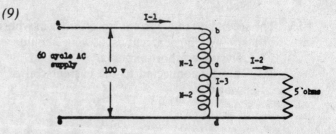

9. An auto transformer whose primary is bd is connected across a 100-volt a.c. supply as shown in the above diagram. The load of 5 ohms is connected across points c and d. If it is assumed that N-1=N-2, (that is, point o is the midpoint of the winding) current I-1, in amperes, is approximately equal to

(A) 5   (B) 10
(C) 15   (D) 20.

10. In reference to question No. 9, current I-2, in amperes, is approximately equal to
(A) 5   (B) 10
(C) 15   (D) 20.

11. In reference to question No. 9, current I-3, in amperes, is approximately equal to
(A) 5   (B) 10
(C) 15   (D) 20.

12. A Wye-delta transformer bank of 3 single-phase transformers is to be used for step down operation between circuits with voltages between lines of 23000 and 2300. The ratio of each individual transformer should be approximately
(A) 5.8 to 1
(B) 7.05 to 1
(C) 10 to 1
(D) 14.1 to 1
(E) 17.3 to 1.

13. A single-phase a.c. potential of 60 volts is required for test purposes. A 600-volt a.c. source and two identical transformers with 600-volt primary windings and 120-volt secondary windings are available. For this purpose, the transformers should be connected with
(A) primaries in parallel, secondaries in parallel
(B) primaries in series, secondaries in parallel
(C) primaries in parallel, secondaries in series
(D) primaries in series, secondaries in series.

(14)

To 3-phase - 2400 Volt Supply

T-1   T-2   T-3

b   c

a

14. The above figure represents a transformer bank composed of 3 single-phase transformers each having a ratio of transformation equal to 20/1. The primary is already connected to the voltage supply, as shown in the diagram, while the secondary side is only "partly connected."

It is desired to connect the secondary of this transformer bank in delta. Before connecting a to d, the combination of voltages should correspond to one of the following:
(A) Vab=120, Vbc=120, Ved=120 and Vad=0
(B) Vab=120, Vbc=120, Ved=120 and Vad=120
(C) Vab=120, Vbc=120, Ved=120 and Vad=208
(D) Vab=208, Vbc=208, Ved=208 and Vad=0.

15. With reference to question No. 14, assuming that the combination of voltages read as follows: Vab=120 volts, Vbc=120 volts, Vcd=120 volts, Vad=240 volts and Vbd=208 volts, before connecting a to d for a delta connection
(A) do nothing as the transformer bank is already phased out
(B) secondary winding of T-1 should be reversed by interchanging its leads
(C) secondary winding of T-2 should be reversed by interchanging its leads
(D) secondary winding of T-3 should be reversed by interchanging its leads.

16. The sketch shows two step-down transformers with 120-volt secondaries connected in a phasing test with two 120-volt lamps to determine which connections to make for paralleling the secondaries. If leads 1 and 3 are of the same polarity, then
(A) lamp X will be bright and lamp Y dark
(B) lamp Y will be bright and lamp X dark
(C) both lamps will be bright
(D) both lamps will be dark.

(16)

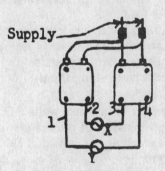

Supply

1   2   3   4

Answer Key

Problems

1. D	5. B	8. A	11. A	14. A
2. B	6. B	9. A	12. A	15. D
3. B	7. C	10. B	13. B	16. C
4. C				

GENERATORS & BATTERIES

Generators

1. The frequency of the alternating current generated by a synchronous generator is governed by the speed and the
   (A) field excitation
   (B) load
   (C) power factor
   (D) number of poles.

2. A leather belt is used to drive a 3 kw DC generator by a 5 hp 3-phase induction motor. Adjustments for proper belt tension, with the generator running at full load, can be made with the aid of a
   (A) 50-lb. weight as wide as the belt
   (B) voltmeter and an ammeter
   (C) power factor meter
   (D) 3-phase wattmeter.

3. Compound D.C. generators are usually wound so as to be somewhat over compounded. The degree of compounding is usually regulated by
   (A) shunting more or less current from the series field
   (B) shunting more or less current from the shunt field
   (C) connecting it short-shunt
   (D) connecting it long-shunt.

4. With reference to a shunt wound D.C. generator, if the resistance of the field is increased to a value exceeding its critical field resistance, the generator
   (A) output may exceed its name plate rating
   (B) may burn out when loaded to its name plate rating
   (C) output voltage will be less than its name plate rating
   (D) cannot build up.

5. A D.C. shunt generator has developed some trouble. You found that there is an open armature coil. As a temporary measure you should

(A) use new brushes having a thickness of at least 3 commutator segments
(B) bridge the two commutator bars across which the open coil is connected
(C) use new brushes having a thickness of at least 4 commutator segments
(D) disconnect the open coil from the commutator.

6. If, after the installation of a self-excited DC generator, it fails to build up on first trial run, the first thing to do is
   (A) increase the field resistance
   (B) check the armature insulation resistance
   (C) reverse the connections to the shunt field
   (D) decrease the speed of the prime mover.

7. In reference to question 6, if the generator still fails to build up, you should make sure that the
   (A) resistance of the field rheostat is all in
   (B) diverter is in series with the armature
   (C) resistance of the field circuit is sufficiently small
   (D) diverter is in parallel with the armature.

8. In reference to questions 6 and 7, if the generator still fails to build up now, you most probably would have to separately excite the
   (A) field for a few minutes with the battery
   (B) armature for a few minutes with the battery
   (C) armature with AC current
   (D) field with AC current.

9. The output of a 6-pole DC generator is 360 amperes at 240 volts. If its armature is simplex lap-wound, the current per path, in amperes, through the armature is
   (A) 52.5   (B) 60
   (C) 105   (D) 210.

10. In reference to question No. 9, the voltage per path, in volts, is
    (A) 120
    (B) 420
    (C) 60
    (D) 240.

11. In reference to question No. 9, the kilowatt rating of the machine is approximately
    (A) 86
    (B) 50
    (C) 14
    (D) 7.

12. A probable cause for a turbo-generator tripping out on overspeed is a sudden
    (A) loss of field excitation
    (B) large increase in load
    (C) total loss of load
    (D) loss of steam pressure.

13. Except for the power limitation of the turbine the maximum load carried by a generator is limited by the
    (A) relay settings
    (B) generator voltage
    (C) field current
    (D) temperature rise.

14. Differential relays are used on generators to guard against
    (A) unbalanced phase currents
    (B) an open in the ground neutral
    (C) large load fluctuations
    (D) reactive currents.

15. A 60 cycle synchronous generator will run at the greatest possible speed if it is wired for
    (A) 8 poles
    (B) 6 poles
    (C) 4 poles
    (D) 2 poles.

16. Equalizer connections are required when paralleling two
    (A) synchronous generators
    (B) series generators
    (C) shunt generators
    (D) compound generators.

17. A six-pole D.C. generator has developed an open circuit in one of its 6 shunt field coils. To locate the defective coil the field is connected across a 120-volt source and voltmeter readings taken across each coil. The defective coil will be the one across whose ends the voltage is
    (A) 120
    (B) 100
    (C) 20
    (D) 0.

18. The frequency of the alternating current generated by a synchronous generator is governed by the speed and the
    (A) field excitation
    (B) load
    (C) power factor
    (D) number of poles.

Answer Key

(You'll learn more by writing your own answers before comparing them with these.)

Generators

1. D	5. B	9. B	13. D	17. A
2. D	6. C	10. D	14. A	18. D
3. A	7. C	11. A	15. D	
4. D	8. A	12. C	16. D	

Batteries

THEORY AND MAINTENANCE

1. The term "ampere-hours" is associated with
   (A) motors
   (B) transformers
   (C) electromagnets
   (D) storage batteries.

2. In an installation used to charge a storage battery from a motor-generator you would *least* expect to find
   (A) a rectifier
   (B) a rheostat
   (C) a voltmeter
   (D) an ammeter.

3. Lead is the metal commonly used for
   (A) transformer cores
   (B) storage battery plates
   (C) knife-switch blades
   (D) power station panel boards.

4. When the liquid in a lead acid storage cell is low it is usually proper to
   (A) add a special weak acid solution
   (B) add only distilled water
   (C) empty out the cell and replace the solution
   (D) do nothing until the voltage has dropped in half.

5. Should the a.c. supply to a bulb type (Tungar) battery charger fail, the battery will not discharge through the charger because
   (A) a reverse current relay will open the d.c. circuit
   (B) the rectifier bulb is a conductor for current in one direction only
   (C) the transformer will not conduct d.c.
   (D) a current limiting resistance is provided to prevent discharge of the battery.

6. It is objectionable to leave a lead-acid storage battery in a discharged state for a long time mainly because the
   (A) terminals will corrode
   (B) acid will evaporate
   (C) electrolyte will attack the container
   (D) plates will become sulphated.

7. When completing the charging of a lead-acid battery the charging rate should be lowered to prevent violent gassing. The main reason for this is because
   (A) violent gassing tends to loosen the active material on the positive plates
   (B) the gases given off are explosive
   (C) evaporation of the acid weakens the electrolyte
   (D) the cell containers are subjected to excessive gas pressure.

8. Routine specific gravity readings taken of a lead-acid storage battery pilot cell are usually corrected for electrolyte temperature. The main reason for doing this is to
   (A) allow the readings to be "rounded off" to the nearest 0.001
   (B) lower the value of the specific gravity if the temperature is too high
   (C) minimize the effect of errors in taking readings
   (D) permit a true comparison of the reading with other readings.

9. When mixing sulphuric acid and water to prepare new electrolyte for a lead-acid battery, the acid should be poured into the water to avoid
   (A) making the initial mixture too strong
   (B) corrosion of the mixing vessel
   (C) generation of excessive heat
   (D) the use of too much concentrated acid.

10. Sediment which collects at the bottom of a lead-acid battery cell is mainly due to
    (A) precipitation from the electrolyte
    (B) dust particles from the atmosphere
    (C) active material dropped from the plates
    (D) disintegration of the container.

11. Overcharging a storage battery will *not* cause
    (A) water loss
    (B) excessive gassing
    (C) overtemperature
    (D) sulphation of the plates.

12. A partially discharged lead storage battery may be brought back to full charge by recharging with
    (A) sulphuric acid
    (B) distilled water
    (C) direct current
    (D) alternating current.

13. An accumulation of hard salts blocking the valve in the filler cap of a storage cell might result in
    (A) bulging of the case
    (B) limiting the charge to less than a full charge
    (C) buckling of the plates
    (D) corrosion of the terminals.

14. A battery is "floating" on the battery bus when the
    (A) battery is supplying all the load
    (B) battery voltage is higher than the bus voltage
    (C) charger is shut down
    (D) battery voltage is equal to the charger voltage.

15. The advantage a storage battery has over a dry cell is that the storage battery
    (A) is cheaper
    (B) is easier to use
    (C) can be recharged
    (D) can be portable.

16. During discharge, the internal resistance of a storage battery
    (A) increases
    (B) remains the same
    (C) decreases
    (D) is negative.

17. The terminal voltage of eight cells connected in series is
    (A) the product of the voltages of each cell
    (B) the sum of the voltages of each cell
    (C) the difference between the largest and smallest individual voltages
    (D) the same as the voltage of any cell.

18. Of the following, the best indication of the condition of the charge of a lead acid battery is the
    (A) specific gravity
    (B) open circuit cell voltage
    (C) level of the electrolyte
    (D) temperature of the electrolyte.

19. Cable connections to lead acid storage batteries can be most economically kept free from corrosion by
    (A) the application of petroleum jelly
    (B) frequent cleaning with a wire brush
    (C) painting with lacquer
    (D) continuous charging.

20. The plates of a lead acid storage battery are most likely to be short circuited if
    (A) the electrolyte evaporates
    (B) the battery is charged too slowly
    (C) sediment collects on the bottom of the battery
    (D) too much water is added.

21. The active materials on the positive and negative plates of a fully charged acid storage cell in good condition are, respectively
    (A) lead peroxide and pure lead
    (B) pure lead and lead sulphate
    (C) lead peroxide and lead sulphate
    (D) pure lead and pure lead.

22. In an ungrounded control battery circuit an accidental ground on one leg should be removed as soon as possible because while this condition exists
    (A) the battery is supplying a heavy load
    (B) a ground on the other leg would short the battery
    (C) the closing and trip coils of OCB's will not function
    (D) difficulty will be experienced in charging the battery.

23. In connection with storage batteries, water is decomposed forming an explosive mixture of hydrogen and oxygen when a battery is
    (A) left standing while fully charged
    (B) discharging
    (C) being charged
    (D) left standing while completely discharged.

Answer Key

Theory and Maintenance

1. D	6. D	11. D	16. A	21. A
2. A	7. A	12. C	17. B	22. B
3. B	8. D	13. A	18. A	23. C
4. B	9. C	14. D	19. A	
5. B	10. C	15. C	20. C	

PROBLEMS

1. In a storage battery installation consisting of twenty 2-volt cells connected in series, a leak develops in one of the cells and all the electrolyte runs out of it. The terminal voltage across the twenty cells will now be
   (A) 40   (B) 38
   (C) 2   (D) 0.

2. A lead cell storage battery having a 75 ampere-hour capacity is 1/3 charged. After this battery has been charged at an average rate of 10 amperes for 2 1/2 hours, it will be approximately
   (A) 2/5 charged   (B) 1/2 charged
   (C) 2/3 charged   (D) 3/4 charged.

3. The number of fresh dry cells that should be connected in series to obtain 12 volts is
   (A) 2   (B) 6
   (C) 8   (D) 12.

Items 4 to 8 inclusive in Column I are supply voltages each of which can be obtained by one of the dry cell battery connections in Column II. For each voltage in Column I, select the proper battery connections from Column II.

COLUMN I
(supply voltages)
4. 1½ volts   5. 3 volts
6. 4½ volts   7. 6 volts
8. 9 volts

COLUMN II
(battery connections)
Note: Each dry cell—1½ volts.

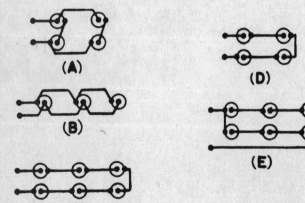

(A)

(B)

(C)

(D)

(E)

9. The number of 1½-volt dry cells that must be connected in series to obtain 9 volts is
   (A) 3   (B) 4
   (C) 6   (D) 9.

10. A battery cell having an e.m.f. of 2.2 volts and an internal resistance of 0.02 ohm is connected to an external resistance of 0.2 ohm. The current, in amperes, of the battery under this condition is approximately
    (A) 15   (B) 10
    (C) 2.5   (D) 1.

11. In reference to Question 10, the efficiency, in percent, of the battery under this condition is most nearly
    (A) 70   (B) 80
    (C) 90   (D) 100.

12. The group of 1½-volt dry cells which is properly connected to deliver 6 volts is number
    (A) 1   (B) 2
    (C) 3   (D) 4.

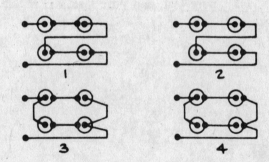

Answer Key

(You'll learn more by writing your own answers before comparing them with these.)

Problems

1. D	3. C	5. A	7. D	9. C
2. C	4. B	6. E	8. C	10. B
	11. C	12. B		

ELECTRICIAN

PART THREE

Previous Examination for Practice

3

ELECTRICIAN'S HELPER

I. PREVIOUS EXAM

DIRECTIONS FOR ANSWERING QUESTIONS

Each question has four suggested answers, lettered
A, B, C, and D. Decide which is the best answer
and underline it. You may check your answers with
the answer key which appears at the end of the test.
Do not do so until you have completed the entire test.

Time allowed 3½ hours.

1. The one of the following which is a unit of inductance is the

   (A) millihenry   (B) microfarad   (C) kilohm   (D) weber.

2. Of the following, the best conductor of electricity is

   (A) aluminum   (B) copper   (C) silver   (D) iron.

3. A voltage of 1000 microvolts is the same as

   (A) 1,000 volts   (B) 0.100 volts   (C) 0.010 volts   (D) 0.001 volts.

4. The function of a rectifier is similar to that of

   (A) an inverter   (C) a commutator
   (B) a relay   (D) a transformer.

5. A 9-ohm resistor rated at 225 watts is used in a 120-volt circuit. In order
   not to exceed the rating of the resistor, the maximum current, in amperes, which
   can flow through the circuit is

   (A) 2   (B) 3   (C) 4   (D) 5.

6. The number of circular mils in a conductor 0.036 inch in diameter is

   (A) 6   (B) 36   (C) 72   (D) 1296.

7. The color of the label on most commerically available 250-volt cartridge fuses
   of 15-amperes or less capacity is

   (A) green   (B) blue   (C) red   (D) yellow.

8. Assume that a two-microfarad capacitor is connected in parallel with a three-microfarad capacitor. The resulting capacity, in microfarads, is

(A) 2/3   (B) 6/5   (C) 3/2   (D) 5.

9. The speed of the rotating magnetic field in a 12-pole 60-cycle stator is

(A) 1800 rpm   (B) 1200 rpm   (C) 720 rpm   (D) 600 rpm.

10. The transformer connection generally used to convert from three-phase to two-phase by means of two transformers is the

(A) Scott or T   (C) Wye- Delta
(B) V or Open delta   (D) Delta-Wye

11. The conductance, in mhos, of a circuit whose resistance is one ohm is

(A) 1/10   (B) 1   (C) 10   (D) 100.

12. Assume that a 220-volt, 25 cycle, A.C., e.m.f. is impressed across a circuit consisting of a 25-ohm resistor in series with a 30-microfarad capacitor. The current in this circuit, in amperes, is most nearly

(A) 0.5   (B) 0.8   (C) 1.0   (D) 1.5.

13. An ammeter has a full scale deflection with a current of 0.010 amperes and an internal resistance of 20 ohms. In order for the ammeter to have a full scale deflection with a current of 10 amperes and not damage its movement, a shunt should be used having a value of

(A) 10 ohms   (B) 0.2 ohms   (C) 0.02 ohms   (D) 0.01 ohms.

14. American Wire Gage (A.W.G.) wire size numbers are set so that the resistance of wire per 1,000 ft. doubles with every increase of

(A) one gage number   (C) three gage numbers
(B) two gage numbers   (D) four gage numbers.

15. In an ideal transformer for transforming or "stepping down" the voltage from 1200 volts to 120 volts, the turns ratio is

(A) 10:1   (B) 12:1   (C) 1:12   (D) 1:10.

16. When a lead-acid battery is fully charged, the negative plate consists of

(A) lead peroxide   (C) lead sulfate
(B) lead sponge   (D) lead dioxide.

17. Improving the commutation of a D.C. generator is most often done by using

(A) a rheostat in series with the equalizer
(B) an equalizer alone
(C) a compensator
(D) interpoles.

18. In a wave-wound armature, the minimum number of commutator brushes necessary is

(A) two times the number of poles
(B) two, regardless of the number of poles
(C) one-half times the number of poles
(D) four, regardless of the number of poles.

19. A three-phase induction motor runs hot with all stator coils at the same temperature. The trouble which would cause this condition is that
    (A) the motor is running single phase
    (B) the motor is overloaded
    (C) a part of the motor windings is inoperative
    (D) the rotor bars are loose.

20. Where constant speed is required, the one of the following motors that should be used is a
    (A) wound-rotor motor
    (B) series motor
    (C) compound motor
    (D) shunt motor.

21. To reverse the direction of rotation of a 3-phase induction motor
    (A) the field connections should be reversed
    (B) the armature connections should be reversed
    (C) any two line leads should be interchanged
    (D) the brushes should be shifted in the direction opposite to that of the armature rotation.

22. The speed of a wound-rotor motor may be increased by
    (A) decreasing the resistance in the secondary circuit
    (B) increasing the resistance in the secondary circuit
    (C) decreasing the shunt field current
    (D) increasing the series field resistance.

23. The one of the following methods which can be used to increase the slip of the rotor in a single-phase shaded-pole motor is the
    (A) reversal of the leads of the field winding
    (B) addition of capacitors in series with the starting winding
    (C) reduction of the impressed voltage
    (D) addition of more capacitors in parallel with the starting winding.

24. The direction of rotation of a single-phase A.C. repulsion motor may be reversed by
    (A) interchanging the two line leads to the motor
    (B) interchanging the leads to the main winding
    (C) interchanging the leads to the starting winding
    (D) moving the brushes to the other side of the neutral position.

25. The torque developed by a D.C. series motor is
    (A) inversely proportional to the square of the armature current
    (B) proportional to the square of the armature current
    (C) proportional to the armature current
    (D) inversely proportional to the armature current.

26. The one of the following which is most commonly used to clean a commutator is
    (A) emery cloth
    (B) graphite
    (C) a smooth file
    (D) fine-grit sandpaper.

27. The type of motor which requires both A.C. and D.C. for operation is the
    (A) compound motor
    (B) universal motor
    (C) synchronous motor
    (D) squirrel-cage motor.

28. Compensators are used for starting large
    (A) shunt motors
    (B) series motors
    (C) induction motors
    (D) compound motors.

29. The device most frequently used to correct low lagging power factor is
    (A) a solenoid
    (B) an induction regulator
    (C) an induction motor
    (D) a synchronous motor.

30. Of the following motors, the one with the highest starting torgue is the
    (A) compound motor   (C) shunt motor
    (B) series motor   (D) split phase motor.

31. The approximate efficiency of a 60-cycle, 6-pole induction motor running at 1050 rpm and having a synchronous speed of 1200 rpm is
    (A) 67.0 per cent   (C) 87.5 per cent
    (B) 78.5 per cent   (D) 90.0 per cent.

32. The main contributing factor to motor starter failures usually is
    (A) overloading (B) dirt   (C) bearing trouble   (D) moisture.

33. The neutral or grounded conductors in branch circuit wiring must be identified by being colored
    (A) black or brown   (C) white with black traces
    (B) black with white traces   (D) white or natural gray.

34. The smallest radius for the inner edge of any field bend in a 1-inch rigid or flexible conduit when type R wire is being used is
    (A) 3 inches   (B) 5 inches   (C) 6 inches   (D) 10 inches.

35. Thermal cutouts used to protect a motor against overloads may have a current rating of not more than
    (A) the starting current of the motor
    (B) 125% of the full-load current rating of the motor
    (C) the full-load current of the motor
    (D) the current-carrying capacity of the branch circuit conductors.

36. The maximum size of EMT permitted is
    (A) 4 inches   (B) 3 1/2 inches   (C) 3 inches   (D) 2 inches.

37. The type of equipment which is defined in the Code as a set of conductors originating at the load side of the service equipment and supplying the main and/or one or more secondary distribution centers is a
    (A) sub-feeder   (B) feeder   (C) main   (D) service cable.

38. The smallest size rigid conduit that may be used in wiring is
    (A) 3/8 inches   (B) 1/2 inches   (C) 3/4 inches   (D) 1 inch.

39. An enclosed 600-volt cartridge fuse must be of the knife-blade contact type if its ampere rating is
    (A) 20   (B) 40   (C) 60   (D) 80.

40. An insulated ground for fixed equipment should be color coded
    (A) yellow   (C) blue or blue with a yellow stripe
    (B) green or green with a yellow stripe   (D) black.

41. Of the following, the meter that <u>cannot</u> be used to measure A.C. voltage is the
    (A) electrodynamic voltmeter   (C) D'Arsonval voltmeter
    (B) electrostatic voltmeter   (D) thermocouple voltmeter.

42. Of the following, an instrument frequently used to measure high insulation resistance is
    (A) a tong-test ammeter   (C) an ohmmeter
    (B) a megger   (D) an electrostatic voltmeter.

43. When using a voltmeter in testing an electric circuit, the voltmeter should be placed in
    (A) series with the circuit
    (B) parallel with the circuit
    (C) parallel or in series with a current transformer, depending on the current
    (D) series with the active element.

44. The minimum number of wattmeters necessary to measure the power in the load of a balanced 3-phase, 4-wire system is
    (A) 1   (B) 2   (C) 3   (D) 4.

45. An instrument that measures electrical energy is the
    (A) current transformer   (C) dynamometer
    (B) watthour meter   (D) wattmeter.

46. The one of the following items which can be used to properly test an armature for a shorted coil is a
    (A) neon light   (C) growler
    (B) megger   (D) pair of series test lamps

47. The instrument that measures loads at the load terminals, averaged over specified time periods, is the
    (A) coulomb meter   (C) demand meter
    (B) wattmeter   (D) var-hour meter.

48. A multiplier is usually used to increase the range of a
    (A) voltmeter   (B) watthour meter   (C) wheatstone bridge   (D) Nernst bridge.

49. The instrument used to indicate the phase relation between the voltage and the current of an A.C. circuit is called a
    (A) power factor meter   (C) phase indicator
    (B) synchroscope   (D) var-hour meter.

50. Except where busways are entering or leaving service or distribution equipment, the bottom of the busway enclosure for all horizontal busway runs should be kept at a minimum height above the floor of
    (A) 4 feet   (B) 6 feet   (C) 8 feet   (D) 10 feet.

51. The lubricant commonly used to make it easier to pull braid-covered cable into a duct is
    (A) soapstone   (B) soft soap   (C) heavy grease   (D) light oil.

52. Of the following, the conductor insulation which may be used in wet locations is type
    (A) RH   (B) RHH   (C) RHW   (D) RUH.

53. Assume that at a certain distribution point you, an electrician's helper, notice that among several of the conductors entering the same raceway, some have a half-inch band of yellow tape, while the others do not. The conductors with the yellow tape are all
    (A) grounded   (B) ungrounded   (C) A.C.   (D) D.C.

54. Conductors of the same length, same circular mil area and type of insulation may be run in multiple
    (A) under no circumstances
    (B) if each conductor is #4 or larger
    (C) if each conductor is #2 or larger
    (D) if each conductor is #1/0 or larger.

55. In order to keep conduits parallel where several parallel runs of conduit of varying size are installed through 45 or 90 degree bends, it is best to
    (A) bend conduit on the job
    (B) use standard factory-made elbows
    (C) use flexible connectors to adjust runs
    (D) bend conduit at the factory.

56. The best way to join two lengths of conduit which cannot be turned is to
    (A) use a split adapter
    (B) use a conduit union ("Erickson")
    (C) cut running threads on one end of one length of the conduit
    (D) cut running threads on the ends of both lengths of conduit.

57. When an electrical splice is wrapped with both rubber tape and friction tape, the main purpose of the friction tape is to
    (A) protect the rubber tape
    (B) provide additional insulation
    (C) build up the insulation to the required thickness
    (D) increase the strength of the splice.

58. Assume that explosion-proof wiring is required in a certain area. Conduits entering an enclosure in this area which contains apparatus that may produce arcs, sparks or high temperature, shall be provided with
    (A) a cable terminator
    (B) an approved sealing compound
    (C) couplings with three full threads engaged.
    (D) insulated bushings.

59. If installed in dry locations, wireways may be used, for circuits of not more than
    (A) 208 volts   (B) 440 volts   (C) 600 volts   (D) 1100 volts.

60. An interior wiring circuit has two conductors, one white and one black. Assume that it becomes necessary to add a third conductor as a switch leg. The color of the third conductor should be
    (A) blue   (B) red   (C) green   (D) natural gray.

61. Keyless lampholders rated at 1500 watts have bases which are classed as
    (A) Intermediate   (B) Medium   (C) Mogul   (D) Admedium.

62. In precast cellular concrete floor raceways, the largest conductor which may be installed, except by special permission, is
    (A) No. 2   (B) No. 0   (C) No. 00   (D) No. 000.

63. The conductor insulation which may be used for fixture wire is type
    (A) TF   (B) TW   (C) TA   (D) RW.

64. Multiple fuses are permissible
    (A) under no circumstances   (C) for conductors larger than 2/0
    (B) for conductors longer than 1/0 (D) for conductors larger than 4/0.

65. In loosening a nut, a socket wrench with a ratchet handle should be used in preference to other types of wrenches if
    (A) the nut is out of reach
    (B) the turning space for the handle is limited
    (C) the nut is worn
    (D) greater leverage is required.

66. Solders used for **electrical** connections are **alloys** of

    (A) tin and lead   (C) lead and zinc
    (B) tin and zinc   (D) tin and copper.

67. Another name for a pipe wrench is a

    (A) crescent wrench   (B) torque wrench (C) Stillson wrench (D) monkey wrench.

68. The tool used to cut raceways is a hacksaw with fine teeth, commonly called a

    (A) crosscut saw   (B) keyhole saw   (C) rip saw   (D) tube saw.

69. Lead expansion anchors are most commonly used to fasten conduit to a

    (A) wooden partition wall   (C) solid concrete wall
    (B) plaster wall   (D) gypsum wall.

70. The use of "running" threads when coupling two sections of conduit is

    (A) always good pratice
    (B) good practice only when installing enameled conduit
    (C) good practice only if it is impossible to turn one of the conduits
    (D) always poor practice.

71. A quick-break knifeswitch is often used rather than a standard knifeswitch
    of the same rating because the quick-break knife switch

    (A) resists burning due to arcing at the contact points
    (B) is easier to install and align
    (C) is simpler in construction
    (D) can carry a higher current without over heating.

72. The tip of a soldering iron is made of copper **because**

    (A) copper is a very good conductor of heat
    (B) solder will not stick to other metals
    (C) it is the cheapest metal available
    (D) the melting point of copper is very high.

73. Good practice requires that cartridge fuses be removed from their clips by using
    a fuse puller rather than the bare hand. The reason for using the fuse puller
    is that the

    (A) bare hand may be burned or otherwise injured
    (B) fuse is less likely to break
    (C) fuse clips may be damaged when pulled
    (D) use of the bare hands slows down removal of fuse and causes arcing.

74. The frame of a portable electric tool should be grounded in order to
    (A) reduce leakage from the winding
    (B) prevent short circuits
    (C) reduce the danger of overheating
    (D) prevent the frame from becoming alive to ground.

75. Small cuts or injuries should be

    (A) cared for immediately because infection may result
    (B) ignored because they are seldom important
    (C) cared for at the end of the day
    (D) ignored unless they are painful.

76. The least desirable device for measuring the dimensions of an electrical equipment cabinet containing live equipment is a

    (A) wooden yardstick
    (B) six-foot folding wooden ruler
    (C) twelve inch plastic ruler
    (D) six-foot steel tape.

77. A commonly recommended safe distance between the foot of an extension ladder and the wall against which it is placed is

    (A) 3 feet for ladders less than 18 feet in height
    (B) between 3 feet and 6 feet for ladders less than 18 feet in length
    (C) 1/8 the length of the extended ladder
    (D) 1/4 the length of the extended ladder.

78. The first thing to do when a person gets an electric shock and is still in contact with the supply is to

    (A) treat the person for burns
    (B) start artificial respiration
    (C) remove the victim from the contact by using a dry stick or dry rope
    (D) cut the power if it can be done in 5 or 6 minutes.

79. When applying the back pressure-arm lift (Holger-Nielsen) method of artificial respiration the victim should first be placed

    (A) in a face down position
    (B) on his back
    (C) in a sitting position
    (D) on his left side.

80. The best type of fire extinguisher for electrical fires is the

    (A) dry chemical extinguisher
    (B) foam extinguisher
    (C) carbon monoxide extinguisher
    (D) baking soda-acid extinguisher.

Answer Key

(Please try to answer the questions on your own before looking at our answers. You'll do much better on your test if you follow this rule.)

1.A	11.B	21.C	31.C	41.C	51.A	61.C	71.A
2.C	12.C	22.A	32.B,D	42.B	52.C	62.B	72.A
3.D	13.C	23.C	33.D	43.B	53.D	63.A	73.A
4.C	14.C	24.D	34.C	44.A	54.D	64.A	74.D
5.D	15.A	25.B	35.B	45.B	55.A	65.B	75.A
6.D	16.B	26.D	36.D	46.C	56.B	66.A	76.D
7.B	17.D	27.C	37.B	47.C	57.A	67.C	77.D
8.D	18.B	28.C	38.B	48.A	58.B	68.D	78.C
9.D	19.B	29.D	39.D	49.A	59.C	69.C	79.A
10.A	20.D	30.B	40.B	50.C	60.B	70.D	80.A

ELECTRICIAN

II. PREVIOUS EXAM

DIRECTIONS FOR ANSWERING QUESTIONS

Each question has four suggested answers, lettered
A, B, C, and D. Decide which is the best answer
and underline it. You may check your answers with
the answer key which appears at the end of the test.
Do not do so until you have completed the entire test.

Time allowed 3½ hours.

1. Five 100-watt, 120-volt lamps connected in series across a 600-volt circuit, will draw
   a current, in amperes of most nearly

   (A) 4.2   (B) .8   (C) .6   (D) .4.

2. For a given level of illumination in a certain lighting installation the cost of
   electrical energy using fluorescent lighting fixtures as compared with incandescent
   lighting fixtures is

   (A) more   (B) less   (C) the same   (D) dependent on the load.

3. Assume that three 20.8 ohm resistances are connected in delta across a 208-volt,
   3-phase circuit. The line current in amperes will be most nearly

   (A) 20.8   (B) 17.3   (C) 10.4   (D) 8.6.

4. Assume that three 10-ohm resistances are connected in wye across a 208-volt, 3-phase
   circuit. The power in watts dissipated in this resistance load will be most nearly

   (A) 4320   (B) 1440   (C) 2160   (D) 720.

5. A tungsten incandescent lamp has its greatest resistance when the lamp is

   (A) cold   (B) burning at full brilliance   (C) burning at half brilliance
   (D) burning at one quarter brilliance.

6. Direct current can be converted to alternating current by means of a/an

    (A) inverter   (B) rectifier   (C) filter   (D) selsyn.

7. The direction of rotation of a D.C. shunt motor can be reversed by

    (A) interchaning the line terminals   (B) reversing the field and armature current
    (C) reversing the field or armature current   (D) reversing the current in any one
    of the commutating pole windings.

8. The insulation resistance of the conductors of an electrical installation is measured
   or tested with a/an

    (A) strobe   (B) ammeter   (C) Q-meter   (D) megger.

9. In dealing with Electrician's Helpers, it is most important that the Electrician be

    (A) stern   (B) fair   (C) blunt   (D) chummy.

10. If an electrician does not understand the instructions that are given to him by his
    foreman, the best thing to do is to

    (A) work out the solution to the problem himself   (B) do the job the way he thinks
    is best   (C) get one of the other electricians to do the job   (D) ask that the
    instructions be repeated and clarified.

11. Assume that a group of D.C. shunt motors is 500 ft. from a power panel and is supplied
    by two 350,000 c.m. conductors with a maximum load for this circuit of 190 amps. If
    the resistance of 1000 feet of 350,000 c.m. conductor is 0.036 ohm, and the voltage at
    the power panel is 230 volts, the voltage at the load will be most nearly

    (A) 217   (B) 220   (C) 223   (D) 229.

12. The power in a three-phase, three wire circuit is measured by means of the two-watt
    meter method. When the reading of one watt meter is exactly the same as the reading
    of the other watt meter, the power factor will be

    (A) 1   (B) .866   (C) .5   (D) 0.

13. Assume that a fluorescent lamp blinks "on" and "off". This may

    (A) in time result in injury to the ballast   (B) cause a fuse to blow   (C) be
    due to a shorted switch   (D) be caused by an abnormally high voltage.

14. The one of the following troubles which is not a cause of sparking at the commutator
    of a D.C. motor is

    (A) a short circuited armature coil   (B) an open circuited armature coil
    (C) vibration of the machine   (D) running below rated speed.

15. The current in amperes of a 220-volt, 10-H.P., D.C. motor having an efficiency of 90%
    is approximately

    (A) 37.6   (B) 34   (C) 28.6   (D) 40.5.

16. The grid controlled gas-type electronic tube most often used in motor control
    circuits is the

    (A) ignitron   (B) thyratron   (C) strobostron   (D) magnetron.

17. With reference to electronic control work, the vacuum tube element or electrode which is placed in the electron stream and to which a control voltage may be applied is the

   (A) plate   (B) grid   (C) filament   (D) cathode.

18. Full wave rectifiers

   (A) may be built with one tungar bulb   (B) produce A.C. current which contains some D.C.   (C) are used to change D.C. current to A.C.   (D) must have at least two tungar bulbs.

19. Assume that two batteries are connected in multiple. If the voltage and internal resistance of one battery are 6 volts and 0.2 ohms respectively and the voltage and internal resistance of the other battery are 3 volts and 0.1 ohm respectively, the circulating current, in amperes, will be approximately

   (A) 2   (B) 5   (C) 10   (D) 30.

20. In a single phase motor the temporary production of a substitute for a two phase current so as to obtain a makeshift rotating field in starting is commonly called

   (A) phase splitting   (B) phase spread   (C) phase transformation   (D) phantom circuit.

21. If a solenoid is grasped in the right hand so that the fingers point in the direction in which the current is flowing in the wires, the thumb, extended, will point in the direction of the

   (A) negative pole   (B) positive pole   (C) south pole   (D) north pole.

22. The junction of two dissimilar metals produces a flow of current when the junction is

   (A) wet   (B) heated   (C) highly polished   (D) placed in a D.C. magnetic field.

23. The active material in the positive plates of a charged lead acid storage battery is

   (A) lead carbonate   (B) lead acetate   (C) lead peroxide   (D) sponge lead.

24. The negative plates of a charged lead acid storage battery are composed of

   (A) lead carbonate   (B) lead acetate   (C) lead peroxide   (D) sponge lead.

25. A constant horse power, two speed squirrel cage induction motor may be made to run at the higher speed by

   (A) changing the connections to make it an eight pole motor   (B) decreasing the rotor resistance   (C) changing the connections so that the motor has the lesser number of poles   (D) changing the connections so that the motor has the greater number of poles.

26. A constant horsepower two speed squirrel cage induction motor has its stator coils and the line wires connected so as to form a series delta connection. Assume that the connections of the stator coils and the lines are now changed so as to form a parallel-wye connection. Under these conditions the motor will now have

   (A) fewer poles and higher speed   (B) fewer poles and lower speed   (C) more poles and higher speed   (D) more poles and lower speed.

27. Assume that a circuit carrying 8 amperes of D.C. current and 6 amperes of A.C. current is connected to a hot wire ammeter. The reading, in amperes, of this meter will be most nearly

   (A) 16   (B) 14   (C) 12   (D) 10.

28. To start a 20 H.P., 3 phase, 208 volt plain induction motor it is good practice to use a

    (A) compensator   (B) 3-point box   (C) rotor box   (D) 4-point box.

29. A 25 ampere, 50 millivolt D.C. shunt has a resistance, in ohms, of approximately

    (A) 0.002   (B) 0.02   (C) 0.5   (D) 5.

30. When a relay coil is energized by applying the rated voltage across its terminals, a certain time, in seconds, must elapse from the moment the circuit is completed before the current attains approximately 2/3 of its full strength. This elapsed time is

    (A) entirely dependent on the coil resistance   (B) entirely dependent on the coil inductance   (C) proportional to the coil resistance divided by the coil inductance   (D) proportional to the coil inductance divided by the coil resistance.

31. For proper operation, all gas discharge lamps require

    (A) a series resistor   (B) a parallel resistor   (C) some sort of ballast
    (D) a starter.

32. To obtain proper short circuit protection for a service, one should use a

    (A) limiting resistor   (B) time delay breaker   (C) time delay relay
    (D) current limiting fuse.

33. A neon test lamp can be used by an electrician to test

    (A) the phase rotation of a source of supply   (B) the power factor of a source of supply   (C) a source of supply to see if it is A.C. or D.C.   (D) the field intensity of a relay magnet.

34. A D.C. milliammeter may be adapted for A.C. measurements by using with it a/an

    (A) paper condenser   (B) instrument shunt   (C) instrument transformer
    (D) selenium rectifier.

35. A static capacitor used for power factor correction, is connected to the line in

    (A) parallel with a machine drawing lagging current   (B) series with a machine drawing lagging current   (C) parallel with a machine drawing leading current
    (D) series with a machine drawing leading current.

36. To start a squirrel cage induction motor with an across-the-line starter, without undue disturbance to the line voltage, the capacity of the motor in H.P. should not exceed

    (A) 100   (B) 75   (C) 50   (D) 5.

37. The type of A.C. motor most commonly used where considerable starting torque is required, is the

    (A) squirrel cage induction motor   (B) wound rotor induction motor   (C) shunt motor   (D) synchronous motor.

38. On direct current controllers where it is necessary to remove or replace blow-out coils it is important to

    (A) see that the positive pole is facing down   (B) see that the negative pole is facing up   (C) insert the blow-out coils to give the proper polarity   (D) cross the coil leads before connecting them.

39. The size of the fuse to be used in a circuit depends upon the

    (A) connected load   (B) size of wire   (C) voltage of the line   (D) size and rating of the switch.

40. Assume that a D.C. contactor coil has two turns short circuited. In operation, it will

   (A) burn out   (B) hum excessively   (C) continue to operate at reduced efficiency   (D) vibrate due to the high induced current.

41. The primary purpose of oil in an oil circuit breaker is to

   (A) quench the arc   (B) lubricate the contacts   (C) reduce the reluctance of the core   (D) lubricate between the windings and the case.

42. Assume that an auto transformer has a ratio of 2 to 1. With a primary voltage of 100 volts, 60 cycles, A.C. and a secondary load of 5 ohms, the current in the load is most nearly

   (A) 20   (B) 15   (C) 10   (D) 5.

43. Assume that an auto transformer has a ratio of 2 to 1, with a primary voltage of 100 volts, 60 cycles A.C. and a load of 5 ohms placed across the secondary. Under the above conditions, the current in the secondary coil, of the auto transformer, is most nearly

   (A) 20   (B) 15   (C) 10   (D) 5.

44. In fire extinguishers used to fight electrical fires, the chemical used as the fire extinguishing agent is

   (A) H_2O (B) K_OH (C) CO_2 (D) $C C_14$.

45. At a frequency of 60 cycles the reactance in ohms of a condenser having a capacitance of 10 microfarads is most nearly

   (A) 26.6   (B) 37.7   (C) 266   (D) 377.

46. Transformation of 3 phase to 2 phase systems can be obtained by using two special transformers. The common method used for connecting these transformers is called a/an

   (A) open delta   (B) zig-zag   (C) differential y on z   (D) Scott or T.

47. The electrolyte for a lead acid storage battery is properly prepared by pouring the

   (A) sulphuric acid into the water   (B) water into the sulphuric acid
   (C) potassium hydroxide into the water   (D) water into the potassium hydroxide.

48. The full-wave rectifier has a ripple frequency that is

   (A) one-half that of the half-wave rectifier   (B) double that of the half-wave rectifier   (C) four times that of the half-wave rectifier   (D) equal to that of the half-wave rectifier.

49. Of the following, the one type of resistance wire which has an extremely low temperature co-efficient of resistance is known as

   (A) Replevin   (B) Ribbon   (C) Maganin   (D) Bifilar.

50. In an A.C. dynamometer-type voltmeter, the deflections depend upon the square of the voltage. It can correctly be said that this instrument reads

   (A) average values   (B) peak values   (C) effective values   (D) maximum values.

51. The Dobrowolsky method used for three-wire generator systems is a very efficient means of obtaining a/an

(A) neutral   (B) V or open delta   (C) two-phase system   (D) three-phase system.

52. Direct current armatures, wound with coils having fractional-pitch windings, have

(A) a coil span which is less than the pole pitch   (B) a coil span which is greater than the pole pitch   (C) more than 4 poles   (D) less than 4 poles.

53. To measure the current in a conductor without breaking into the conductor you would use a/an

(A) ampback   (B) amprobe   (C) ampule   (D) ampclip.

54. If two identical coils each having an inductance of one henry are connected in series aiding, the combined inductance, in henries is

(A) exactly two   (B) greater than two   (C) exactly one   (D) less than one.

55. In a simplex lap winding there are as many paths through the armature as there are

(A) armature slots   (B) poles   (C) commutator segments   (D) armature coils.

56. In a wave winding the minimum number of commutator brushes required is

(A) four   (B) two   (C) dependent on the number of commutator segments
(D) dependent on the armature coils.

57. Some electricians have the faculty of knowing when there is work to be done and do not have to be prompted to do it. These electricians may be said to have

(A) initiative   (B) individuality   (C) virtue   (D) discrimination.

58. The number of threads per inch on a 1/4" diameter screw, having American Standard coarse threads, is most nearly

(A) 20   (B) 18   (C) 14   (D) 13.

59. For general field or shop work, the proper tap drill size to use for a 6/32 machine screw is most nearly number

(A) 50   (B) 40   (C) 36   (D) 21.

60. Graphical electrical symbols used on architectural plans are those recommended by the A. S. A. The abbreviation A.S. A. refers to the

(A) American Society of Architects   (B) American Standards Association.
(C) Architectural Standards Association   (D) Architectural Standards of America.

61. Of the following, the best course of action to take if a motor bearing runs dangerously hot is to

(A) cool it quickly with cold water then rapidly decrease motor speed and oil the bearing freely   (B) oil the bearing freely and increase speed of motor
(C) decrease speed of motor until bearing cools sufficiently then stop the motor and check for oil level and any damage to bearing   (D) add #40 SAE oil before increasing the load.

62. Ten graduations on the barrel of a micrometer indicates an opening, in inches, of most nearly

(A) 0.010   (B) 0.050   (C) 0.250   (D) 0.270.

63. The type of motor that may be designed to run on both A.C. or D.C. is the

(A) shunt motor   (B) repulsion motor   (C) compound motor   (D) series motor.

64. Assume that the cost of a certain wiring installation is broken down as follows: Materials $1,200, Labor $800 and Rental of equipment $400. The percentage of the total cost of the job that can be charged to Labor is most nearly

    (A) 12.3   (B) 33.3   (C) 40.0   (D) 66.6.

65. Assume that it takes 4 electrician's helpers 6 days to do a certain job. Working at the same rate of speed, the number of days it will take 3 electrician's helpers to do the same job is

    (A) 6   (B) 7   (C) 8   (D) 9.

66. Assume that a 120-volt, 25-cycle magnetic coil is to be rewound to operate properly on 60-cycles at the same voltage. If the coil at 25-cycles has 1,000 turns, at 60-cycles the number of turns should be most nearly

    (A) 2,400   (B) 1,200   (C) 416   (D) 208.

67. A coil having 50 turns of #14 wire as compared with a coil of the same diameter but having only 25 turns of #14 wire has

    (A) a smaller inductance   (B) a larger inductance   (C) the same inductance
    (D) the same impedance.

The following 13 questions numbered 68 to 80 inclusive are to be answered in accordance with the requirements of the N.Y.C. Electrical Code.

NOTES:
    1. Unless otherwise stated, the word "Code" refers to the Electrical Code of the City of New York (Title B of Chapter 30 of the Administrative code).

    2. Questions are to be answered assuming normal procedures, as given in the Code. Do not use exceptions which are granted by special permission.

68. For elevator control wiring, conductors of 1/64 insulation may be used. The number of such conductors that may be installed in a conduit should be such that the sum of the cross-sectional area of all the conductors expressed as a percentage of the interior cross-sectional area of the conduit, should not exceed

    (A) 20%   (B) 30%   (C) 40%   (D) 60%.

69. Assume that the internal diameter of a two-inch conduit is 2.067 inches. The interior cross-sectional area, in square inches, of this conduit is most nearly

    (A) 3.36   (B) 4.79   (C) 7.38   (D) 9.90.

70. No. 2 type R conductors in vertical raceways must be supported at intervals not greater than

    (A) 50 feet   (B) 60 feet   (C) 80 feet   (D) 100 feet.

71. A unit of an electrical system, other than a conductor, which is intended to carry but not consume electrical energy is called a/an

    (A) device   (B) circuit   (C) appliance   (D) equipment.

72. Three #4 A.W.G. Rubber covered, type R, conductors require a conduit having a diameter, in inches, of not less than

    (A) 1/2   (B) 3/4   (C) 1   (D) 1¼.

73. For control conductors between motors and controllers, the maximum number of #10 type R conductors that may be put into a 1¼" conduit or tubing is

(A) 10   (B) 13   (C) 15   (D) 17.

74. The type of wire commonly used for switchboard wiring is classified by type letter or letters

(A) TF   (B) CF   (C) TA   (D) R.

75. Wires in conduit (approved as to insulation and location) are required to have stranded conductors if they are

(A) No. 8 or larger   (B) No. 6 or larger   (C) No. 6 or smaller
(D) No. 8 or smaller.

76. Bends of rigid conduit should be so made that the conduit will not be injured. Where rubber conductors are used, the radius of the curve of the inner edge of any field bend should be not less than

(A) 15 times the internal diameter of the conduit   (B) 10 times the internal diameter of the conduit   (C) 6 times the internal diameter of the conduit
(D) 4 times the internal diameter of the conduit.

77. In Class I hazardous locations, when a conduit leads from a hazardous location to a non-hazardous location, the conduit should be sealed off with a sealing compound which is not affected by the surrounding atmosphere and has a melting point of not less than

(A) 200°F   (B) 150°F   (C) 100°F   (D) 75°F.

78. Feeders should be of such size that the voltage drop up to the final distribution point should not exceed

(A) 6%   (B) 4½%   (C) 3%   (D) 2½%.

79. For not more than three conductors in raceway (based on room temperature of 30°C or 86°F) the current carrying capacity in amperes of #10 type R insulated aluminum conductor is

(A) 10   (B) 15   (C) 25   (D) 35.

80. The maximum number of No. 12 wires terminating in a 1½" x 3¼" octagonal junction box should be

(A) 20   (B) 15   (C) 10   (D) 5.

Answer Key

(Please make every effort to answer the questions on your own before look-ing at these answers. You'll make faster progress by following this rule.)

1. B	11. C	21. D	31. C	41. A	51. A	61. C	71. A
2. B	12. A	22. B	32. D	42. C	52. A	62. C	72. D
3. B	13. A	23. C	33. C	43. D	53. B	63. D	73. B
4. A	14. D	24. D	34. D	44. C	54. B	64. B	74. C
5. B	15. A	25. C	35. A	45. C	55. B	65. C	75. B
6. A	16. B	26. D	36. D	46. D	56. B	66. C	76. C
7. C	17. B	27. D	37. B	47. A	57. A	67. B	77. A
8. D	18. D	28. A	38. C	48. B	58. A	68. C	78. D
9. B	19. C	29. A	39. B	49. C	59. C	69. A	79. C
10. D	20. A	30. D	40. C	50. C	60. B	70. D	80. D

ELECTRICIAN'S HELPER

III. PREVIOUS EXAM

DIRECTIONS FOR ANSWERING QUESTIONS

Each question has four suggested answers, lettered
A, B, C, and D. Decide which is the best answer
and underline it. You may check your answers with
the answer key which appears at the end of the test.
Do not do so until you have completed the entire test.

Time allowed 3½ hours.

1. If three equal resistance coils are connected in parallel, the resistance of this combination is equal to

   (A) 1/3 the resistance of one coil   (B) the resistance of one coil
   (C) three times the resistance of one coil   (D) nine times the resistance of one coil.

2. The voltage to neutral of a 3-phase 4-wire system is 120 volts. The line-to-line voltage is

   (A) 208 volts   (B) 220 volts   (C) 230 volts   (D) 240 volts.

3. Three 6-ohm resistances are connected in Y across a 3-phase circuit. If a current of 10 amperes flows through each resistance, the total power in watts drawn by this load is most nearly

   (A) 600   (B) 1200   (C) 1800   (D) 2400.

4. A conduit in an outlet box should be provided with a

   (A) locknut on the outside and bushing on the inside   (B) locknut and bushing on the inside   (C) locknut on the inside and bushing on the outside   (D) locknut and bushing on the outside.

5. If the current in a single-phase 120-volt circuit is 10 amperes and a wattmeter in this circuit reads 1080 watts, the power factor is most nearly

   (A) 1.11   (B) .9   (C) .8   (D) .7

6. It is poor practice to use a file without a handle because

   (A) the file may be dropped and damaged   (B) the unprotected end may mar the surface being filed   (C) the user may be injured   (D) the file marks will be too deep.

195

7. If a 60-cycle, 4-pole squirrel cage induction motor has a slip of 5%, its speed is most nearly

   (A) 1800 rpm   (B) 1795 rpm   (C) 1750 rpm   (D) 1710 rpm.

8. The proper way to reverse the direction of rotation of a 3-phase wound rotor induction motor is to

   (A) reverse two leads between the rotor and the control resistances
   (B) shift the brushes   (C) reverse two supply leads   (D) open one rotor lead.

9. Sulphuric acid should always be poured into the water when new electrolyte for a lead-acid battery is prepared. The reason for this precaution is to

   (A) avoid splattering of the acid   (B) avoid explosive fumes   (C) prevent corrosion of the mixing vessel   (D) prevent clotting of the acid.

10. The direction of rotation of a D.C. shunt motor can be reversed properly by

    (A) reversing the two supply leads   (B) shifting the position of the brushes
    (C) reversing the connections to both the armature and the field
    (D) reversing the connections to the field.

The following 3 questions numbered 11 to 13 inclusive refer to the excerpt from the N.Y.C. Electrical Code on the subject of grounding electrodes which is quoted below.

   "Each buried plate electrode shall present not less than two square feet of surface to the exterior soil. Electrodes of plate copper shall be at least .06 inch in thickness. Electrodes of iron or steel plate shall be at least one-quarter inch in thickness. Electrodes of iron or steel pipe shall be galvanized and not less than three-quarter inch in internal diameter. Electrodes of rods of steel or iron shall be at least three-quarter inch minimum cross section dimension ..... Driven electrodes of pipes or rods ..... shall be driven to a depth of at least eight feet regardless of the size or number of electrodes used ..... Each electrode used shall be separated at least six feet from any other electrode including those used for signal circuits, radio, lightning rods or any other purpose".

11. According to the above paragraph, all grounding electrodes must

    (A) be of plate copper   (B) be of iron pipe   (C) be at least three-quarter inch minimum cross section dimension   (D) be separated at least six feet from any other electrode.

12. According to the above paragraph, the one of the following electrodes which meets the code requirements is

    (A) a copper plate 12" x 18" x .06"   (B) a steel plate 14" x 24" x .06"
    (C) a copper plate 12" x 24" x .06"   (D) an iron plate 12" x 18" x .25"

13. According to the above paragraph, the one of the following electrodes which meets the code requirements is

    (A) plain iron pipe, 1" in internal diameter, driven to a depth of 10 feet
    (B) galvanized iron pipe, 3/4" in internal diameter, driven to a depth of 6 feet
    (C) plain steel pipe, 1" in internal diameter, driven to a depth of 7 feet
    (D) galvanized steel pipe, 3/4" in internal diameter, driven to a depth of 9 feet.

14. With reference to armature windings, lap windings are often called

    (A) ring windings   (B) multiple windings   (C) series windings
    (D) toroidal windings.

The following question refers to the diagram.

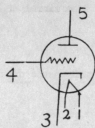

15. The element numbered 4 is usually called the

    (A) plate   (B) grid   (C) filament   (D) cathode.

16. To properly mount an outlet box on a concrete ceiling, it is best to use

    (A) expansion screw anchors   (B) wooden plugs   (C) wood screws   (D) masonry nails.

17. A D.C. motor takes 30 amps. at 110 volts and has an efficiency of 90%. The horsepower available at the pulley is approximately

    (A) 5   (B) 4   (C) 3   (D) 2.

18. If the armature current drawn by a series motor doubles, the torque

    (A) remains the same   (B) doubles   (C) becomes 4 times as great
    (D) becomes 8 times as great.

19. The full load current, in amperes, of a 110-volt, 10 HP, D.C. motor having an efficiency of 80% is approximately

    (A) 62   (B) 85   (C) 99   (D) 133.

20. The heat dissipation, W, in a resistor having a resistance of R ohms connected across a supply of E volts is proportional to $\frac{E^2}{R}$. If R is reduced to one-half of its former value and E is doubled, the heat dissipation in this resistor is now

    (A) 8 W   (B) 2 W   (C) 4 W   (D) 1/2 W.

The following 2 questions numbered 21 and 22 shall be answered in accordance with the diagram below.

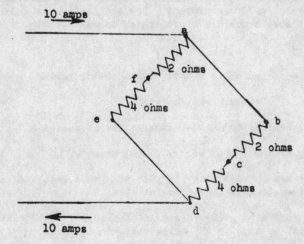

21. With reference to the above diagram, the voltage difference between points c and f is most nearly

    (A) 40 volts   (B) 20 volts   (C) 10 volts   (D) 0 volts.

22. With reference to the above diagram, the current flowing through the resistance c d is most nearly

    (A) 10 amperes   (B) 5 amperes   (C) 4 amperes   (D) 2 amperes.

The following 4 questions numbered 23 to 26 inclusive refer to the diagram below.

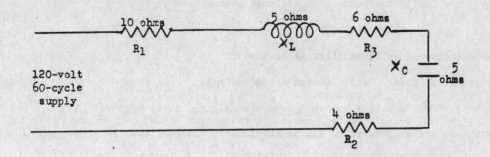

23. The value of the impedance in ohms of the above circuit is most nearly

    (A) 60   (B) 30   (C) 25   (D) 20.

24. The current, in amperes, flowing in the above circuit is most nearly

    (A) 2   (B) 3   (C) 6   (D) 8.

25. The potential drop, in volts, across R_3 is most nearly

    (A) 12   (B) 18   (C) 36   (D) 48.

26. The power, in watts, consumed in the above circuit is most nearly

    (A) 1080   (B) 720   (C) 180   (D) 80.

27. Solder commonly used for electrical work is composed, most likely, of

    (A) lead and tin   (B) antimony and zinc   (C) lead and zinc   (D) silver and antimony.

28. A condenser having a capacitance of 3 microfarads is connected in parallel with a condenser having a capacitance of 2 microfarads. The combination is equal to a single condenser having a capacitance, in microfarads, of most nearly

    (A) 5/6   (B) 6/5   (C) 5   (D) 6.

29. Of the following units, the one which is a unit of inductance is the

    (A) maxwell   (B) henry   (C) weber   (D) oersted.

30. The tool commonly used for bending conduit of small sizes is called a

    (A) mandrel   (B) bending wrench   (C) hickey   (D) kinker.

31. If a cartridge fuse clip makes contact with its fuse with much less than normal spring tension, the result would most likely be that the

    (A) fuse will immediately burn out   (B) voltage at the supply will be high
    (C) voltage at the load will be high   (D) clips will become warm.

32. Of the following units, the one which is a unit of work or energy is the

    (A) Joule   (B) Faraday   (C) Coulomb   (D) Farad.

33. The one of the following substances which is the best conductor of electricity is

    (A) iron   (B) aluminum   (C) tin   (D) copper.

34. The formula for the resistance of one branch of a wye which is equivalent to a given delta is $R_a = \dfrac{A\ B}{A + B + C}$

    If $A = B = C = 3$, the value of R_a is most nearly

    (A) 1   (B) 3   (C) 6   (D) 9.

35. When a splice is soldered, flux is used to

    (A) act as a binder   (B) lubricate the surfaces   (C) keep the surfaces clean
    (D) prevent rapid loss of heat.

36. A 2000 ft. cable which has an insulation resistance of 180 megohms is cut in half. The insulation resistance of one of the 1000-ft. lengths will be most nearly

    (A) 720 megohms   (B) 360 megohms   (C) 90 megohms   (D) 45 megohms.

37. The area in circular mils of a piece of bare copper wire whose diameter is 0.1" is most nearly

    (A) 780   (B) 1,000   (C) 7,800   (D) 10,000.

38. The resistance of a piece of copper wire is

    (A) directly proportional to its diameter   (B) inversely proportional to its length
    (C) directly proportional to the square of its diameter   (D) inversely proportional
    to its cross-sectional area.

39. If an incandescent lamp is operated at a voltage which is higher than its rated voltage, the

    (A) lumens output will be less than rated value   (B) current drawn will be less
    than rated value   (C) power consumed will be less than rated value
    (D) life of the lamp will be less than rated value.

40. The one of the following that is best suited to fight electrical fires is a

    (A) CO_2 fire extinguisher   (B) soda-acid fire extinguisher   (C) foam fire
    extinguisher   (D) very fine spray of water.

41. In order to get maximum power output from a battery, the external resistance should equal

    (A) zero   (B) one-half of the internal resistance of the battery   (C) the internal
    resistance of the battery   (D) twice the internal resistance of the battery.

42. A voltmeter with a scale range of 0-5 has a resistance of 500 ohms. The resistance, in ohms, of a multiplier for this instrument which will give it a range of 0 to 150 volts is most nearly

    (A) 750   (B) 2,500   (C) 14,500   (D) 75,000.

43. The one of the following items which is commonly used to increase the range of a D.C. ammeter is a

    (A) ceramicon   (B) shunt   (C) current transformer   (D) bridging transformer.

44. Continuity of the conductors in an electrical circuit can be determined conveniently in the field by means of

    (A) a bell and battery set   (B) a Maxwell bridge   (C) a Preece test
    (D) an ammeter.

45. The one of the following items which is used to test the electrolyte of a battery is

    (A) a manometer   (B) a hydrometer   (C) an electrometer   (D) a hygrometer.

The following 6 questions numbered 46 to 51 inclusive refer to the symbols of the A.S.A. which are listed below.

1. Ⓓ	6. 𝔽⊸	11 Ⓦ	16. ⑂⑂⑂
2. ⊖	7. ⊡	12. WH	17. Ⓒ
3. Ⓕ	8. S₂	13. Ⓑ	18. ▭⊐
4. ⊙	9. 𝔽	14 ─╫╫─	19. SC
5. ⊖₃	10. ⊠	15 P	20. Sₘc

46. A push button is designated by the symbol numbered

    (A) 4   (B) 7   (C) 13   (D) 15

47. A fire alarm station is designated by the symbol numbered

    (A) 3   (B) 6   (C) 9   (D) 10

48. A duplex convenience outlet is designated by the symbol numbered

    (A) 1   (B) 2   (C) 5   (D) 17

49. A battery is designated by the symbol numbered

    (A) 10   (B) 13   (C) 16   (D) 18

50. A double pole switch is designated by the symbol numbered

    (A) 1   (B) 2   (C) 8   (D) 15.

51. The designation for a 3-wire circuit is numbered

    (A) 3   (B) 5   (C) 11   (D) 14.

52. The one of the following instruments which **cannot** be used to measure the current in both A.C. circuits and D.C circuits without additional equipment is a/an

    (A) D'Arsonval galvanometer   (B) hot wire ammeter   (C) iron vane ammeter
    (D) electro dynamometer type ammeter

53. A growler is commonly used to test

    (A) relays   (B) armatures   (C) cable joints   (D) rectifiers.

54. In cutting a large stranded copper cable with a hacksaw, the primary reason for using a blade with fine teeth rather than one with coarse teeth is

    (A) that using a coarse blade overheats the copper   (B) to avoid making too wide a cut   (C) that the coarse blade bends too easily   (D) to avoid snagging or pulling the strands.

55. Toggle bolts are most commonly used to fasten an outlet box to a

    (A) solid brick wall   (B) solid concrete wall   (C) plaster or tile wall
    (D) wooden partition wall

56. Laminated sheet steel is usually used to make up transformer cores in order to minimize

    (A) copper loss   (B) weight   (C) hysterisis loss   (D) eddy current loss.

The following 3 questions numbered 57 to 59 inclusive refer to the diagram below.

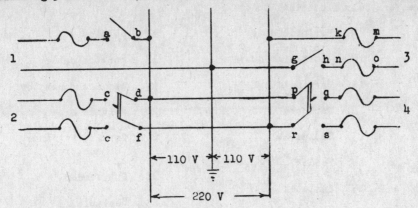

57. Circuit No. 3 in the above diagram

(A) supplies 220 volts to the load   (B) would be correctly wired if there were a direct connection instead of a fuse between points k and m   (C) would be correctly wired if there were a direct connection instead of a fuse between points n and o
(D) would be correctly wired if the switch and fuse were eliminated and replaced by a direct connection between g and o.

58. Circuit No. 4 in the above diagram

(A) is not properly fused as it should have only one fuse in the hot leg
(B) supplies 220 volts to the load   (C) is grounded if, with the switch open, test lamps light when placed between points p and r   (D) is shorted if, with the switch open, test lamps light when placed between points p and r.

59. Circuit No. 1 in the above diagram

(A) supplies 220 volts to the load   (B) is grounded if a pair of test lamps light when placed between point b and ground   (C) is not properly fused as it should have a fuse in each leg   (D) is shorted if, with the switch open, a pair of test lamps light when placed between points a and b.

60. An ideal transformer which has 1 ampere in the primary and 10 amperes in the secondary **must** have

(A) 10 volt amperes in the primary   (B) a ratio of primary turns to secondary turns of 1 to 10   (C) 10 volt amperes in the secondary   (D) a ratio of primary turns to secondary turns of 10 to 1.

61. In soldering electric wires, rosin is used in preference to acid as a flux primarily because rosin is

(A) a dry powder   (B) non-conducting   (C) non-corrosive   (D) a strong electrolyte.

62. The one of the following items which should be used to test whether a circuit is A.C. or D.C. is a

(A) pair of test lamps   (B) hot wire ammeter   (C) psychrometer   (D) neon light.

63. An ideal transformer has 200 volts impressed across its primary. If the primary current is 10 amperes,

(A) the ratio of primary turns to secondary turns is 20 to 1   (B) the ratio of primary turns to secondary turns is 1 to 20   (C) there are approximately 2 KVA in the secondary   (D) the secondary voltage is 20 volts.

64. To control a lamp independently from five locations, the one of the following groups of switches which is required is

(A) four 3-way switches and one 4-way switch   (B) three 3-way and two 4-way switches
(C) two 3-way and three 4-way switches   (D) two single-pole, single throw switches and three 4-way switches

The following 6 questions numbered 65 to 70 inclusive refer to the terms listed below which are defined in the New York City Electrical Code.

1. Appliance	9. Periodic duty	17. Service
2. Branch circuit	10. Short time duty	18. Service cable
3. Connected load	11. Varying duty	19. Service conductor
4. Concealed	12. Enclosed	20. Service drop
5. Computed load	13. Equipment	21. Service Entrance conductors
6. Device	14. Feeder	22. Sub-feeder
7. Demand factor	15. Isolated	23. Sealable
8. Intermittent duty	16. Mains	24. Rating

65. The one term in the above which is defined as "A unit of an electrical system other than a conductor which is intended to carry but not consume electrical energy" is numbered
(A) 1   (B) 6   (C) 13   (D) 19.

66. The one term in the above which is defined as "That portion of the wiring system extending beyond the final overcurrent device protecting the circuit" is numbered
(A) 2   (B) 14   (C) 16   (D) 22.

67. The one term in the above which is defined as "That portion of the overhead service conductors between the last pole and the first point of attachment to the building" is numbered
(A) 17   (B) 18   (C) 20   (D) 21.

68. The one term in the above which is defined as "Rendered inaccessible by the structure or finish of the building" is numbered
(A) 4   (B) 12   (C) 15   (D) 23.

69. The one term in the above which is defined as "A requirement of service that demands operation at loads, and for intervals of time, both of which may be subject to wide variation" is numbered
(A) 8   (B) 9   (C) 10   (D) 11.

70. The one term in the above which is defined as "The sum of the continuous ratings of the load consuming apparatus connected to the system or part of the system under consideration" is numbered
(A) 3   (B) 5   (C) 7   (D) 24.

Answer Key

(Please make every effort to answer the questions on your own before looking at these answers. You'll make faster progress by following this rule.

1. A	10. D	19. B	28. C	36. B	44. A	53. B	62. D
2. A	11. D	20. A	29. B	37. D	45. B	54. D	63. C
3. C	12. C	21. D	30. C	38. D	46. B	55. C	64. C
4. A	13. D	22. B	31. D	39. D	47. C	56. D	65. B
5. B	14. B	23. D	32. A	40. A	48. B	57. D	66. A
6. C	15. B	24. C	33. D	41. C	49. C	58. B	67. C
7. D	16. A	25. C	34. A	42. C	50. C	59. D	68. A
8. C	17. B	26. B	35. C	43. B	51. D	60. D	69. D
9. A	18. C	27. A			52 A	61. C	70. A

ELECTRICIAN'S HELPER

IV. PREVIOUS EXAM

DIRECTIONS FOR ANSWERING QUESTIONS

Each question has four suggested answers, lettered
A, B, C, and D. Decide which is the best answer
and underline it. You may check your answers with
the answer key which appears at the end of the test.
Do not do so until you have completed the entire test.

Time allowed 3½ hours.

1. The property of an electric circuit tending to prevent the flow of current and at
    the same time causing electric energy to be converted into heat energy is called

    (A) conductance   (B) inductance   (C) resistance   (D) reluctance.

2. If a certain length of copper wire is elongated by stretching its volume does not
    change, it then can be said that for a fixed volume, the resistance of this
    conductor varies directly as

    (A) the square of its length   (C) the cube of its length
    (B) its length   (D) the square root of its length.

3. The property of a circuit or of a material which tends to permit the flow of an
    electric current is called

    (A) conductance   (B) inductance   (C) resistance   (D) reluctance.

4. The equivalent resistance in ohms of a circuit having four resistances,
    respectively 1, 2, 3 and 4 ohms in parallel is

    (A) 14.8   (B) 10   (C) 4.8   (D) .48.

5. The area in square inches of one circular mil is

    (A) $(\pi/4)(0.001)^2$ (B) $4\pi(.01)$ (C) $(0.001)^2$ (D) $(0.01)^2$.

6. The current through a field rheostat is 5 amperes and its resistance is 10 ohms. The power lost as heat in the rheostat is approximately

   (A) 500 watts   (B) 250 watts   (C) 125 watts   (D) 50 watts.

7. A D.C. motor takes 30 amps at 220 volts and has an efficiency of 80%. The horsepower available at the pulley is approximately

   (A) 10   (B) 7   (C) 5   (D) 2.

8. A tap is a tool commonly used to

   (A) remove broken screws   (C) cut external threads
   (B) cut internal threads   (D) smooth the ends of conduit.

9. Lead covering is used on conductors for

   (A) heat prevention   (C) grounding
   (B) explosion protection   (D) moisture proofing.

10. The one of the following tools which is run through a conduit to clear it before wire is pulled through is a (an)

    (A) auger   (B) borer   (C) stop   (D) mandrel.

11. A pothead as used in the trade is a

    (A) pot to heat solder
    (B) cable terminal
    (C) protective device used for cable splicing
    (D) type of fuse.

12. Resistance measurements show that an electro-magnet coil consisting of 90 turns of wire having an average diameter of 8 inches is shorted. The length of wire in feet required to rewind this coil is approximately

    (A) 110   (B) 190   (C) 550   (D) 2280.

13. An inexpensive and portable instrument commonly used for detecting the presence of static electricity is the

    (A) neon-tube electrical circuit tester
    (B) gauss meter
    (C) photo-electric cell
    (D) startometer.

14. A coil of wire is connected to an A.C. source of supply. If an iron bar is placed in the center of this coil, it will affect the magnetic circuit in such a way that the

    (A) inductance of the coil will increase
    (B)   power taken by the coil will increase
    (C) coil will draw more current
    (D) impedance of the coil will decrease.

15. The electrolyte used with the Edison nickel-iron-alkaline cell is

    (A) sulphuric acid   (C) potassium hydroxide
    (B) nitric acid   (D) lead peroxide.

16. The D'Arsonval galvanometer principle used in sensitive current measuring instruments is nothing more than

    (A) the elongation of a wire due to the flow of current
    (B) two coils carrying current reacting with one another
    (C) the dynamic reaction of an aluminum disc due to eddy currents
    (D) a coil turning in a magnetic field.

17. With reference to armature windings, lap windings are often called

    (A) series windings
    (B) cascade windings
    (C) multiple or parallel windings
    (D) ring windings.

18. With reference to armature windings, wave windings are often called

    (A) series windings
    (B) cascade windings
    (C) multiple or parallel windings
    (D) ring windings.

19. Polarization in a dry cell causes the reduction in the current capacity of the cell after it has delivered current for some time. A remedy for polarization is to bring oxidizing agents into intimate contact with the cell cathode. A chemical agent commonly used for this purpose is

    (A) potash
    (B) manganese dioxide
    (C) lead carbonate
    (D) acetylene.

20. The e.m.f. induced in a coil is greatest where the magnetic field within the coil is

    (A) constant
    (B) increasing
    (C) decreasing
    (D) changing most rapidly.

21. The brightness of incandescent lamps is commonly rated in

    (A) foot candles   (B) kilowatts   (C) lumens   (D) watts.

22. The effect of eddy currents in A.C. magnetic circuits may be reduced by

    (A) laminating the iron used
    (B) making the magnet core of solid steel
    (C) making the magnet core of solid cast iron
    (D) inserting brass rings around the magnet core.

23. The direction of rotation of a single phase repulsion induction motor can be reversed by

    (A) reversing two supply leads
    (B) shifting the position of the brushes
    (C) changing the connections to the field
    (D) changing the connections to the armature.

24. Underexciting the D.C. field of a synchronous motor will cause it to

    (A) slow down
    (B) speed up
    (C) draw lagging current
    (D) be unable to carry full normal load.

25. A certain 6-pole 60-cycle induction motor has a slip of 5% when operating at a certain load. The actual speed of this motor under these conditions is most nearly

    (A) 1200 rpm   (B) 1140 rpm   (C) 570 rpm   (D) 120 rpm.

26. The direction of rotation of a 3-phase wound rotor induction motor can be reversed by

    (A) interchanging the connections to any two rotor terminals
    (B) interchanging the connections to any two stator terminals
    (C) interchanging the connections to the field
    (D) shifting the position of the brushes.

Questions numbered 27 to 30 inclusive, refer to the diagram below.

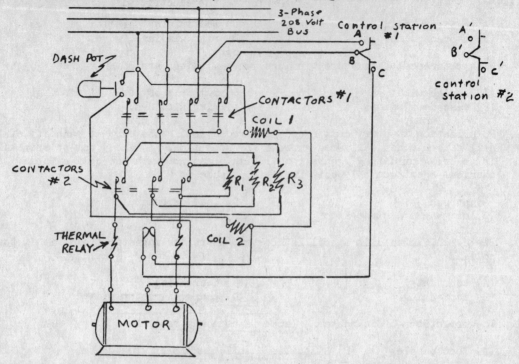

The above is a wiring diagram of a resistance starting controller for A.C. motors. This type of starter limits the starting current by means of equal resistances in each line wire leading to the motor.   These resistances are automatically shunted out after the motor has gained full speed connecting the motor directly across the lines.

Station #2 may be added to Station #1 by connecting the start buttons in parallel and the stop buttons in series.

27. When the starting button is pressed

   (A) contactor coil #1 is immediately energized causing contactors #1 to close
   (B) contactor coil #2 is immediately energized causing contactors #2 to close
   (C) contactor coil #1 is energized but contactors #1 close only after contactors#2 close
   (D) both contactors #1 and contactors #2 close at the same time.

28. The motor shown in the above diagram is a 3-phase

   (A) wound rotor induction motor
   (B) squirrel cage induction motor
   (C) capacitator type induction motor
   (D) synchronous motor

29. When the motor current becomes excessive the thermal relay will actuate and cause

   (A) contactors #1 to open first
   (B) contactors #2 to open first
   (C) contactors #1 and contactors #2 to open simultaneously
   (D) the dash pot to energize coil #2.

30. To add control station #2 to the circuit

   (A) A is connected to A^1, lead to C is disconnected and connected to C^1 and C is connected to B^1
   (B) A is connected to A^1, C to C^1 and B to B^1
   (C) lead to B is disconnected and connected to B^1, A^1 to B and C to C^1
   (D) A is connected to B^1, A^1 to B and C to C^1.

Questions numbered 31 to 38 inclusive refer to the electric wiring plan below.

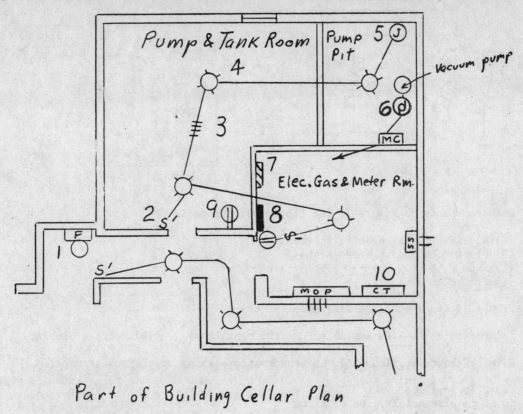

Part of Building Cellar Plan

31. Symbol numbered 1 represents a

    (A) local fire alarm gong
    (B) bell

    (C) buzzer
    (D) local fire alarm station.

32. Symbol numbered 2 represents a

    (A) 3-way switch
    (B) 2-way switch

    (C) single pole switch
    (D) push button switch and pilot.

33. Symbol numbered 3 represents

    (A) flexible conduit
    (B) the number of phases

    (C) the number of conductors in the conduit
    (D) the size of wire in the conduit.

34. Symbol numbered 4 represents a

    (A) drop cord   (B) lamp holder   (C) floor outlet   (D) ceiling outlet.

35. Symbol numbered 5 represents a

    (A) telephone jack
    (B) junction box

    (C) Jandus fixture
    (D) convenience outlet.

36. Symbol numbered 6 represents a

    (A) doorbell   (B) drop cord   (C) transformer   (D) motor

37. Symbol numbered 7 represents a (an)

    (A) power panel
    (B) telephone box

    (C) interconnection cabinet
    (D) voltmeter

38. Symbol numbered 8 represents a (an)

    (A) meter panel
    (B) interconnection cabinet

    (C) lighting panel
    (D) underfloor duct.

Questions numbered 39 to 42 inclusive refer to the diagram below.

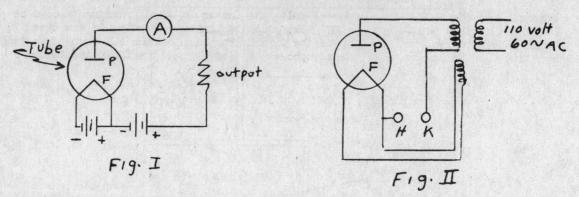

39. With reference to Figure I, the flow of electrons is

   (A) blocked by the negative filament
   (B) blocked by the negative plate
   (C) from F to P
   (D) from P to F.

40. Figure II represents the diagram of a (an)

   (A) rectifier   (B) amplifier   (C) oscillator   (D) voltage doubler.

41. With reference to Figure II, under normal operating conditions terminal

   (A) H is negative
   (B) H is alternately plus or minus
   (C) K is positive
   (D) H is positive.

42. The tube in the above diagram (Figure I) is a commonly used symbol for a

   (A) tetrode   (B) heptode   (C) pentode   (D) diode.

43. A 10" pulley revolving at 950 rpm is belted to a 20" pulley. The rpm of the 20" pulley is most nearly

   (A) 1900   (B) 1425   (C) 950   (D) 475.

44. A battery composed of 5 cells each having an e.m.f. of 1.5 volts and an internal resistance of (.1) ohm is connected to a .5 ohm resistance. If the cells are all in parallel, the current in amperes drawn from the battery is most nearly

   (A) 2.88   (B) 3.00   (C) 12.50   (D) 14.50.

45. The maximum power delivered by a battery is obtained when the external resistance of the battery is made

   (A) two times as large as its internal resistance
   (B) one half as large as its internal resistance
   (C) one quarter as large as its internal resistance
   (D) equal to its internal resistance.

46. A voltmeter is connected across the terminals of a certain battery. The difference between the open-circuit voltage and the voltage when current is taken from the battery is the

   (A) internal voltage drop in the battery
   (B) external voltage drop of the battery
   (C) emf of the battery
   (D) drop in voltage across the load resistance.

The questions numbered 47 and 48 relate to the following information:

According to the N.Y. City electrical code, the number of wires, running through or terminating in an outlet or junction box, shall be limited according to the free space within the box and the size of the wires. For combinations NOT found in a table provided for the selection of junction boxes, the code gives the following table:

Size of Conductor	Free Space Within Box For Each Conductor
No. 14	2 cubic inches
No. 12	2.25 cubic inches
No. 10	2.5 cubic inches
No. 8	3 cubic inches

47. In accordance with the above information, the minimum size of box, in inches, for 9 No. 12 wires is

(A) $1\frac{1}{2}$ x 4 square   (B) $1\frac{1}{2}$ x 3 square   (C) 2 x 3 square   (D) 2 x 4 square.

48. With reference to the above information, the minimum size of box, in inches, for 4 No. 8 wires and 4 No. 10 wires is

(A) $1\frac{1}{2}$ x 4 square   (B) $1\frac{1}{2}$ x 3 square   (C) 2 x 3 square   (D) 2 x 4 square.

Questions numbered 49 to 52 inclusive refer to the diagram below.

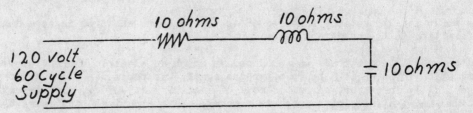

49. The value of the impedance, in ohms, of the above circuit is most nearly

(A) 30   (B) 10   (C) 3.33   (D) 1.73.

50. The current, in amperes, flowing in the above circuit is most nearly

(A) 4   (B) 6   (C) 12   (D) 18.

51. The power, in watts, consumed in the above circuit is most nearly

(A) 480   (B) 635   (C) 720   (D) 1440.

52. The voltage drop across the 10 ohm resistance is most nearly

(A) 10V   (B) 40V   (C) 60V   (D) 120V.

53. The current, in amperes, drawn from a battery cell having an e.m.f. of 3 volts and an internal resistance of 0.02 ohm when connected to an external resistance of 0.28 ohm is most nearly

(A) 5   (B) 10   (C) 15   (D) 20.

The following four questions numbered 54 to 57 inclusive are to be answered in accordance with the paragraph below.

Men engaged in industrial electrical work have a _significant_ responsibility and opportunity for service in securing the success of industrial undertakings. Viewed in this light, industrial men from top to bottom have _inherent_ importance that should inspire _maximum_ cooperation with other departments and with the executive branches.

54. The word _significant_, as used in the above paragraph, means

    (A) important   (B) accidental   (C) meaningless   (D) doubtful.

55. The word _inherent_, as used in the above paragraph, means

    (A) separable   (B) alienable   (C) loose   (D) natural.

56. The word _maximum_, as used in the above paragraph, means

    (A) steepest   (B) lowest   (C) greatest   (D) sharpest.

57. The above paragraph means most nearly that

    (A) industrial undertakings are the concern of executives only
    (B) the success of industrial undertakings is affected to an important degree by industrial electrical workers
    (C) executives rarely cooperate with industrial workers
    (D) industrial electrical workers are of little importance.

The following 2 questions numbered 58 to 59 are to be answered in accordance with the information in the paragraph below.

In the year 1914 a circuit was produced in which an electric current showed no diminution in strength 5 hours after the e.m.f. was removed. The current was induced magnetically in a short-circuited coil of lead wire at $-270°C$, produced by liquid helium, and the inducing source was removed. This experiment indicates that the resistance of lead was practically zero at this extremely low temperature.

58. In accordance with the above paragraph, the current in the short circuited lead wire must have been

    (A) electro-static current   (C) leading current
    (B) induced current   (D) lagging current.

59. According to the above paragraph, the resistance of lead

    (A) is practically zero at $-270°C$
    (B) is practically infinity at $-270°C$
    (C) varies inversely with the temperature
    (D) varies in direct proportion to the square of the temperature.

60. The term _open circuit_ means that

    (A) the wiring is exposed
    (B) the fuse is located outdoors
    (C) the circuit has one end exposed
    (D) all parts of the circuit (or path) are not in contact.

61. A form of metal suitable for carrying electrical current, such as a wire or cable, is called a (an)

    (A) raceway   (B) trough   (C) conductor   (D) appliance.

62. In accordance with the N.Y. City Electrical Code, the minimum size of the wire used on a 15 ampere circuit is

    (A) No. 16   (B) No. 14   (C) No. 12   (D) No. 10.

63. In cutting conduit, the pressure applied on a hacksaw should be on

    (A) the forward stroke only
    (B) the return stroke only
    (C) the forward and return strokes equally
    (D) either the forward or return stroke depending on the material.

64. To measure the diameter of wire most accurately it is best to use a

    (A) wire gauge   (B) depth gauge   (C) micrometer   (D) microtome.

65. To measure the speed of an armature directly in rpm, it is best to use a

    (A) tachometer   (B) chronometer   (C) bolometer   (D) manometer.

66. The primary purpose for the use of oil in certain transformers is

    (A) for lubrication
    (B) to reduce the permeability
    (C) to provide insulation and aid in cooling
    (D) as a rust inhibitor.

67. A single-throw switch should be mounted in such a way that to open the switch the blade must move

    (A) to the right   (B) upward   (C) to the left   (D) downward.

68. Of the following, the metal most commonly used as a filament in electric lamps is

    (A) platinum   (B) tungsten   (C) manganin   (D) constantin.

69. Of the following tools, the one most commonly used to cut holes in masonry is the

    (A) star drill   (B) auger   (C) router   (D) reamer.

70. Resistance coils having a small resistance temperature coefficient, are made with a wire of a metal alloy called

    (A) mallacca   (B) massicot   (C) manganin   (D) malachite.

71. For lead-acid type storage batteries, the normal battery potential is calculated on the basis of

    (A) 12 volts per cell   (C) 3 volts per cell
    (B) 6 volts per cell   (D) 2 volts per cell.

72. Fluorescent lamps, while designed for alternating-current operation, can be used on a direct-current circuit if a

    (A) specially designed D.C. auxiliary and parallel condenser of correct value are employed
    (B) specially designed D.C. auxiliary and series condenser of correct value are employed
    (C) specially designed D.C. auxiliary and parallel resistance of correct value are employed
    (D) specially designed D.C. auxiliary and series resistance of correct value are employed.

73. A transformer bank composed of three single phase transformers is to be connected delta-delta. The primary side is first connected, but before making the last secondary connection, the transformer should be

    (A) tested for an open-circuit
    (B) tested for a grounded-circuit
    (C) tested for a cross-circuit
    (D) tested for the proper phase relation.

74. As a safety measure, water should not be used to extinguish fires involving electrical equipment. The main reason is that water

    (A) is ineffective on electrical fires
    (B) may transmit current and shock to the user
    (C) may destroy the insulation property of wire
    (D) may short-circuit the equipment.

75. The smallest number of wires necessary to carry 3-phase current is

    (A) 2 wires   (B) 3 wires   (C) 4 wires   (D) 5 wires.

76. A 5 ampere D.C. ammeter may be safely used on a 50-ampere circuit provided the

    (A) correct size current transformer is used
    (B) proper size shunt is used
    (C) proper circuit series resistance is used
    (D) proper size multiplier is used.

77. As used in the N.Y. City electrical code, the term "device" refers to

    (A) an electrical appliance which does not have moving parts
    (B) a unit of an electrical system other than a conductor which is intended to carry but not consume electrical energy
    (C) current consuming equipment
    (D) an accessory which is intended primarily to perform a mechanical rather than an electrical function.

78. The difference of electrical potential between two wires of a circuit is its

    (A) voltage   (B) resistance   (C) amperage   (D) wattage.

79. On long straight horizontal conduit runs it is good practice to use

    (A) expansion joints   (C) isolation joints
    (B) universal joints   (D) insulation joints.

80. A set of conductors originating at the load side of the service equipment and supplying the main and/or one or more secondary distribution centers is commonly called a

    (A) circuit   (B) line   (C) cable   (D) feeder.

81. A 5 microfarad condenser is charged by putting 100 volts D.C. across its terminals. If this condenser is now placed across another condenser which has the same capacity rating and is identical in every other respect, the new voltage across these two condensers is most nearly

    (A) 100   (B) 75   (C) 50   (D) 25.

82. A synchronous condenser, so far as construction and appearance is concerned, closely resembles a (an)

    (A) electrolytic condenser   (C) synchroscope
    (B) synchronous motor   (D) wound rotor induction motor.

83. In an electric spot welding machine, the primary winding contains 200 turns of #10 wire and the secondary contains one turn made up of laminated copper sheeting. When the primary current is 5 amperes, the current, in amperes, passing through the metal to be welded is approximately

    (A) 100   (B) 200   (C) 500   (D) 1000.

84. With reference to an electric spot welding machine, the metal best suited to be united by spot welding is

    (A) copper   (B) zinc   (C) lead   (D) iron.

85. Two steel bars "G" and "H" have equal dimensions but one of them is a magnet and the other an ordinary piece of soft steel. In order to find out which one of the two bars is the magnet, you would touch the point midway between the ends of bar "G" with one end of bar "H". Then if bar "H" tends to

    (A) pull bar "G", bar "H" is not the magnet
    (B) pull bar "G", bar "H" is the magnet
    (C) repel bar "G", bar "H" is the magnet
    (D) repel bar "G", bar "H" is not the magnet.

86. The <u>main</u> purpose of a cutting fluid used in threading electrical conduits is to

    (A) prevent the formation of electrolytic pockets
    (B) improve the finish of the thread
    (C) wash away the chips
    (D) prevent the eventual formation of rust.

87. If a certain electrical job requires 212 ft. of $\frac{1}{2}$" rigid conduit, the number of lengths that you should requisition is

    (A) 16   (B) 18   (C) 20   (D) 22.

88. The number of threads per inch commonly used for $\frac{1}{2}$" electrical conduit is

    (A) 15   (B) 14   (C) 13   (D) 12.

89. For mounting a heavy pull box on a hollow tile wall, it is best to use

    (A) lag screws   (C) toggle bolts
    (B) masonry nails   (D) expansion shields.

90. For mounting an outlet box on a concrete ceiling, it is best to use

    (A) ordinary wood screws   (C) expansion screw anchors
    (B) masonry nails   (D) toggle bolts.

91. The N.Y. City electrical code states that "Incandescent lamps shall not be equipped with medium bases if above 300 watts rating nor mogul bases if above 1500 watts, special approved bases or other devices shall be used." In accordance with the above statement, the lamp base that you should use for a 750 watt incandescent lamp is the

    (A) medium base   (C) intermediate base
    (B) candelabra base   (D) mogul base.

92. In order to remove rough edges after cutting, all ends of conduit should be

    (A) filed   (B) sanded   (C) reamed   (D) honed.

93. Where a conduit enters a box, in order to protect the wire from abrasion, you should use an approved

    (A) coupling   (B) close nipple   (C) locknut   (D) bushing.

94. The maximum number of No. 10 type R conductors permitted in a 3/4" conduit is

    (A) 8   (B) 6   (C) 4   (D) 2.

95. A large switch which opens automatically when the current exceeds a predetermined limit is called a

    (A) disconnect   (C) circuit breaker
    (B) contactor   (D) limit switch.

96. The flux commonly used for soldering electrical wires is

    (A) rosin   (B) borax   (C) zinc chloride   (D) tallow.

97. The cost of the electrical energy consumed by a 50 watt lamp burning for 100 hours as compared to that consumed by a 100 watt lamp burning for 50 hours is

    (A) four times as much   (C) twice as much
    (B) three times as much   (D) the same.

98. Pneumatic tools are run by

    (A) electricity   (B) steam   (C) compressed air   (D) oil.

99. It is required to make a right angle turn in a conduit run in which there are already   3 quarter bends following the last pull box. The fitting best suited to properly do this is a (an)

    (A) cross   (B) tee   (C) union   (D) ell.

100. A 10,000 ohms resistance in an electronic timing switch burned out and must be replaced. The service manual states that this resistance should have an accuracy of 5%. This means that the value of the new resistance should differ from 10,000 ohms by not more than

    (A) 50 ohms   (B) 150 ohms   (C) 300 ohms   (D) 500 ohms.

Answer Key

(Please make every effort to answer the questions on your own before looking at these answers. You'll make faster progress by following this rule.)

1. C	14. A	27. A	39. C	51. D	63. A	75. B	88. B
2. A	15. C	28. B	40. A	52. D	64. C	76. B	89. C
3. A	16. D	29. C	41. D	53. B	65. A	77. B	90. C
4. D	17. C	30. A	42. D	54. A	66. C	78. A	91. D
5. A	18. A	31. A	43. D	55. D	67. D	79. A	92. C
6. B	19. B	32. C	44. A	56. C	68. B	80. D	93. D
7. B	20. D	33. C	45. D	57. B	69. A	81. C	94. C
8. B	21. C	34. D	46. A	58. B	70. C	82. B	95. C
9. D	22. A	35. B	47. A	59. A	71. D	83. D	96. A
10. D	23. B	36. D	48. A	60. D	72. D	84. D	97. D
11. B	24. C	37. A	49. B	61. C	73. D	85. B	98. C
12. B	25. B	38. C	50. C	62. C	74. B	86. B	99. D
13. A	26. B					87. D	100. D

ELECTRICIAN

V. PREVIOUS EXAM

DIRECTIONS FOR ANSWERING QUESTIONS

Each question has four suggested answers, lettered
A, B, C, and D. Decide which is the best answer
and underline it. You may check your answers with
the answer key which appears at the end of the test.
Do not do so until you have completed the entire test.

Time allowed 3½ hours.

1. For a given level of illumination, the cost of electrical energy with fluorescent lighting fixtures as compared with incandescent lighting fixtures is

   (A) less
   (B) the same
   (C) more
   (D) dependent on the utility rate.

2. The initial current of an incandescent lamp (tungsten) as compared with its normal operating current is

   (A) less
   (B) the same
   (C) more
   (D) dependent on the system frequency.

3. According to the N.Y.C. electrical code, fixtures in which the wiring may be exposed to temperatures in excess of 140°F. (60°C)

   (A) are prohibited
   (B) shall be wired with type AF fixture wires
   (C) shall be so designed or ventilated and installed to operate at temperatures which will not cause deterioration of the wiring
   (D) shall have suitable thermal insulation between the fixture and any adjacent combustible material.

4. The direction of rotation of a D.C. shunt motor can be reversed by

   (A) reversing the line terminals
   (B) reversing the field and armature
   (C) reversing the field or armature
   (D) flashing the field.

5. A starting device which will limit the starting current of a D.C. motor is generally required because

   (A) the counter e.m.f. is maximum at standstill
   (B) the inertia of the driven load causes excessive starting current
   (C) the counter e.m.f. is zero at standstill
   (D) decreased starting current increases the starting torque.

6. According to the N.Y.C. electrical code, the controller for an A.C. motor shall be capable of interrupting

   (A) twice the full load current of the motor
   (B) three times the full load current of the motor
   (C) five times the full load current of the motor
   (D) the stalled rotor current.

7. According to the N.Y.C. electrical code, motor disconnecting means shall be located

   (A) within 10 feet of the motor
   (B) within sight of the controller
   (C) within 15 feet of the motor
   (D) where convenient.

8. According to the N.Y.C. electrical code, motor disconnecting means shall have a continuous duty rating, in percent of the name plate current rating of the motor, of at least

   (A) 100%   (B) 115%   (C) 150%   (D) 200%.

9. The lumens per watt taken by a lamp varies with the type and size of lamp. Given that a one candle power light source emits 12.57 lumens, the lumens per watt taken by a 75 candle power lamp drawing 40 watts is approximately

   (A) 1.9   (B) 6.7   (C) 23.6   (D) 240.

10. A 230-volt, 25-cycle magnetic brake coil is to be rewound to operate properly on 60 cycles at the same voltage. Assuming that the coil at 25-cycles has 1800 turns, at 60 cycles the number of turns should be

   (A) reduced to 750   (C) reduced to 420
   (B) increased to 2400   (D) increased to 3000.

11. Nichrome wire having a resistance of 200 ohms per 1000 feet is to be used for a heater requiring a total resistance of 10 ohms. The length, in feet, of wire required is

   (A) 5   (B) 15   (C) 25   (D) 50.

12. The main reason for grounding conduit is to prevent the conduit from becoming

   (A) corroded by electrolysis
   (B) magnetized
   (C) a source of radio interference
   (D) accidentally energized at a higher potential than ground.

13. A feeder consisting of a positive and a negative wire supplies a motor load. The feeder is connected to bus-bars having a constant potential of 230 volts. The feeder is 500 ft. long and consists of two 250,000 circular-mil conductors. The maximum load on the feeder is 170 amps. Assume that the resistance of 1000 ft. of this cable is 0.0431 ohm. The voltage, at the motor terminals is most nearly

   (A) 201 V (B) 209 V (C) 213 V (D) 217.V.

14. With reference to question 13, the efficiency of transmission, in percent, is most nearly

   (A) 83% (B) 87% (C) 91% (D) 97%.

15. With reference to A.C. motors, in addition to overload, many other things cause fuses to blow. The fuse will blow if, in starting an A.C. motor, the operator throws the starting switch of the compensator to the running position

   (A) too slowly
   (B) too quickly
   (C) with main switch in open position
   (D) with main switch in close position.

16. A change in speed of a D.C. motor of 10 to 15 percent can usually be made by

   (A) rewinding the armature
   (B) rewinding the field
   (C) decreasing the number of turns in the field coils
   (D) increasing or decreasing the gap between the armature and field.

17. In order to check the number of poles in a 3-phase wound rotor induction motor, it is necessary to check the no-load speed. The no-load speed is obtained by running the motor with load disconnected and with

   (A) the rotor resistance short-circuited
   (B) the rotor resistance all in
   (C) the rotor resistance half in
   (D) the rotor resistance one third in.

18. A group of industrial oil burners are equipped with several electric pre-heaters which can be used singly or in combination to heat the #6 oil for the burners. Electric preheater "A" alone can heat a certain quantity of oil from 70° to 160° in 15 minutes and preheater "B" alone can do the same job in 30 minutes. If both preheaters are used together, they will do the job in

   (A) 12 minutes   (B) 11 minutes   (C) 10 minutes   (D) 9 minutes.

19. With reference to armature windings, in a wave winding, regardless of the number of poles, only

   (A) two brushes are necessary   (C) six brushes are necessary
   (B) four brushes are necessary   (D) eight brushes are necessary.

20. The minimum number of overload devices required for a 3-phase A.C. motor connected to a 120/208 volt, 3-phase, 4 wire system is

   (A) 1   (B) 2   (C) 3   (D) 4.

21. According to the N.Y.C. electrical code, an externally operable switch may be used as the starter for a motor of not over 2 horsepower (and not over 300 volts) provided it has a rating of at least

   (A) 2 times the stalled rotor current of the motor
   (B) 2 times the full load current of the motor
   (C) 115% of the full load current of the motor
   (D) 150% of the stalled rotor current of the motor.

22. According to the N.Y.C. electrical code, a single disconnecting means may serve a group of motors provided

    (A) all motors are ½ HP or less
    (B) all motors are within a short distance from each other
    (C) all motors are locaed within a single room and within sight of the disconnecting means
    (D) one half of the motors are located within a single room and within sight of the disconnecting means.

23. In a 3-phase system with 3 identical loads connected in delta, if the line voltage is 4160 volts, the line to neutral voltage is

    (A) indeterminate   (B) 7200 volts   (C) 2400 volts   (D) 2000 volts.

24. If the current in each line is 100 amperes, the currents in each of the individual loads is (under the conditions as set forth in question 23)

    (A) indeterminate   (B) 57.7 amps   (C) 173 amps   (D) 50.0 amps.

25. In a 3-phase system with 3 identical loads connected in wye, if the line to neutral voltage is 115 volts, the line voltage is

    (A) indeterminate   (B) 208 volts   (C) 200 volts   (D) 220 volts.

26. A circuit composed of a 6 ohm resistance, a 10 ohm capacitative reactance, and an 18 ohm inductive reactance connected in series is energized by a 120 volt A.C. supply. The current, in amperes, flowing in this circuit is

    (A) 0   (B) 12   (C) 35   (D) 20.

27. With reference to question 26, the power, in watts, used in this circuit is

    (A) 0   (B) 1440   (C) 420   (D) 864.

28. With reference to question 26, the power factor, in per cent, is

    (A) 100   (B) 60   (C) 80   (D) 90.

29. With reference to question 26, the total impedance, in ohms, of the circuit is

    (A) 10   (B) 34   (C) 14   (D) 28.

30. A triode does not have a

    (A) cathode   (B) screen grid   (C) control grid   (D) plate.

31. An industrial plant in New York City utilizes acetone as a solvent in one area. All wiring in this area must be

    (A) vaportight   (C) explosionproof
    (B) watertight   (D) of normal construction.

32. In an area where explosionproof wiring is required, each conduit entering an enclosure containing apparatus which may produce arcs, sparks or high temperatures shall be provided with

    (A) insulating bushings   (C) an approved sealing compound
    (B) a cable terminator   (D) double locknuts

33. Decreasing the bias voltage on the control grid of a triode (making it less negative with respect to the cathode) causes the plate current to

    (A) not change   (B) increase   (C) decrease   (D) oscillate.

The following 13 questions numbered 34 to 46 inclusive are to be answered in accordance with the provisions of the Electrical Code of the City of New York.

34. The minimum size of wire for signalling systems is

   (A) #14AWG   (B) #16AWG   (C) #18AWG   (D) #19AWG.

35. The minimum size of service entrance conductors is

   (A) #2AWG   (B) #4AWG   (C) #6AWG   (D) #8AWG.

36. The maximum number of individual sets of service equipment which can be supplied from one set of service entrance conductors is

   (A) 1   (B) 2   (C) 4   (D) 6.

37. Service switches of ratings larger than 1,200 amperes

   (A) are prohibited
   (B) shall be of the pressure contact type
   (C) shall be of the air circuit breaker type
   (D) shall be remotely operable.

38. The rating of service switches shall be not less than

   (A) the computed load current
   (B) twice the computed load current
   (C) one and a half times the computed load current
   (D) one and a quarter times the computed load current.

39. The allowable current carrying capacity of conductors in raceway or cable

   (A) is independent of the number of conductors
   (B) shall be reduced to 70% of table values if more than three conductors are contained within the raceway or cable
   (C) shall be reduced to 50% of the table values if more than six conductors are contained in the raceway or cable
   (D) shall be reduced to 80% for 4-6 conductors and to 70% for 7-9 conductors in the same raceway or cable.

40. The maximum number of conductors for general light and power in a single raceway is

   (A) 6   (B) 9   (C) 15   (D) unlimited.

41. The number of signal wires in a conductor raceway shall

   (A) be the same as for lighting and power conductors
   (B) be the maximum number which can be easily installed
   (C) be such that their total cross sectional area shall not exceed 50% of the cross sectional area of the conduit or raceway
   (D) be such that their total cross sectional area shall not exceed 40% of the cross sectional area of the conduit or raceway.

42. Lightning arrestors for receiving station antennas shall operate at a voltage of not more than

   (A) 100 volts   (B) 200 volts   (C) 500 volts   (D) 1000 volts.

43. The minimum size of copper ground connection to lightning arrestors for receiving antennas shall be

   (A) #14AWG   (B) #10AWG   (C) #6AWG   (D) #16AWG.

44. Only motor generator sets having a generated voltage of 65 volts or less **may** be protected by

   (A) one protective device in the generator armature circuit
   (B) a protective device in each armature lead
   (C) the over current protective devices in the motor circuit set to trip when the generators are delivering not more than 150% of their full load rated current
   (D) the motor running protective devices of the motor.

45. Single pole protective devices for direct current generators must be activated by

   (A) the total generated current, including all field current
   (B) total current except that in the shunt field
   (C) separate elements in each brush lead
   (D) separate elements in each line lead.

46. Motor control equipment for hazardous locations must

   (A) not produce sparks
   (B) be contained in an enclosure which is vapor tight
   (C) be capable of withstanding an external explosion
   (D) be of a type specifically approved for the installation.

47. A room is 20 feet wide and is to be provided with 4 rows of lighting outlets symmetrically spaced. The distance from the wall to the center line of the first fixture row will be

   (A) 5'-0"   (B) 10'-0"   (C) 7'-6"   (D) 2'-6".

48. A fixture mounting height of 9'-6" is specified for a room with a ceiling height of 12'-0", utilizing fixtures with a height of 6". The size of stem required is most nearly

   (A) 3'-0"   (B) 2'-6"   (C) 2'-0"   (D) 1'-6".

49. Specifications for a project require that 40W, T-12, RS/CW lamps be installed in a given group of fixtures. The type of lamp required is

   (A) 40 watt, type 12, reflector spot, clear white, incandescent
   (B) 40 watt, single pin, relay start, code white, fluorescent
   (C) 40 watt, bi-pin, rapid start, cool white, fluorescent
   (D) type 12, medium base, recessed spot, clear white, incandescent.

50. Specifications for a project require the use of indirect type of lighting fixtures. The one of the following types that will meet this requirement is

   (A) RCM dome fixture
   (B) concentric ring fixture with silverbowl lamp
   (C) downlight with par 38 spot
   (D) opal glass bowl.

51. The list of symbols for the plans for a project gives and defines the following symbol:

   O_{A5C} – Incandescent lighting fixture, letters and number indicate fixture type per specifications, circuit number and controlling switch, respectively.

   The symbol for a fixture connected to circuit 8, controlled by a switch designated "e", and conforming to the requirements of a type D fixture would be

   (A) O_{E8d} (B) O_{d8E} (C) O_{D8e} (D) O_{8eD}.

The following 4 questions numbered 52 to 55 inclusive shall be answered in accordance with the diagram below.

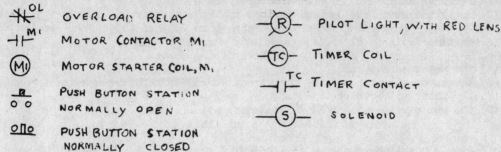

LIST OF SYMBOLS

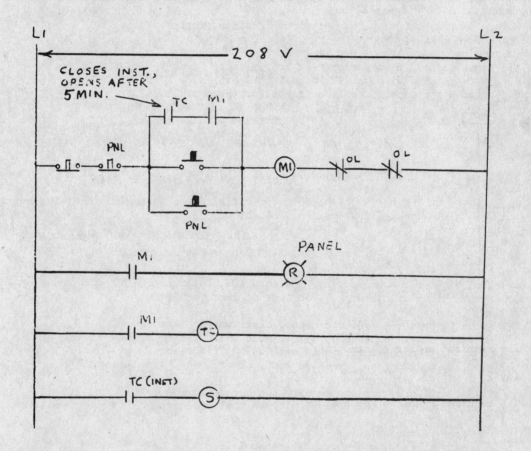

52. The above schematic diagram indicates a desired control scheme for a pump motor. The number of locations the motor can be started from, is/are

   (A) 1   (B) 2   (C) 3   (D) 4

53. Of the following, the one which contains the most complete and correct list of possible operations which will cause the already started motor, to stop is

   (A) pressing of stop PB after 5 minutes have elapsed since motor started, or operation of OL.
   (B) a lapse of 5 minutes since starting of motor, or pressing of stop PB, or operation of OL.
   (C) the passing of 5 minutes from the time of starting, or pressing of stop PB, or operation of OL, or loss of voltage
   (D) loss of voltage after 5 minutes have elapsed since starting motor, or operation of OL.

54. The solenoid will be energized

    (A) as long as the motor starter is energized
    (B) only as long as the start P.B. is depressed
    (C) for five minutes
    (D) until the stop P.B. is depressed.

55. If the timer fails to close its associated contact

    (A) the motor cannot run
    (B) the motor will run only as long as the start P.B. is depressed
    (C) the motor will run continuously
    (D) the motor will run for five minutes.

The following 3 questions numbered 56 to 58 inclusive should be answered in accordance with the diagram below.

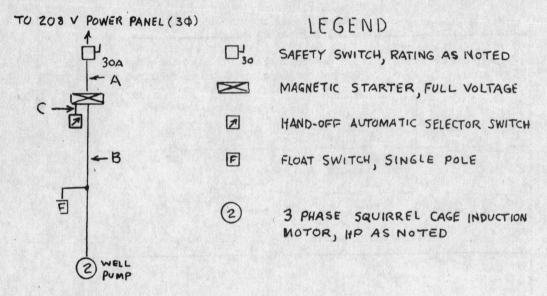

56. The required number of conductors at point "A" is

    (A) 2   (B) 3   (C) 4   (D) 5.

57. The required number of conductors at point "B" is

    (A) 2   (B) 3   (C) 4   (D) 5.

58. The required number of conductors at point "C" is

    (A) 2   (B) 3   (C) 4   (D) 5.

59. The least number of single-phase wattmeters that can be used to measure the power in an unbalanced 3-phase 4-wire A.C. circuit is

    (A) 1   (B) 2   (C) 3   (D) 4.

60. A note on a plan states: "All runs shall be 3/4" conduit with 2#12AWG conductors or number of #12 conductors indicated by hatchmarks unless otherwise designated." A run is shown as follows: —————///—————
This run consists of

    (A) 2#12, ½"C   (B) 3#12, ½"C   (C) 3#12-3/4"C   (D) 2#12-3/4"C.

61. Specifications for a particular project call for a system of empty conduits and outlet boxes for public telephones, with a galvanized steel wire installed in each conduit. The one of the following reasons for providing this wire which is most acceptable is

   (A) to ensure that the conduit is clear
   (B) to permit pulling in of wire at a later date
   (C) to ground the system
   (D) to limit corrosion of the interior surfaces of the conduit.

62. An interior auxiliary fire alarm system to be installed in a building is to be of the coded city connected shunt-trip type. The one of the following which best describes the operation of this system is

   (A) operating any station sounds a coded signal on all bells and uses local power to trip a city box
   (B) operating any station operates the city box only
   (C) operating any station trips a city box using municipal system power and simultaneously sounds a coded signal on interior bells
   (D) operating any station operates interior gongs only.

63. A magnetic motor starter is to be controlled with momentary start-stop push-buttons at two locations. The number of control wires required respectively in the conduit between the controller and the first station and in the conduit between the two stations is

   (A) 3 and 3   (B) 4 and 4   (C) 3 and 4   (D) 2 and 4.

64. If the voltage on a 3-phase squirrel cage induction motor is reduced to 90% of its rating, the starting current

   (A) increases slightly   (C) decreases 10%
   (B) is unchanged   (D) decreases 20%.

65. If the voltage on a 3-phase squirrel case induction motor is reduced to 90% of its rating, the full load current

   (A) decreases slightly   (C) increases 10%
   (B) is unchanged   (D) increases 20%.

66. A 3-conductor cable is used to provide a "hot" leg, switch leg and neutral between two outlets. The individual conductors are most commonly connected as follows:

   (A) red is hot, white is neutral, black is switch
   (B) red is switch, white is hot, black is neutral
   (C) red is neutral, white is switch, black is hot
   (D) red is switch, white is neutral, black is hot.

67. To obtain A.C. current from a D.C. source of supply, it is best to use a (an)

   (A) inverter   (B) diode   (C) rectifier   (D) shunt generator.

68. Insulation resistance is commonly measured by means of a (an)

   (A) ammeter   (B) varmeter   (C) capacitance bridge   (D) megger.

69. A specification requires the installation if five pole, four wire, grounded 250 volt, 15 amp receptacles for 120/208 volt 3ϕ 4 wire service, with matching plug and 15 foot #14AWG portable heavy duty cord. The number of conductors which the required cord must have is

   (A) 3   (B) 4   (C) 5   (D) not clearly specified.

The following two questions numbered 70 and 71 are to be answered in accordance with the information given below.

To get equivalent delta from wye	To get equivalent wye from delta

$$A = \frac{ab+bc+ac}{a} \qquad\qquad a = \frac{BC}{A+B+C}$$

$$B = \frac{ab+bc+ac}{b} \qquad\qquad b = \frac{AC}{A+B+C}$$

$$C = \frac{ab+bc+ac}{c} \qquad\qquad c = \frac{AB}{A+B+C}$$

The above formula indicates the relationship between equivalent wye and delta net works.

70. If in a delta the branches are resistors such that A = 5 ohms, B = 10 ohms and C = 10 ohms, the resistor of branch "a" of the equivalent wye is

    (A) 5 ohms   (B) 10 ohms   (C) 2 ohms   (D) 4 ohms.

71. In the problem 70 above, the resistor of branch "b" of the equivalent wye is

    (A) 10 ohms   (B) 4 ohms   (C) 2 ohms   (D) 5 ohms.

The following 2 questions numbered 72 and 73 should be answered in accordance with the paragraph below.

Insulation resistance tests are best made with a direct-reading Megger. These tests can also be made with a high-resistance voltmeter and a source of D.C. supply. Assume that a direct reading instrument is not available but you have on hand a 100 volt voltmeter having a sensitivity of 5000 ohms per volt and a 100 volt battery. The battery is connected in series with the voltmeter. One free battery lead is connected to the wire whose insultation resistance is to be measured, and the other free lead to the grounded conduit. With this hookup the voltmeter reads 50 volts.

72. The insultation resistance, in ohms, of the above conductor is

    (A) 500   (B) 5,000   (C) 250,000   (D) 500,000.

73. The resistance, in ohms, of the above mentioned voltmeter is

    (A) 500   (B) 5,000   (C) 250,000   (D) 500,000.

74. An ammeter and voltmeter are connected through instrument transformers to measure the KVA of a balanced three phase load connected to a 2400 volt, 3-phase, 3 wire system. The PT is rated 2400/120 volts and the CT is rated 200/5 amperes. If the ammeter reads 4 amps. and the voltmeter 100 volts, the load, in KVA, is approximately

    (A) 0.4   (B) 6.8   (C) 320   (D) 555.

75. A note on a lighting plan states: "All fluorescent fixtures shall be symmetrically spaced and oriented so that the major axis of the fixture is parallel to the major axis of the room." For a room 20' long by 16' wide, with four-four foot fixtures the desired arrangement is:

    (A) fixtures parallel with and centered 4' from 20' wall, 5' from 16' wall
    (B) fixtures parallel with and centered 5' from 20' wall, 4' from 16' wall
    (C) fixtures parallel with and centered 4' from 16' wall, 5' from 20' wall
    (D) fixtures parallel with and centered 5' from 16' wall, 4' from 20' wall.

The following 6 questions numbered 76 to 81 inclusive are to be answered in accordance with the provisions of the Electrical Code of the City of New York.

76. Individual conductors of multi-conductor control cables shall be

(A) color coded
(B) clearly tagged at each end
(C) identified by painting
(D) stranded.

77. Terminals of motor starting rheostats shall be

(A) suitable for solderless external connections only
(B) clearly marked to indicate wire to which they are to be connected
(C) equipped with barriers
(D) brought out to a suitable terminal block.

78. Incandescent lamps can be used for control resistors

(A) under no circumstances
(B) as protective resistances provided they do not carry the main current
(C) for loads less than 1000 watts
(D) if mounted in porcelain receptacles.

79. Wiring in battery rooms shall

(A) utilize lead covered cable
(B) be installed in rigid steel conduit
(C) be installed in Greenfield
(D) be enclosed in non-corrodible conduit or be exposed.

80. Control switches for emergency lights in a theater shall be located

(A) where convenient to operating personnel
(B) in the lobby where accessible to authorized persons
(C) on the stage switchboard
(D) in the projection booth.

81. Signal wires of sizes #18 or #16 shall be considered as properly protected by fuses rated at

(A) 15 amps   (B) 20 amps   (C) 25 amps   (D) 30 amps.

82. If the voltage of a 3 phase squirrel cage induction motor is reduced to 90% of its rating, the power factor

(A) increases slightly
(B) is unchanged
(C) decreases slightly
(D) decreases 10 points.

83. To reverse the direction of rotation of a wound rotor 3 phase induction motor

(A) interchange all line wires
(B) interchange all rotor connections
(C) interchange any 2 rotor connections
(D) interchange any 2 line wires.

The following 3 questions numbered 84 to 86 inclusive relate to the diagram below.

LEGEND

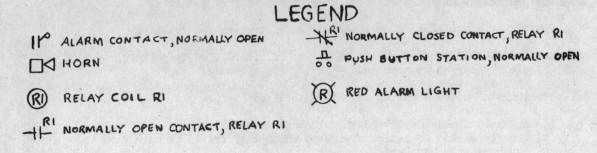

ALARM CONTACT, NORMALLY OPEN

HORN

RELAY COIL R1

NORMALLY OPEN CONTACT, RELAY R1

NORMALLY CLOSED CONTACT, RELAY R1

PUSH BUTTON STATION, NORMALLY OPEN

RED ALARM LIGHT

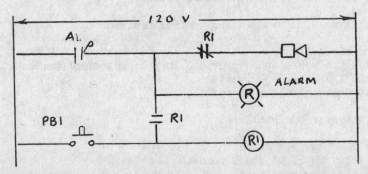

The above diagram represents a simple alarm panel. Note that closing of the alarm contact causes the horn to sound and alarm lamp to light.

84. Assume that the alarm contact has closed. Then pressing the P.B.

    (A) causes the red alarm light to go out only as long as the button is depressed
    (B) causes the horn to be silenced until the alarm contact opens and closes again
    (C) tests the alarm light
    (D) tests the alarm horn.

85. The alarm light is illuminated

    (A) only when the push button is depressed
    (B) only after the horn is silenced
    (C) as long as the alarm contact is closed
    (D) continuously.

86. The relay R_1 has the following contacts:

    (A) 2 N.O.   (B) 2 N.C.   (C) 1 N.O. & 1 N.C.   (D) 2 N.O. & 1 N.C.

87. A blind hickey is used

    (A) to cap a spare conduit
    (B) in lieu of a fixture stud
    (C) in lieu of a fixture extension
    (D) to hang a lighting fixture on a gas outlet.

The following 4 questions numbered 88 to 91 inclusive are to be answered in accordance with the diagram below.

Legend

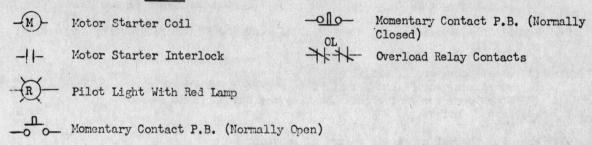

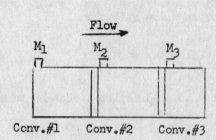

NOTE: This diagram represents the wiring diagram for a three-section conveyor, with interlocks

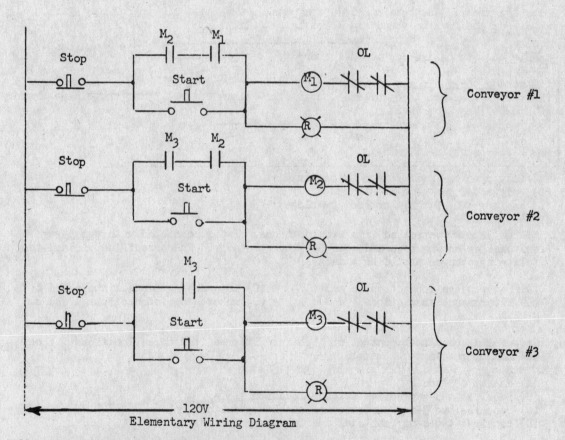

Elementary Wiring Diagram

88. For continuous operation of all conveyors

    (A) conveyor #1 must be started first
    (B) conveyor #2 must be started first
    (C) conveyor #3 must be started first
    (D) conveyors can be started in any order.

89. Stopping of conveyor #3 will

(A) not affect other conveyors   (C) stop conveyor #1
(B) stop conveyor #2   (D) stop conveyors #1 and #2.

90. Momentarily depressing the start P.B. of conveyor #2 before starting conveyor #3 or #1 will

(A) start conveyors #1 and #2
(B) start conveyor #2 and permit it to run continuously
(C) start conveyor #2 for only the time the button is depressed
(D) have no effect.

91. When the thermal overload relays of conveyor #2 open,

(A) motor #2 only stops   (C) motors #1, #2, and #3 will stop
(B) motors #1 and #2 will stop   (D) an alarm will sound.

92. An Erickson coupling is used

(A) to join sections of EMT
(B) to connect EMT to flexible conduit
(C) to connect two sections of rigid conduit when one section cannot be turned
(D) as a substitute for all thread.

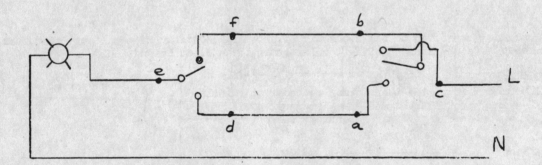

93. A light is to be controlled from two locations. It is connected with two 3-way switches as shown above and does not work properly. To correct the wiring, the following changes should be made:

(A) interchange connections e and f   (C) interchange connections a and b
(B) interchange connections b and c   (D) interchange connections a and c.

94. Proper and economical control of lighting fixtures from three locations without the use of relays

(A) cannot be done
(B) requires a 3-way switch at each location
(C) requires two 3-way switches and one 4-way switch
(D) requires two 4-way switches and one 3-way switch.

95. The outside diameter of a certain rigid steel conduit is measured to be approximately 2" (to the nearest 1/8 inch). The nominal trade size is

(A) 2"   (B) $1\frac{1}{2}$"   (C) $1\frac{1}{4}$"   (D) $2\frac{1}{2}$".

96. Electrical equipment can be secured to concrete walls by means of

    (A) toggle bolts   (C) cut nails
    (B) wooden plugs and screws   (D) lead shields.

97. Continuity of an electrical circuit can conveniently be determined in the field by means of a (an)

    (A) smoke test   (C) ammeter
    (B) bell and battery set   (D) Wheatstone Bridge.

98. The speed of a motor can be measured by means of a

    (A) potentiometer   (C) tachometer
    (B) megger   (D) thermocouple.

99.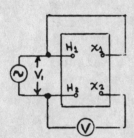
A test for transformer polarity is made on a transformer rated 2400-240 volts, by applying a voltage $V_1 = 120$ volts to the high voltage terminals H_1 and H_2 and measuring the voltage between terminals H_2 and X_2. (See diagram to the left.)

If the transformer is of subtractive polarity, the voltmeter will read approximately

    (A) 132 volts   (B) 12 volts   (C) 108 volts   (D) 0 volts.

100. An ammeter connected to the secondary of an energized metering transformer requires repairs. Before disconnecting the instrument, the electrician should

    (A) open the secondary circuit
    (B) short circuit the transformer secondary terminals
    (C) short circuit the transformer primary terminals
    (D) remove the transformer secondary fuses.

Answer Key

(Please make every effort to answer the questions on your own before looking at these answers. You'll make faster progress by following this rule.)

1. A	14. D	27. D	39. D	51. C	63. C & A	75. A	88. C
2. C	15. B	28. B	40. B	52. B	64. C	76. A	89. D
3. C	16. D	29. A	41. D	53. C	65. C	77. B	90. C
4. C	17. A	30. B	42. C	54. A	66. D	78. B	91. B
5. C	18. C	31. C	43. C	55. B	67. A	79. D	92. C
6. D	19. A	32. C	44. C	56. B	68. D	80. B	93. B
7. B	20. B	33. B	45. B	57. D	69. C	81. A	94. C
8. B	21. B	34. D	46. D	58. B	70. D	82. A	95. B
9. C	22. C	35. B	47. D	59. C	71. C	83. D	96. D
10. A	23. C	36. D	48. C	60. C	72. D	84. B	97. B
11. D	24. B	37. B	49. C	61. B	73. D	85. C	98. C
12. D	25. C	38. D	50. B	62. C	74. D	86. C	99. C
13. D	26. B					87. D	100. B

ELECTRICIAN

VI. PREVIOUS EXAM

DIRECTIONS FOR ANSWERING QUESTIONS

Each question has four suggested answers, lettered
A, B, C, and D. Decide which is the best answer
and underline it. You may check your answers with
the answer key which appears at the end of the test.
Do not do so until you have completed the entire test.

Time allowed 3½ hours.

NOTE: Whenever the term "The Code" appears in this test
it means only the New York City Electrical Code.

1. Two copper conductors have the same length but the cross section of one is
twice that of the other. If the resistance of the one having a cross section
of twice the other is 10 ohms, the resistance of the other conductor, in ohms,
is

   (A) 5   (B) 10   (C) 20   (D) 30.

2. Assuming that copper weighs 0.32 lbs. per cubic inch, the weight, in lbs., of
a bus bar 10' long and having a cross section 2" x 1/2" is

   (A) 120   (B) 32   (C) 3.2   (D) 38.4.

3. In a two-phase, three-wire system, the voltage between the common wire and
either of the other two wires is 200 volts. The voltage between these other
two wires is then approximately

   (A) 200 volts   (B) 283 volts   (C) 141 volts   (D) 100 volts.

4. Three 30-ohm resistances are connected in delta across a 208-volt, 3-phase circuit. The line current, in amperes, is approximately

(A) 6.93 (B) 13.86 (C) 120 (D) 12.

5. A storage battery consists of three lead cells connected in series. On open circuit the emf of the battery is 6.4 volts. When it delivers a current of 80 amperes its terminal voltage drops to 4.80 volts. Its internal resistance, in ohms, is approximately

(A) 0.01 (B) 0.02 (C) 0.03 (D) 0.04.

6. In reference to question No. 5, the terminal voltage, in volts, when the battery delivers 50 amperes is approximately

(A) 5.9 (B) 5.4 (C) 4.9 (D) 4.4.

7. In order to magnetize a steel bar, a magnetomotive force of 1000 ampere turns is necessary. The voltage that must be applied to a coil of 100 turns and 10 ohms resistance is

(A) 1 (B) 10 (C) 100 (D) 1000.

8. Rosin is preferable to acid as a flux for soldering wire because rosin is

(A) a nonconductor   (B) a dry powder   (C) a better conductor
(D) noncorrosive.

9. If, in tracing through an armature winding, all of the conductors are encountered before coming back to the starting point, there is but one closure and the winding is

(A) doubly reentrant   (B) singly reentrant   (C) triply reentrant
(D) quintuply reentrant.

10. A power factor meter is connected to a single-phase 2-wire circuit by means of

(A) 2 wires   (B) 3 wires   (C) 4 wires   (D) 5 wires.

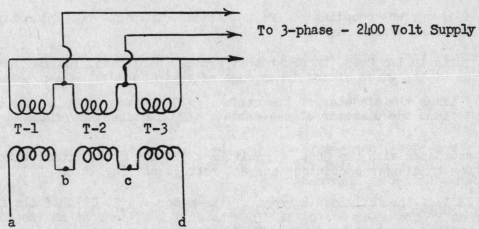

To 3-phase - 2400 Volt Supply

11. The above figure represents a transformer bank composed of 3 single-phase

transformers each having a ratio of transformation equal to 20/1. The primary is already connected to the voltage supply, as shown in the diagram, while the secondary side is only "partly connected."

It is desired to connect the secondary of this transformer bank in delta. Before connecting a to d, the combination of voltages should correspond to one of the following:

(A) Vab = 120, Vbc = 120, Vcd = 120 and Vad = 0

(B) Vab = 120, Vbc = 120, Vcd = 120 and Vad = 120

(C) Vab = 120, Vbc = 120, Vcd = 120 and Vad = 208

(D) Vab = 208, Vbc = 208, Vcd = 208 and Vad = 0.

12. With reference to question No. 11, assuming that the combination of voltages read as follows: Vab = 120 volts, Vbc = 120 volts, Vcd = 120 volts, Vad = 240 volts and Vbd = 208 volts, before connecting a to d for a delta connection

(A) do nothing as the transformer bank is already phased out
(B) secondary winding of T-1 should be reversed by interchanging its leads
(C) secondary winding of T-2 should be reversed by interchanging its leads
(D) secondary winding of T-3 should be reversed by interchanging its leads.

13. The torque of a shunt motor varies as

(A) the armature current   (B) the square of the armature current
(C) the cube of the armature current   (D) the cube of the field current.

14. The armature of a synchronous converter has

(A) 3 slip rings for the AC and 2 slip rings for the DC   (B) 4 slip rings, 2 for the AC and 2 for the DC   (C) a commutator and slip rings
(D) no slip rings.

15. An electrical device that transmits rotation from a driving to a driven member without mechanical contact — with stepless adjustable control and with almost instantaneous response — is the

(A) eddy current coupling   (B) universal coupling   (C) planetary coupling
(D) coupling transformer.

16 According to the Code, in order that armored cable will not be injured, the radius of the curve of the inner edge of any bend must be not less than

(A) 3 times the diameter of the cable   (B) 5 times the diameter of the cable
(C) 7 times the diameter of the cable   (D) 10 times the diameter of the cable.

17. In accordance with the Code, circuit breakers for motor branch circuit protection shall have continuous current ratings not less than

(A) 110% of the full load current of the motor   (B) 115% of the full load current of the motor   (C) 120% of the full load current of the motor
(D) 125% of the full load current of the motor.

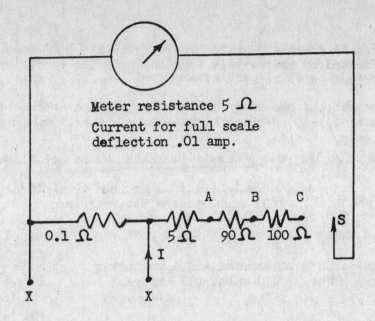

Meter resistance 5 Ω
Current for full scale
deflection .01 amp.

18. The above diagram represents the circuit of a multi-range ammeter. X - X is connected in series with an electric circuit for the purpose of measuring the current in that circuit. When slider S is connected to point B, the current I, in amperes, that will cause the meter to read full scale is approximately

(A) 30   (B) 20   (C) 10   (D) 1.

19. In reference to question No. 18, when slider S is connected to point C, the current I, in amperes, that will cause the meter to read full scale is approximately

(A) 30   (B) 20   (C) 10   (D) 1.

20. The Code states that feeders over 40' in length supplying two branch circuits shall be not smaller than

(A) 2 No. 14 AWG   (B) 2 No. 12 AWG   (C) 2 No. 10 AWG
(D) 2 No. 8 AWG.

21. Speed control by a method that requires two wound rotor induction motors with their rotors rigidly connected together is called speed control by

(A) change of poles   (B) field control   (C) concatenation
(D) voltage control.

22. Before connecting an alternator to the bus bars and in parallel with other alternators, it is necessary that its voltage and frequency be the same as that of the bus bars but that

(A) the rotor revolve at synchronous speed   (B) the voltage be in phase opposition as well   (C) its power factor be not less than unity
(D) its power factor be greater than unity.

23. A leather belt is used to drive a 3 kw DC generator by a 5 hp 3-phase induction motor. Adjustments for proper belt tension, with the generator running at full load, can be made with the aid of a

(A) 50-lb. weight as wide as the belt   (B) voltmeter and an ammeter
(C) power factor meter   (D) 3-phase wattmeter.

24. The cold resistance of a 120 volt 100 watt Tungsten incandescent lamp is

(A) greater than its hot resistance   (B) smaller than the hot resistance
(C) approximately 100 ohms   (D) equal to the hot resistance.

25. The correct value of the resistance of a field coil can be measured by using

(A) a Schering bridge   (B) an ammeter and a voltmeter
(C) a Kelvin double bridge   (D) a Maxwell bridge.

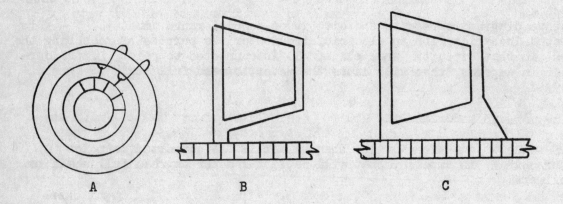

26. The three windings shown above belong respectively to the

(A) ring, lap, and wave types of closed-coil windings
(B) ring, lap, and wave types of open-coil windings
(C) ring, lap, and wave types of reverse-coil windings
(D) ring, lap, and wave types of cumulative-coil windings.

27. Simplex lap windings have as many armature circuits as there are

(A) commutator bars   (B) number of coils   (C) number of active conductors
(D) poles.

28. The power factor of a single phase alternating current motor may be found by using one of the following sets of AC instruments:

(A) one voltmeter and one phase-rotation meter   (B) one voltmeter and one ammeter   (C) one voltmeter, one ammeter, and one wattmeter   (D) one voltmeter, one ammeter, and one watt-hour meter.

29. When connecting wattmeters to AC motor circuits consuming large amounts of current, it is necessary to use

(A) current transformers   (B) potential transformers   (C) power shunts
(D) isolation transformers.

30. To control a lamp independently from five different points you would use

(A) two 3-way and three 4-way switches   (B) four 3-way switches and one 4-way switch   (C) three 3-way and two 4-way switches   (D) three 4-way and two S.P.S.T. switches.

31. The average life of a 100 watt incandescent light bulb is approximately

(A) 100 hrs.   (B) 400 hrs.   (C) 1000 hrs.   (D) 10,000 hrs.

32. The efficiency in lumens per watt of a 40 watt fluorescent lamp

(A) is less than that of a 40 watt incandescent lamp   (B) is the same as that of a 40 watt incandescent lamp   (C) is greater than that of a 40 watt incandescent lamp   (D) may be greater or less than that of a 40 watt incandescent lamp, depending on the manufacturer.

33. In order to use fluorescent lighting in a building which has only a 110 volt DC supply, it is necessary to use

(A) fluorescent lamps designed for DC   (B) fluorescent fixtures with an approved DC auxiliary or inductance unit and a series resistance of the correct value   (C) fluorescent fixtures ordinarily used on AC
(D) fluorescent fixtures ordinarily used on AC but equipped with a rectifier.

34. Electrical contacts are opened or closed when the electrical current energizes the coils of a device called a

(A) reactor   (B) transtat   (C) relay   (D) thermostat.

35. Transformer cores are composed of laminated sheet steel in order to keep the

(A) hysteresis loss to a minimum   (B) windage loss to a minimum
(C) eddy current loss to a minimum   (D) copper loss to a minimum.

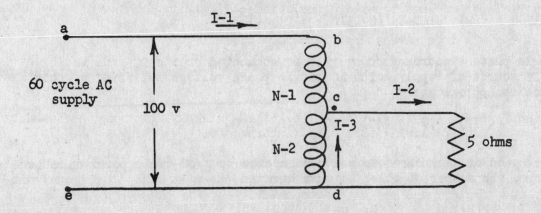

36. An auto transformer whose primary is bd is connected across a 100-volt AC supply as shown in the above diagram. The load of 5 ohms is connected across points c and d. If it is assumed that N-1 = N-2, (that is, point c is the midpoint of the winding) current I-1, in amperes, is approximately equal to

(A) 5   (B) 10   (C) 15   (D) 20.

37. In reference to question No. 36, current I-2, in amperes, is approximately equal to

(A) 5   (B) 10   (C) 15   (D) 20.

38. In reference to question No. 36, current I-3, in amperes, is approximately equal to

(A) 5   (B) 10   (C) 15   (D) 20.

39. The transformer is based on the principle that energy may be effectively transferred by induction from one set of coils to another by a varying magnetic flux, provided both sets of coils

(A) are not on a common magnetic circuit   (B) have the same number of turns   (C) are on a common magnetic circuit   (D) do not have the same number of turns.

40. In a transformer the induced emf per turn in the secondary winding is

(A) equal to the induced emf per turn in the primary winding
(B) not equal to the induced emf per turn in the primary winding
(C) equal to the induced emf per turn in the primary winding multiplied by the ratio N-1/N-2
(D) equal to the induced emf per turn in the primary winding divided by the ratio N-1/N-2.

41. A spool of wire consisting of 400 turns has an average diameter of 3 inches. The approximate total length of wire, in feet, is

(A) 1200   (B) 3140   (C) 314   (D) 120.

42. A single phase synchronous converter is connected on its DC side to 141.4 volt DC source of supply. The AC single phase voltage delivered by this machine is approximately

(A) 300   (B) 200   (C) 150   (D) 100.

43. If the speed of a synchronous motor connected to a 60-cycle power line is 1200 rpm, the number of poles it must have is

(A) 2   (B) 4   (C) 6   (D) 8.

44. Under load, the current in the armature conductors of a DC dynamo give rise to an independent excitation which alters both the magnitude and distribution of the flux produced by the field alone. This magnetizing action of the armature is called

(A) armature reaction   (B) dynamic breaking   (C) field reaction
(D) radial excitation.

45. The voltage induced in a loop of wire rotating in a magnetic field is

(A) DC   (B) pulsating DC   (C) rectified AC   (D) AC.

46. The relative polarity of the windings of a transformer is determined by

(A) open circuit test   (B) phasing out   (C) short circuit test
(D) polarimeter test.

47. If the field of a shunt motor while running under no load opens, the motor will

(A) stop running immediately   (B) continue to run at a very slow speed
(C) run away   (D) gradually slow down until it stops.

48. If, after the installation of a self-excited DC generator, it fails to build up on first trial run, the first thing to do is

(A) increase the field resistance   (B) reverse the connections to the shunt field   (C) check the armature insulation resistance   (D) decrease the speed of the prime mover.

49. In reference to question No. 48, if the generator still fails to build up, you should make sure that the

(A) resistance of the field rheostat is all in   (B) diverter is in series with the armature   (C) resistance of the field circuit is sufficiently small   (D) diverter is in parallel with the armature.

50. In reference to questions No. 48 and 49, if the generator still fails to build up now, you most probably would have to separately excite the

(A) field for a few minutes with a battery   (B) armature for a few minutes with a battery   (C) armature with AC current   (D) field with AC current.

51. Toggle bolts are most commonly used to fasten an outlet box to a

(A) solid concrete wall   (B) plaster or tile wall
(C) solid brick wall   (D) wooden partition wall.

Questions (52) to (55) refer to the diagram below:

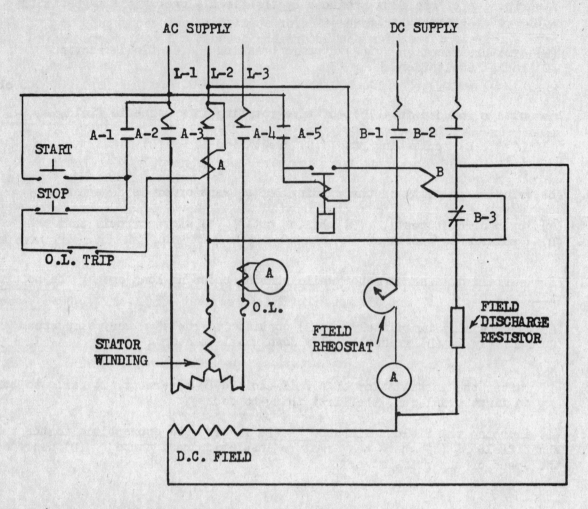

52. The above sketch represents a starter diagram of a

(A) synchronous motor (B) DC series motor (C) wound rotor induction
motor (D) squirrel cage induction motor.

53. When start P.B. is pressed

(A) Contactor A-1, A-2, A-3, A-4, A-5, B-1 and B-2 will close at once
(B) Contactor A-1, A-2, A-3, A-4 and A-5 will close at once
(C) Contactor A-2, A-3, A-4 and B-3 will close at once
(D) Contactor A-2, A-3 and A-4 only will close at once.

54. After the start button is pressed

(A) the motor will run but will stop unless field is energized
(B) the DC field is energized at once
(C) the DC field is energized after a definite time
(D) the motor will not run until the DC field is energized.

55. The field discharge resistor acts to

(A) steady the DC field during start period (B) improve the power factor
(C) dissipate the energy stored in the field after the DC field supply is
cut off (D) quench the arc.

56. In accordance with the Code all wiring is to be installed so that when completed, the system will be free from shorts or grounds. A circuit installation of #12 wire with all safety devices in place, but lamp-holders, receptacles, fixtures and/or appliances not connected, shall have a resistance between conductors and between all conductors and ground not less than

(A) 10,000 ohms   (B) 100,000 ohms   (C) 250,000 ohms   (D) 1,000,000 ohms.

57. The Code states that wires, cables and cords of all kinds except weather-proof wire shall have a

(A) distinctive marking so that the maker may be readily identified
(B) tag showing the minimum working voltage for which the wire was tested or approved   (C) tag showing the maximum current passed through the conductor under test   (D) tag showing the ultimate tensile strength.

58. The Code states that conductors supplying an individual motor shall have a minimum carrying capacity of

(A) 110% of the motor full load current   (B) 120 % of the motor full load current   (C) 125% of the motor full load current   (D) 135% of the motor full load current.

59. For not more than three conductors in raceway, "based on a room temperature of 86°F" the allowable current carrying capacity, in amperes, of a No. 12, AWG type R conductor is

(A) 15   (B) 20   (C) 30   (D) 40.

60. A 41740 CM Class A stranded copper conductor is composed of 7 wires. The diameter, in mils, of one wire is approximately

(A) 109.3   (B) 97.4   (C) 86.7   (D) 77.2.

61. In accordance with the Code, the number of No. 14 AWG type R conductors running through or terminating in a 1-1/2" x 3-1/4" octagonal outlet or junction box, should not be greater than

(A) 5   (B) 6   (C) 7   (D) 8.

62. The part of a circuit which melts when the current abnormally exceeds the allowable carrying capacity of the conductor is called

(A) circuit breaker   (B) thermo cutout   (C) overload trip   (D) fuse.

63. Defects in wiring which permit current to jump from one wire to another before the intended path has been completed are called

(A) grounds   (B) shorts   (C) opens   (D) breaks.

64. In accordance with the Code, a grounding conductor for a direct current system shall have a current carrying capacity not less than that of the largest conductor supplied by the system and in no case less than that of

(A) No. 12 copper wire   (B) No. 10 copper wire   (C) No. 8 copper wire
(D) No. 6 copper wire.

65. In accordance with the Code, the grounding connection for interior metal raceways and armored cable shall be made at a point

   (A) not greater than 5 feet from the source of supply   (B) not greater than 10 feet from the source of supply   (C) as far as possible from the source of supply   (D) as near as practicable to the source of supply.

66. In accordance with the Code, motors

   (A) may be operated in series multiple   (B) may be operated in multiple series   (C) shall not be operated in series multiple   (D) shall not be operated in multiple

67. Boxes and fittings intended for outdoor use should be of

   (A) weatherproof type   (B) stamped steel of not less than No. 16 standard gauge   (C) stamped steel plated with cadmium   (D) ample strength and rigidity.

68. Two 1/4 h.p. motors, under the protection of a single set of over-current devices and with or without other current consuming devices in the current, are considered as being sufficiently protected if the rating or setting of the over-current device does not exceed

   (A) 15 amperes at 250 volts   (B) 15 amperes at 125 volts
   (C) 30 amperes at 125 volts   (D) 30 amperes at 250 volts.

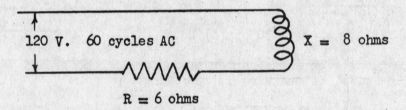

120 V.   60 cycles AC   X = 8 ohms

R = 6 ohms

69. A relay circuit is connected to a 120 volt 60 cycle AC supply as shown above. The current flowing in the circuit is

   (A) 20 amperes   (B) 15 amperes   (C) 12 amperes   (D) 8.57 amperes.

12 ohms

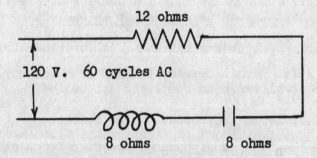

120 V.   60 cycles AC

8 ohms   8 ohms

70. In the above AC circuit, the capacitive reactance is equal to the inductive reactance. Under these conditions the current is

   (A) a minimum   (B) 10 amperes   (C) 6 amperes   (D) 4 amperes.

71. In a balanced three-phase **wye** connected load the

(A) line to neutral voltage equals the line voltage   (B) line to neutral
voltage equals the line voltage multiplied by the square root of three
(C) line voltage equals the line to neutral voltage divided by the square
root of three   (D) line voltage equals the line to neutral voltage
multiplied by the square root of three.

Questions No. 72 and No. 73 Refer To Diagram Below:

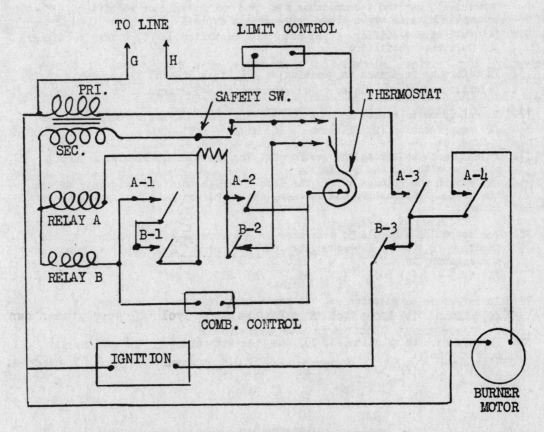

DIAGRAM OF PROTECTOR RELAY FOR OIL BURNER

72. When the thermostat calls for heat

(A) relay A is energized bringing in the motor only   (B) relay A is energized bringing in the ignition only   (C) relay A is energized bringing in
the motor and ignition   (D) relay B is first energized.

73. Momentary power failure while burner is in operation causes

(A) both relays to drop out   (B) relay A to drop out only
(C) relay B to drop out only   (D) the relay to go out on safety.

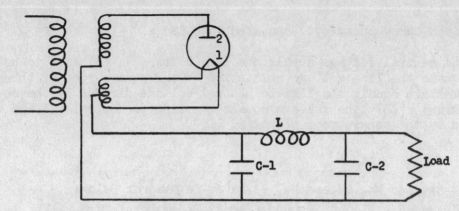

74. In order to furnish DC for the operation of relays and control circuits, where only a source of AC is available and the use of batteries is not convenient, gas and vacuum tubes are used extensively as rectifiers. The schematic diagram shown above represents a typical
    (A) full wave rectifier   (B) push pull rectifier   (C) bridge rectifier
    (D) half wave rectifier.

75. In reference to sketch in question No. 74, tube element 1 represents the
    (A) filament   (B) plate   (C) suppressor   (D) grid.

76. In reference to sketch in question No. 74, tube element 2 represents the
    (A) suppressor   (B) filament   (C) grid   (D) plate.

77. In reference to sketch in question No. 74, the circuit element marked L together with C-1 and C-2 act to
    (A) smooth the voltage across the load   (B) change the frequency across the load   (C) rectify the incoming AC   (D) maintain the factor K cos ϕ intact.

78. The output of a 6-pole DC generator is 360 amperes at 240 volts. If its armature is simplex lap-wound, the current per path, in amperes, through the armature is
    (A) 52.5   (B) 60   (C) 105   (D) 210.

79. In reference to question No. 78, the voltage per path, in volts, is
    (A) 120   (B) 420   (C) 60   (D) 240.

80. In reference to question No. 78, the kilowatt rating of the machine is approximately
    (A) 86   (B) 50   (C) 14   (D) 7.

Answer Key

(Please make every effort to answer the questions on your own before look-ing at these answers. You'll make faster progress by following this rule.)

1. C	11. A	21. C	31. C	41. C	51. B	61. A	71. D
2. D	12. D	22. B	32. C	42. D	52. A	62. D	72. C
3. B	13. A	23. D	33. B	43. C	53. B	63. B	73. A
4. D	14. C	24. B	34. C	44. A	54. C	64. C	74. D
5. B	15. A	25. B	35. C	45. D	55. C	65. D	75. A
6. B	16. B	26. A	36. A	46. B	56. D	66. C	76. D
7. C	17. B	27. D	37. B	47. C	57. A	67. A	77. A
8. D	18. C	28. C	38. A	48. B	58. C	68. B	78. B
9. B	19. B	29. A	39. C	49. C	59. B	69. C	79. D
10. B-C	20. C	30. A	40. A	50. A	60. D	70. B	80. A

ELECTRICIAN

VII. PREVIOUS EXAM

DIRECTIONS FOR ANSWERING QUESTIONS

Each question has four suggested answers, lettered
A, B, C, and D. Decide which is the best answer
and underline it. You may check your answers with
the answer key which appears at the end of the test.
Do not do so until you have completed the entire test.

Time allowed 3½ hours.

1. In order to operate satisfactorily in parallel, two single phase
    transformers must have

    (A) equal turn ratios, equal resistance drops, equal voltage ratings
         and be connected so as to have opposite polarity
    (B) equal turn ratios, equal impedance drops, equal K.V.A. ratings and
         be connected so as to have the same polarity
    (C) equal turn ratios, equal impedance drops, equal voltage ratings and
         be connected so as to have the same polarity
    (D) equal turn ratios, equal resistance drops, equal K.V.A. ratings and
         be connected so as to have opposite polarity.

2. Of the following, the primary advantage of the wound rotor induction motor
    over the standard (i.e. NEMA Design A) squirrel cage induction motor is
    that the wound rotor induction motor has a

    (A) higher starting current and a low power factor
    (B) lower starting torque and a unity power factor
    (C) higher starting torque and a lower starting current
    (D) lower starting torque and a higher starting current.

3. The synchronous speed of a 60-cycle A.C. induction motor that has 8 poles
    is most nearly

    (A) 800 rpm   (B) 900 rpm
    (C) 1200 rpm   (D) 1800 rpm.

4. As the load on a synchronous motor increases, its speed

    (A) remains constant until full load is reached and then decreases linearly as the load is increased further
    (B) decreases slowly as the load increases
    (C) remains constant until the "pull-out torque" is exceeded causing the motor to stop
    (D) decreases until the "pull-out torque" is exceeded causing the motor to stop.

5. In the conventional synchronous motor, direct current is applied to the

    (A) stator at standstill
    (B) rotor at standstill
    (C) stator when the motor speed approximates synchronous speed
    (D) rotor when the motor speed approximates synchronous speed.

6. The A.C. motor that would be used when only constant speed is required is the

    (A) synchronous motor
    (B) high-slip squirrel cage motor
    (C) high-torque squirrel cage motor
    (D) wound-rotor motor.

7. The minimum number of commutator brushes required in a wave winding is

    (A) four
    (B) two
    (C) dependent on the armature coil
    (D) dependent on the number of commutator segments.

8. In a simplex lap winding there are as many paths through the armature as there are

    (A) commutator segments   (B) armature coils
    (C) poles   (D) armature slots.

9. A half-wave rectifier has a ripple frequency which is

    (A) half that of the full-wave rectifier
    (B) twice that of the full-wave rectifier
    (C) equal to that of the full-wave rectifier
    (D) one-quarter that of the full-wave rectifier.

10. Blocking capacitors are used for the purpose of

    (A) passing A.C. and D.C.
    (B) passing D.C.
    (C) blocking A.C.
    (D) blocking D.C.

11. A battery that has an emf of two volts and an internal resistance of 0.2 ohm causes a current of one ampere to flow through a load. The terminal voltage of the battery under these conditions is

    (A) 0.2   (B) 0.4
    (C) 1.8   (D) 2.2

12. Resistances of twelve ohms, six ohms and four ohms are connected in parallel with each other. The total resistance in ohms, of the combination is

    (A) 22   (B) 7.2
    (C) 2.0   (D) 0.5

13. In American Wire Gage any wire has double the cross-sectional area of any other wire whose gage number is

    (A) 2 greater than the first wire
    (B) 3 greater than the first wire
    (C) 6 lower than the first wire
    (D) 6 greater than the first wire.

14. As the temperature increases the

    (A) electrical resistances of both carbon and copper increase
    (B) electrical resistance of carbon increases and the electrical resistance of copper decreases
    (C) electrical resistances of both carbon and copper decreases
    (D) electrical resistance of carbon decreases and the electrical resistance of copper increases.

15. The total capacitance, in microfarads, in a two microfarad condenser connected in series with a three microfarad condenser is

    (A) 1.2   (B) 2
    (C) 3.2   (D) 5

16. Two wattmeters are properly connected to read the load on a balanced three-phase, three wire system. One of the wattmeters reads zero. The power factor of the load is

    (A) 1.73   (B) 0.866
    (C) 0.5   (D) 0

17. Assume that you have a coil of 2000 feet of a certain size of bare copper wire which weights one pound and has a resistance of 64ohms, and a coil of 1000 feet of a different size of bare copper wire which also weights one pound. The resistance in ohms, of the second coil of wire is most nearly

    (A) 8   (B) 16
    (C) 32   (D) 64

18. If the allowable current density for copper bus bars is 1000 amperes per square inch, the current carrying capacity, in amperes, of a circular copper bar having a diameter of 2 inches is most nearly

(A) 1050
(B) 2320
(C) 3140
(D) 4260

19. A 10 hp motor is supplying power to a machine by means of a belt drive. If the motor runs at 900 rpm and the diameters of the pulley are 8 inches for the motor and 20 inches for the machine, the speed of the machine is most nearly

(A) 2250 rpm
(B) 1800 rpm
(C) 360 rpm
(D) 40 rpm.

20. Of the following metals the one which has the lowest resistivity at 20° c is

(A) aluminum
(B) nickel
(C) tungsten
(D) soft steel.

21. The root-mean-square value, in volts, of a sine wave with a peak voltage of 100 volts is

(A) 141.4
(B) 70.7
(C) 63.6
(D) 50.0

22. The one of the following which is a unit of inductance is the

(A) joule
(B) henry
(C) hertz
(D) ampere.

23. One maxwell per square centimeter is equal to

(A) a coulomb
(B) an erg
(C) a volt
(D) a gauss.

24. Assume that four inductors, each of a different value, are connected in parallel. The total inductance of the combination is

(A) smaller than that of the smallest inductance
(B) greater than that of the greatest inductance
(C) equal to the average inductance
(D) equal to the reciprocal of the average inductance.

25. If two identical coils, each having an inductance of 1 henry, are tightly coupled and connected in series with fields aiding, the combined inductance, in henrys, is

    (A) greater than two
    (B) slightly less than two
    (C) slightly less than one
    (D) almost zero.

26. A circuit consists of a 0.5-microhenry coil connected in series with a combination of two 0.2-microhenry coils connected in parallel. The total inductance of this circuit, in microhenrys, is most nearly

    (A) 0.9   (B) 0.6
    (C) 0.2   (D) 0.1

27. In the conventional four-point starting box for D.C. motors, the hold-up coil is of

    (A) high resistance and is connected directly across the line
    (B) low resistance and is connected in series with the shunt field
    (C) high resistance and is connected in series with the armature
    (D) low resistance and is connected directly across the line.

28. Of the following, improving the commutation of a D.C. generator is most often done by means of

    (A) a compensator
    (B) interpoles
    (C) an equalizer
    (D) a series rheostat in series with the equalizer.

29. Of the following, the type of motor that may be designed to run on both A.C. or D.C. is the

    (A) shunt motor
    (B) repulsion motor
    (C) compound motor
    (D) series motor.

30. Assume that a 10 h.p., D.C. shunt motor has a counter-emf of 225 volts at full load, an armature resistance of 0.2 ohms, and that its supply voltage is 230 volts. Under these conditions, its armature current, in amperes, is most nearly

    (A) 2.5
    (B) 25.0
    (C) 45.0
    (D) 91.1

31. Compensator starters for polyphase squirrel cage motors are basically

    (A) autotransformers
    (B) delta-wye switches
    (C) QMQB across-the-line switches
    (D) resistance banks.

32.   Design C squirrel-cage induction motors have a

(A)   high-torque and a low-starting-current
(B)   normal-torque and a low-starting-current
(C)   normal-torque and a normal-starting-current
(D)   low-torque and a low-starting-current.

33.   The one of the following statements which is <u>not</u> an valid evaluation
of the advantages of using autotransformers is

(A)   they have a high efficiency
(B)   they have better voltage regulation than two-coil transformer of the
same rating
(C)   they are less expensive than two-coil transformers
(D)   they are safe for stepping down high voltage.

34.   In an induction motor, the slip varies with the load. Doubling the
load will cause the slip to

(A)   double
(B)   halve
(C)   increase slightly
(D)   decrease slightly.

35.   An eight-pole 60 cycle induction motor which runs at 800 rpm has a slip
of most nearly

(A)   5.6%   (B)   8.9%
(C)   11.1%   (D)   12.5%.

36.   Assume that the lead has become disconnected from one of the slip rings
of a 3-phase wound-rotor induction motor. Under these conditions the motor

(A)   cannot run at all
(B)   can run at exactly half-speed when not loaded
(C)   can be started with full load and run at full speed
(D)   can be started at full load and run at two-thirds of its
normal speed.

37.   Assume that a certain D.C. motor and a certain D.C. generator both operate
so that in each case the commutator turns in the clockwise direction as
viewed when facing the commutator end. Neither machine has interpoles but
both have movable brush rigging. To improve commutation in both machines
when the load is increased, one should move the brushes

(A)   clockwise in both the motor and the generator
(B)   counter-clockwise in both the motor and the generator
(C)   clockwise in the motor and counter-clockwise in the generator
(D)   counter-clockwise in the motor and clockwise in the generator.

38.   The tool that is used to align vitrified tile conduit in multiple ducts
is a

(A)   mandrel   (B)   reamer
(C)   hickey   (D)   rod.

39. Of the following, the best fastener to use in a hollow wall is the

(A)   expansion bolt
(B)   carriage bolt
(C)   machine bolt and nut
(D)   toggle bolt.

40. Of the following, the tool which should be used for turning conduit is a

(A)   chain wrench
(B)   crescent wrench
(C)   monkey wrench
(D)   hook spanner.

41. A method commonly used for testing armatures for short circuits and open circuits is the

(A)   segment to segment test
(B)   Varley loop test
(C)   Murray loop test
(D)   Wien-Maxwell method.

42. A capacitor used for power factor connection is connected to the line in

(A)   series with a machine drawing leading current
(B)   series with a machine drawing lagging current
(C)   parallel with a machine drawing leading current
(D)   parallel with a machine drawing lagging current.

43. The one of the following hacksaw blades which should be used for best results in cutting thin tubing is one having

(A)   14 teeth per inch
(B)   18 teeth per inch
(C)   24 teeth per inch
(D)   32 teeth per inch.

44. When pulling wire through conduit, sometimes one conductor crosses another resulting in a hump that will wedge in the conduit. Of the following substances, the best one to use to make pulling easier, is

(A)   powdered soapstone
(B)   powdered carbon
(C)   resin
(D)   oil.

45. The horsepower ratings of motors are based on an observable safe temperature rise above ambient temperature. The ambient temperature is taken as

(A)   60° C
(B)   55° C
(C)   50° C
(D)   40° C.

46. Three single-phase transformers having ratios of 10 to 1 are connected with their primaries in wye and their secondaries in delta. If the low-voltage windings are used as the primaries, and the line voltage on the primary side is 208 volts, then the phase voltage on the secondary side is, in volts

    (A) 3600   (B) 2080
    (C) 1200   (D) 690.

47. Oil is used in many large transformers to

    (A) cool and insulate the transformer
    (B) lubricate the core
    (C) lubricate the coils
    (D) prevent breakdown due to friction.

48. Of the following, the main reason for damping an electrical indicating instrument is to prevent

    (A) excessive oscillation of the needle
    (B) the instrument from being damaged if it is dropped
    (C) the instrument from getting too dry
    (D) the needle from going off scale.

49. Of the following, flashing or excessive arcing from brush to brush in a motor is caused by

    (A) a high voltage on the line
    (B) the brushes being too hard
    (C) the brush pressure being too great
    (D) the brushes being set at the improper angle for the direction of rotation.

50. Of the following groups of lamps, the one which is best for testing a 460/265 volt supply is a group of

    (A) four 120-volt lamps in series
    (B) four 120-volt lamps in parallel
    (C) two 120-volt lamps in parallel
    (D) two 120-volt lamps in series.

51. Of the following, the best way to clean a dirty motor commutator is to rub it with

    (A) emery cloth   (B) sandpaper
    (C) fine steel wool   (D) powdered soapstone.

52. The one of the following which is the proper maintenance procedure to be followed when the liquid level in a lead-acid storage battery is too low is to

    (A) pour out all of the old solution and replace it with new solution
    (B) add enough double strength solution to bring the level up to normal
    (C) add only distilled water until the level is normal
    (D) add weak solution to bring the level back up to normal.

53. Assume that a D.C. ammeter having a resistance of 2.0 ohms and a 0 to 100 scale has a full scale reading when the meter current is .01 amps. The resistance of the shunt that should be used with the ammeter so that it will read 10 amps full scale is, in ohms, most nearly

   (A)   0.0004
   (B)   0.001
   (C)   0.002
   (D)   0.02.

54. The internal diameter of 3/4 inch electrical conduit, in inches, is most nearly

   (A)   0.824
   (B)   0.804
   (C)   0.753
   (D)   0.690

55. The one of the following inspection and maintenance procedures which should be carried out on motors every 6 months, according to various authorities such as the Electrician's Handbook, Westinghouse's Preventive Maintenance, etc., is

   (A)   check oil level in the bearings
   (B)   make sure that the brushes ride freely in the holders and replace any that are more than half worn
   (C)   examine the shaft to see that it is free of oil and grease from the bearings
   (D)   see that the oil rings turn in the shaft.

56. Of the following, the one which is <u>not</u> a type of file is a

   (A)   mill
   (B)   flat
   (C)   tubular
   (D)   half round.

57. The set of a hacksaw blade refers to how much the teeth are pushed out in opposite directions from the side of the blade. The one of the following which is <u>not</u> a type of set is

   (A)   an alternate set
   (B)   a lap set
   (C)   a raker set
   (D)   a wave set.

58. A transformer, having its terminals marked in the standard method so that H_1 and H_2 represent its high voltage terminals and X_1 and X_2 represent its low voltage leads, will have subtractive polarity if

   (A) H_1 and X_2 are adjacent
   (B) H_2 and X_2 are placed diagonally
   (C) H_1 and X_1 are placed diagonally
   (D) H_1 and X_1 are adjacent.

59. The D.C. component of the harmonic composition of the output of a half-wave rectifier tube is

(A) $\frac{2}{\pi}$ times the peak of the alternating voltage applied to the rectifier tube

(B) 2π times the peak of the alternating voltage applied to the rectifier tube

(C) π times the peak of the alternating voltage applied to the rectifier tube

(D) $\frac{1}{\pi}$ times the peak of the alternating voltage applied to the rectifier tube.

60. A widely used device is the SCR semiconductor. Of the following, the initials SCR stand for

(A) Signal Current Relay
(B) Solid Circuit Relay
(C) Semi Conductor Resonator
(D) Silicon Controlled Rectifier.

The following fifteen questions numbered 61 to 75 inclusive are to be answered in accordance with the provisions of the New York City Electrical Code

Notes:

1) Unless otherwise stated, the word "Code" refers to the Electrical Code of the City of New York (Title B of Chapter 30 of the Administrative Code) and Bulletins and Amendments which are in effect at present.

2) Questions are to be answered assuming normal procedures as given in the Code. Do not use exceptions which are granted by special permission.

61. Electrical metallic tubing shall not be used for interior wiring systems of more than

(A) 125 volts (B) 250 volts
(C) 350 volts (D) 600 volts.

62. A cartridge fuse must have a navy blue paper label if its rating is

(A) 600 volts; 30 amperes capacity
(B) 250 volts; 15 amperes or less capacity
(C) 250 volts; over 15 amperes capacity
(D) 250 volts; 30 amperes capacity.

63. Dry cleaning and dyeing plants using any inflammable solvents where the respective processes are carried on are considered hazard locations in Class

(A) I   (B) II
(C) III (D) IV.

64. High potential shall mean a voltage, in volts, of

(A) 350 up to and including 600
(B) over 600, up to and including 5000
(C) over 5000, up to and including 10,000
(D) over 10,000.

65. Overhead from main to building, weatherproof, rubber or thermoplastic covering shall be employed on single wires and rubber or thermoplastic insulation between wires in multiple-conductor cables, used as <u>service drops</u>. These wires, if of copper, shall not be smaller than

   (A) #10 AWG
   (B) #8 AWG
   (C) #6 AWG
   (D) #4 AWG.

66. Electric metallic tubing shall not be used in cinder concrete or fill unless protected on all sides by a layer of non-cinder concrete with a thickness of at least

   (A) 4 inches
   (B) 3 inches
   (C) 2 inches
   (D) 1 inch.

67. Wires or cables shall <u>not</u> approach nearer to buildings over which they pass than

   (A) 15 feet
   (B) 12 feet
   (C) 8 feet
   (D) 6 feet.

68. The maximum number of No. 12 wires that may be run through a deep square outlet or junction box which measures 1¼ x 4 inches is

   (A) 4
   (B) 5
   (C) 6
   (D) 7.

69. Where copper busbars are enclosed in auxiliary gutters and carry D.C. current, the maximum current density shall be, in amperes per square inch

   (A) 600
   (B) 800
   (C) 1000
   (D) 1200.

70. Of the following types of conductor insulation, the one which is used for fixture wire is

   (A) TW
   (B) RH
   (C) TA
   (D) TFF.

71. A flexible cord may not be smaller than number

   (A) 12   (B) 14
   (C) 18   (D) 22.

72. Where an exposed flexible conduit for a branch circuit goes directly from a basement cutout cabinet through the basement ceiling, the exposed portion of the flexible metallic conduit or armored cable may not exceed

    (A)   10 feet
    (B)   6 feet
    (C)   4 feet
    (D)   2 feet.

73. Of the following, the type of conductor insulation used in both dry and wet locations is type

    (A)   AVA
    (B)   AVB
    (C)   AVL
    (D)   AIA.

74. When used exclusively for stair lighting, the maximum number of outlets that may be supplied through a 15-ampere branch circuit is

    (A)   10, provided the load does not exceed 1380 va
    (B)   10, provided the load does not exceed 1800 va
    (C)   20, provided the load does not exceed 1380 va
    (D)   20, provided the load does not exceed 1800 va.

75. The maximum wattage rating allowed by the Code for an individual appliance with No. 14 wire

    (A)   1200
    (B)   1680
    (C)   1800
    (D)   1380

76. The one of the following which is the first thing to do when a person gets an electric shock and is still in contact with the supply is to

    (A)   start artificial respiration immediately
    (B)   treat for burns
    (C)   cut the power if it takes no more than 5 minutes to locate the switch
    (D)   remove the victim from the contact by using a dry stick or dry rope.

77. A Class A extinguisher should be used for fires in

    (A)   potassium, magnesium, zinc, sodium
    (B)   electrical wiring
    (C)   oil, gasoline
    (D)   wood, paper, and textiles.

78. Before applying the back pressure-arm lift (Holger-Nielsen) method of artificial respiration you should first place the victim

    (A)   on his left side
    (B)   in a sitting position
    (C)   on his back
    (D)   in a face-down position.

79. The one of the following which is <u>not</u> a safe practice when lifting heavy objects is

    (A)   keep the back as nearly upright as possible
    (B)   if the object feels too heavy keep lifting until you get help
    (C)   spread the feet apart
    (D)   use the arm and leg muscles.

80. When placing an extension ladder against a wall, the distance between the foot of the ladder and the wall should be

    (A)   always less than 2 feet
    (B)   always more than 2 feet
    (C)   ¼ the length of the extended ladder
    (D)   1/8 the length of the extended ladder.

Answer Key

(Please make every effort to answer the questions on your own before looking at these answers. You'll make faster progress by following this rule.)

1. C	11. C	21. B	31. A	41. A	51. B	61. D	71. C
2. C	12. C	22. B	32. A	42. D	52. C	62. B	72. B
3. B	13. B	23. D	33. D	43. D	53. C	63. A	73. C
4. C	14. D	24. A	34. A	44. A	54. A	64. B	74. C
5. D	15. A	25. A	35. C	45. D	55. B	65. C	75. A
6. A	16. C	26. B	36. B	46. C	56. C	66. C	76. D
7. B	17. B	27. A	37. D	47. A	57. B	67. C	77. D
8. C	18. C	28. B	38. A	48. A	58. D	68. D	78. D
9. A	19. C	29. D	39. D	49. A	59. D	69. C	79. B
10. D	20. A	30. B	40. A	50. A	60. D	70. D	80. C